The only thing necessary for the triumph of evil is for good men to do nothing.

—Edmund Burke (1729–1797)

In Germany, they came first for the communists, and I didn't speak up because I wasn't a communist. Then they came for the Jews, and I didn't speak up because I wasn't a Jew. Then they came for the trade unionists, and I didn't speak up because I wasn't a trade unionist. Then they came for the Catholics, and I didn't speak up because I was a Protestant. Then they came for me, and by that time there was nobody left to speak up.

—Pastor Martin Niemöller (1892–1984)

The world is too dangerous to live in—not because of people who do evil, but because of people who sit and let it happen.

—Albert Einstein (1879–1955)

Let us not forget that violence does not and cannot flourish by itself; it is inevitably intertwined with *lying.* Between them there is the closest, the most profound and natural bond: nothing screens violence except lies, and the only way lies can hold out is by violence. Whoever has once announced violence as his method must inevitably choose lies as his principle. . . . The simple act of an ordinary courageous man is not to take part, not to support lies! Let the lie come into the world, even dominate the world, but not through me.

—Alexander Solzhenitsyn (1918–), Nobel address, 1970

UNSPEAKABLE

UNSPEAKABLE

Facing Up to Evil in
an Age of Genocide and Terror

OS GUINNESS

HarperSanFrancisco
A Division of HarperCollins*Publishers*

HarperCollins books may be purchased for educational, business, or sales
promotional use. For information please write: Special Markets Depart-
ment, HarperCollins Publishers, Inc., 10 East 53rd Street, New York, NY
10022.

HarperCollins Web site: http://www.harpercollins.com

HarperCollins®, ❦®, and HarperSanFrancisco™ are trademarks of
HarperCollins Publishers, Inc.

Chapters 10, 11, and 12 contain material that was first published in *Long
Journey Home: A Guide to Your Search for the Meaning of Life* (Colorado
Springs, Colo.: WaterBrook Press; New York: Doubleday, 2001) and is used
here with the publisher's permission.

FIRST EDITION

Library of Congress Cataloging-in-Publication Data
Guinness, Os
   Unspeakable : facing up to evil in an age of genocide and terror /
Os Guinness.—1st ed.
     p. cm.
   Includes bibliographical references.
   ISBN 0-06-058636-2 (cloth)
    1. Good and evil. 2. Good and evil—Religious aspects—Christianity.
I. Title.
BJ1401.G85 2005
170—dc22   2004054032

05 06 07 08 09 ❦/RRD(H) 10 9 8 7 6 5 4 3 2 1

DOM
and to CJ,
and all in your generation
who have a passion to seek justice
and the courage to take a stand for it.

CONTENTS

NO STRANGER TO EVIL

The date September 11, 2001, was marked down in my calendar for a dinner discussion in Manhattan—on the theme of evil. When the dinner did take place a week after the ruthless terrorist strike, the only other people in the hotel were the survivors from an investment firm that had lost nearly seventy people in the tragedy. One of them, who attended our discussion, had made it down safely from the 104th floor of the second tower and was a harrowing witness to the day of terror. As our host said in introducing the discussion of some key readings on evil, "When I read some of these readings before September 11, I thought they were far too dark. When I read them again after September 11, they weren't nearly dark enough."

The thinking in this book goes back long before September 11 and the lurid incidents around the world since then, such as kidnappings, car bombings, beheadings, mass rapes, and forced starvation, which show clearly that evil is with us still—and will be even when September 11 has faded from our memories as the worst of atrocities eventually do. But the book itself was spurred by the questions and discussions thrown up by that awful day.

Is there anything harder to face and figure out than evil? Evil is quite simply the most serious problem in human life, the most serious problem in the contemporary world, and the most serious problem for our deepest human resort in life—our trust in God or in the universe that is our planet home.

Not surprisingly, there are few things harder to write about. I am not an expert on evil and suffering. There is no such thing, thank God. Evil dwarfs our best discussions and remains a mystery even after our best explorations. And suffering is too individual and deep for recipe approaches and fix-it solutions.

But neither am I a stranger to evil. It has been the horizon of much of my life. None of us, I argue, has the answers to evil all sewn up, and certainly I do not. But I have had to wrestle with the questions for years, because from my earliest days I have somehow repeatedly found myself in situations where the reality of evil was palpable.

To be sure, there are some, like the survivors of the Nazi death camps and the Soviet Gulag, who speak of evil with the authority of those who have gone to hell and back. They have stared evil in the white of the eye and felt its lash on their souls, and the look in their eyes and the tone of their voices speak louder than words. Alexander Solzhenitsyn, I am told by a friend who knows him, is like that. Elie Wiesel, the world's leading witness to the horrors of the Holocaust, certainly is. To talk to him is to be seared by the fires of the camp and by the courage of a human being who has survived and surmounted human evil at its most horrendous.

My parents and grandparents were closer to a world like that. Living in China from the end of the nineteenth century through to the first years of the triumph of Mao Tse-tung, they lived in a crucible made savage by the decay of an ancient dynasty, the corruption and incompetence of its would-be replacement, the savagery of foreign invaders, and the fanatical rage for justice of the revolution that prevailed against them all. Their stories included hair-raising accounts of callous imperial cruelty, the slaughters of the Boxer Rebellion, the arbitrary violence of the early Communist insurgency, the brutality of Japanese invaders, the dangers of life in a war zone circled by not just two but three armies, and the first years of the red terror that became the most murderous regime in all history. For more than fifty years they witnessed the worst of grinding cruelty, savage rapes, random murders, false accusations, rigged trials, unjust executions, brutal repression, and religious persecution.

My own journey has been far safer, though it began in the same dire setting. My first ten years included the cataclysmic forces of war, famine, revolution, and repression—desperate, dangerous times in which my two brothers died and my parents and I were nearly killed on several occasions. Current estimates are that the Japanese alone killed nearly twenty million Chinese in that period, especially with their infamous "three all policy": "loot all, kill all, burn all."

Later we lived in Nanking, China, just a short time and a short distance from the killing grounds of the Japanese "rape of Nanking" in which 300,000 Chinese were slaughtered in a few weeks. Not only was this one of the most sadistic and savage mass rapes and atrocities in all history, but it rivaled the Mongol massacres, appalled even the Nazis who were present, and could not be excused through secrecy because it was splashed across the newspapers of the world. Yet to date it still has not been officially acknowledged by its perpetrators.

So I grew up with firsthand knowledge of raw terror, and I experienced other forms of evil later on—some better masked and even beautiful, but evil still. Having lived at least a decade of my life on each of three continents—Asia, Europe, and America—I am as aware as anyone of deeply different ways of understanding evil and the decisive differences they make.

So I am no expert on evil, but I am someone who has covered a fair bit of the road on the human journey and had the privilege of talking over the issues with many and offering a helping hand to some. Join me, then, on a tough but rewarding journey of exploration into the most urgent and momentous issue of our times.

CHAPTER 1

EVIL AND
THE EXAMINED LIFE

"Where was God when the towers fell?" The ABC reporter's question to me, only two days after the horrific slaughter of the innocent thousands in the World Trade Center on September 11, 2001, went straight for the jugular, and it was meant to. Or as a National Public Radio interviewer asked me the same day, "I saw a woman running through the acrid smoke crying, 'God, are you here?' What should I have said to her?"

With television making the atrocity a local event for untold millions around the world, questions like that must have been asked in countless ways that day—sometimes with heartbreak, sometimes with anger, and sometimes with mute incomprehension. But the concern was surely the same. On a clear blue, peaceful Tuesday morning, the deadly terrorist strike laid bare the two deepest issues of human life: the raw evil of the inhumanity of humanity and the agonizing question of the place of God in human suffering.

These two issues, and the piercing questions they raise, are the central theme of this book. Together they lie at the heart of our human existence. Each requires the other for an adequate response,

1

and both are surrounded by a dangerous ignorance and confusion today. The first can be expressed as: "Why do bad things happen to good people?" And the second: "What does it say of us as human beings that the worst atrocities on planet earth are done by our own species—in other words, by people like us?"

Needless to say, these issues and questions are far older and have far wider application than the events of September 11. For one thing, while thousands died at Ground Zero, thousands of others across New York and hundreds of thousands across the world also died that day—of cancer, stroke, hunger, accidents, murder, AIDS, suicide, and for many other tragic reasons, not to mention old age. Each of these deaths was accompanied by its own grieving family and friends, and each was a dire event that, for them as individuals, was as bad as the terrorist strike was for the United States as a whole.

A basic fact of life is that any of us may suffer and all of us will die.

For another thing, while a televised attack on two of the world's most famous buildings was shockingly extraordinary, and designed to be so, far more people in the world suffer today under the heel of grinding evils that are numbingly ordinary and will never make the newspaper headlines or the television news. Few of us, for instance, give serious thought to the millions of young girls forced into prostitution, to the women abused by their husbands, to the widows driven from their homes and their rightful lands, to the men convicted and imprisoned without justice, or to the millions of families kept for a lifetime in bonded slavery.

Another basic fact of life is that countless human beings live in abject daily fear of evil and the brutal people who abuse power and oppress them. For much of the world, evil is—and always has been— a daily fact of life.

The Lisbon Earthquake of Our Time

These two ancient issues are dark and difficult enough in themselves. But there is a modern twist to the discussion that makes it harder still.

The events of September 11 hit America and the West at large at a time when intellectual and moral responses to evil are weaker, more controversial, and more confused than they have been for centuries. Put simply, we no longer have a shared understanding about whether there is any such thing as *evil*. Some even question whether it is proper to speak of anyone as our *enemy*. The consequences of our uncertainty damage us on all sorts of levels.

Thus, whether September 11 was viewed as a disaster, a tragedy, a crime, an act of war, or a symbolic spectacle on the grandest scale—"the greatest work of art of all time," as the German composer Karlheinz Stockhausen put it—the force of the hijacked planes hit the Western intellectual world as damagingly as it did the World Trade Center. The lethal challenge of evil at the beginning of the twenty-first century exposes the core confusion of modern thinking just as the Great Lisbon earthquake in 1755 challenged traditional European views in the eighteenth century—but in the opposite direction.

In the mid-eighteenth century Lisbon was the capital of the far-flung Portuguese empire and one of the most powerful and beautiful cities in the world. But on November 1, 1755, it was devastated by a triple shock: an offshore earthquake lasting ten minutes that was felt as far away as France, Italy, Switzerland, and North Africa; a gigantic killer wave that unleashed a fifty-foot wall of water pounding across the city; and a series of fires, set off by the tremors, which devastated what was left of the city. The combined death toll of all three disasters was more than 60,000 people, and the shock and horror were felt right across Europe. To the eighteenth century the mention of "Lisbon" was the equivalent of the mention of "Auschwitz" today.

The parallels between New York 2001 and Lisbon 1755 are evident at once: an autumn day; sudden, total, and appalling devastation; buildings destroyed; skies dark and thick with dust; thousands hideously slaughtered; heroic human responses; civilized life drastically disrupted; weeks following filled with a lifetime's worth of grief and funerals; and intense intellectual debates set off around the centers of the educated world.

But the difference between 1755 and 2001 is crucial too. The outcome of the Lisbon earthquake, as interpreted by Voltaire and others, was to weaken traditional faith in God and providence and strengthen the new confidence in Enlightenment progress—God is dead and the future of humankind is one of our own making. Whereas the outcome of September 11 has been to destroy the last threads of the Enlightenment belief that humans are getting better and better. It has also served to reunite the deepest questions about God with the deepest questions about humanity.

For Europeans and many around the world, Auschwitz rather than September 11 is the true counterpoint to Lisbon, though September 11 was the shock that brought evil home for many Americans. But whether we regard Auschwitz or September 11 as pivotal, in a way that is only beginning to sink into current thinking our "post-Auschwitz" or "post 9/11" questions are raising issues that only "pre-Lisbon" answers can address.

Cause for a Pause

Four troubling facts make up the challenge to rethink evil and suffering in our times.

First, *the scale and scope of evil has increased in the modern world.* To anyone who thinks deeper than the morning headlines, the atrocity of September 11 forms part of the wider record of the dark catalog of human evil in modern history and pales beside the worst of the evils. The Ottoman massacre of one and a half million Armenians in World War I and the Rwandan and Sudanese massacres in the 1990s, in which nearly three million people died, are like a pair of grisly bookends that frame the twentieth century as the most murderous century in all history. In between, such atrocities as the Ukraine terror famine, Auschwitz, the rape of Nanking, the Burma railway, the Soviet Gulag, the Chinese Cultural Revolution, the Cambodian killing fields, and the massacres in Bangladesh and Yugoslavia form an indelible stain on our human story. Leaving aside the one hundred

million human beings killed in the century's wars, more than one
hundred million more were killed by their fellow human beings in political repression, massacre, and genocide.

It is sometimes argued that the modern world is more humane
than ever before, and in some ways it is. The paradox, however, is that
we save more victims than ever before and slaughter more victims
than ever before. The Rwandan bloodbath, for example, was one of
the fastest massacres in history. In less than three months, machete-
wielding Hutus ferociously slaughtered more than 800,000 Tutsis—
the clearest case of genocide since the Holocaust, carried out at three
times the speed of Hitler's extermination of the Jews and Gypsies. It
was the equivalent of more than two World Trade Center slaughters
every single day for one hundred days straight. Quite simply, it was
the most devastating mass killing since the bombings of Hiroshima
and Nagasaki in 1945, which slaughtered a third of a million people.
And as with the Holocaust, it was carried out by men and women like
ourselves.

Second, *modern people have demonstrated a consistently poor response
to modern evil*. Part of the uniqueness of our time is that we are the
first to live when it is possible to know of almost all the world's atrocities as they happen. Yet a sad feature of the horrendous evils of the
last century has been that strong leaders and decent people knew
what was happening when it was happening, but did little or nothing.
More than we like to admit, we are all bystanders now. We often
know enough to know that it is better not to know more.

In 2001 the world responded to America's tragedy with an out
pouring of sympathy and aid. "We are all Americans now," the French
said famously. But in 1994, when the defenseless Tutsis cried for help,
the watching world watched and turned away. Not a single country
went to their rescue. And this was the response from the generation
that had coined the word *genocide*, trumpeted the universality of
human rights, and built and visited memorials such as the Holocaust
Museum in Washington, D.C., so that we might never forget.

"Never again," the civilized world intoned solemnly after the Nazi

Holocaust. "You never know" would be more realistic in light of sub-
sequent history. Clearly the responsibility for contemporary evil has
to be shouldered by bystanders as well as by perpetrators.

Third, *modern people have shown a chronic inability to name and judge
evil and to respond effectively.* Deeds such as the terrorist attacks of September 11 caught the Western world as much off guard intellectually
and morally as they did in terms of national security. An act that was
flagrantly evil—in the clear, traditional sense of intending to do
harm—exposed the paralyzed confusion of many who were uncertain whether it was evil, or how to say so, or at least how to justify
their saying so in public terms.

"Today our nation saw evil, the very worst of human nature,"
President George W. Bush solemnly declared the day of the strike.
But his critics at once said that the president and anyone who spoke
openly of evil were simplistic and old-fashioned, that they had a view
of life shaped more by fairy tales and old westerns than by science.
Evil had become so politicized, they said, that it was no longer a
moral term; abusing it this way would lead to self-righteousness,
hypocrisy, a new round of the politics of fear, and more real evil.

But then, as the response to terrorism unfolded, as the casualties
among Iraqi civilians topped the number of New Yorkers killed in the
9/11 attack, and as photographs of American soldiers as happy young
torturers flashed around the world, it was the turn of the president's
supporters to cavil over the term *evil.* Moral indignation was brushed
aside as a spurious form of moral equivalence. Saddam Hussein's bru-
talities were evil; America's were expedient. His were malevolent;
America's were benign. The abuse, sexual humiliation, and tortures
at the Abu Ghraib prison were excused as "fraternity antics" and
"emotional release," understandable responses to the stress of war
and not something over which to "ruin a soldier's life." One Republican senator declared that he was more "outraged by the outrage"
than by the outrages themselves.

That Americans could be this confused over the word *evil,* and the
controversies to which it leads, should not be surprising. The nation
with the most radical view of evil at its core—embedded in the sepa-

ration of powers in the Constitution—has been shown to have current views of evil that are weak, hesitant, contradictory, and far from shared. "Whatever became of sin?" Karl Menninger asked his fellow Americans a generation ago. The tough-minded realism of the traditional American view of evil defined under God as sin has softened into evil defined before the law as crime, and then degenerated further into low self-esteem—the infamous "hole in the soul" that was the poster problem of the eighties and nineties.

Plainly a combination of forces over the past century did their damage and created the sorry state of moral illiteracy and intellectual cowardice in which we find ourselves.

At one level, the confusion is easily explained. Progressivism in philosophy and politics has replaced evil with utopian views of human goodness and led people and whole societies to believe that people are truly getting better and better on an ever-upward march to peace and prosperity.

Psychologism in the form of the therapeutic revolution and its talking cures has claimed to offer alternative explanations and remedies for human dysfunctions that make deeper traditional answers unnecessary.

Polyannaism at the level of popular culture has given many Americans a constitutional propensity to look on the bright side of everything and plaster life with rainbows and smiley buttons. (In Peter Sellers's brilliant film *Being There*, a gang leader pulls a knife on Chance, who in response pulls a television remote control out of his pocket, points it at the young hood, and tries to change channels to something more pleasant.)

And most recently, postmodernism, with its insistence on relativism and its drive to unmask truth claims as disguised bids for power, has spawned legions of people who pronounce all judgments of evil to be judgmental and evil themselves. Some have even acted as if it were worse to judge evil than to do evil.

The confusion, however, goes far deeper. Philosophy has not lived up to its promise of illuminating life with reason, and it has even had to own up to its signal lack of any answers at all. In his essay "Philos-

ophy and Philosophers," the eminent Polish philosopher Leszek Ko-
lakowski surveys the age-old attempt to distinguish the real from the
unreal, the true from the false, and the good from the evil. "There
came a point, however," he concludes, "when philosophers had to
confront a simple, painfully undeniable fact: that of the questions
which have sustained European philosophy for two and a half millen-
nia, not a single one has been answered to general satisfaction."

This dilemma is sharpest over the challenge of evil. Philosophically,
we have reached the very limits of language and reason and are no
nearer to resolving the problem. What was launched after Lisbon as a
challenge to believers to justify their faith in God in the face of evil has
deepened into a challenge to everyone to justify their faith in life in the
face of evil. What began as a probe into God's thinking in allowing evil
has widened into perplexity at our own in committing it.

If there is no God to blame for evil, then we humans are fully responsible. But if evil in the modern world has grown worse rather
than better, are we really capable or worthy of such responsibility?
What is at stake is the rationality of human life in the universe and
our ability to make sense of it and take responsibility for it. Evil has
reduced reason to the mind at the end of its tether.

Ethically, we are no better off. The modern world has witnessed a
grand fading of the power of moral law as moral certainties have
been assaulted and modern evils have exhausted the capacity of our
minds to understand, our hearts to embrace, and our judgments to
resolve. Again and again we find that evil overtaxes our ideals as well
as our emotions, our policies as well as our analyses. One person's response is another's revenge and yet another's grounds for retaliation.
One generation's practices pave the way for the next generation's
precedents and the pretexts of the generation after that. A solution to
one evil becomes the seedbed for others. There is even a direct line-
age in cruelty. The Gestapo becomes the model for the East German
Stasi, and in turn the Stasi train Saddam Hussein's torturers.

Again and again we find ourselves looking into the heart of darkness, and what we see is literally unspeakable—in Joseph Conrad's
famous words, "The horror! The horror!"

Modern evil has called into question modern progress, modern morality, and modern humanity. In her great survey *Evil in Modern Thought*, the philosopher Susan Neiman raises the question, "Can we summarize the changes by saying that humankind lost faith in the world at Lisbon and faith in itself at Auschwitz?" She concludes simply, "Contemporary evil left us helpless."

Fourth—and most controversially—*the worst modern atrocities were perpetrated by secularist regimes, led by secularist intellectuals and in the name of secularist beliefs.* This fact runs directly counter to today's ruling orthodoxy in educated circles in the West. Many actually make the opposite claim. "The great unmentionable evil at the center of our culture is monotheism," Gore Vidal thundered in the Lowell Lecture at Harvard University. "Only the willfully blind," writes Richard Dawkins in *A Devil's Chaplain*, "fail to implicate the divisive force of religion in most, if not all, of the violent enmities of the world today." The "real axis of evil," one British journalist responded in counter to President Bush, is "Judaism, Christianity, and Islam."

Not so fast. Vidal, Dawkins, and many like them overlook the fact that monotheism is the single most influential and constructive belief in human history and that the links between twentieth-century massacres, secularist intellectuals, and secularist beliefs are shocking but undeniable. In this case, September 11 was a break with the worst twentieth-century massacres because the atrocity was done in the name of Allah and by avowed, if extremist, followers of Islam. But the ensuing discussion has become grossly distorted in putting the blame for modern evil solely on religion.

We return to this point in the course of the exploration, but an analysis of modern massacres and genocides—from the Young Turks through Stalin and Mao Tse-tung to Pol Pot—reveals a fact that is stunning yet vital for public discussion in the West: more people in the twentieth century were killed by secularist regimes, led by secularist intellectuals and in the name of secularist ideologies, than in all the religious persecutions in Western history.

If September 11 was a "religious atrocity," as Dawkins and others insist, then these were all "secularist atrocities," and the important debates in our Western public conversation must take into account the full significance of these realities.

A Troubling Invitation

What does it take to get us to consider evil seriously? As a death camp survivor, Primo Levi described himself as acting like the Ancient Mariner in Coleridge's poem—tiresomely waylaying his friends and everyone he met in Turin to tell them the dark tale of his time in Auschwitz. But even he was stumped by the ten-year-old schoolboy he tells of in *The Drowned and the Saved*, who was a die-hard product of the media age. The boy "listened to his description of the camp, then solemnly told him what he should have done to get away—cut a guard's throat, switch off the power to the electric fence—and urged him not to forget his advice if it should happen again."

In the same vein, Arthur Koestler, author of *Darkness at Noon* and a leading protagonist among those exposing Soviet tyranny, wrote an essay, "On Disbelieving Atrocities," published in the *New York Times Magazine* in 1944. He had a recurring dream. It was dark and he was being murdered in some kind of thicket that was only ten yards from a busy road. He screamed and screamed for help, but nobody heard him. The crowd walked past, laughing and chattering. So it is for the survivors, he said. Haunted by their memories, screaming and yelling to the world, they now and then succeed in reaching the ear of the public for a minute. "But it only lasts a minute. You shake yourself like puppies that have got their fur wet; then the transparent screen descends again, and you walk on, protected by the dream barrier which stifles all sound."

All such warnings apply here. On one level, this book is a straightforward invitation to explore and a challenge to engage—an invitation to explore the mystery of evil and suffering in our world and a challenge to engage with evil wherever we find it. As such, this is written not for scholars but for serious people in all walks of life. Such an invitation is a key part of Socrates' "examined life" that every thoughtful person should welcome. But on another level, it is unquestionably a troubling invitation, for naming the unspeakable is troubling not only for our minds and hearts but for our consciences.

The straightforwardness is genuine. Having addressed these issues in countless settings, from private conversations to public discussions at many universities, I believe the best approach is to set out the basic questions in thinking through the challenge of evil and suffering in human life and to point out where different choices may lead to decisively different consequences.

As I said, we need to explore the subject because a simple fact confronts anyone who would live an examined life: for all the soaring greatness of human accomplishments and the precious, inalienable dignity of each man, woman, and child, we are still always and only mortals. Any of us may suffer, and all of us will die.

What is the best approach to thinking through the challenge of evil? Out of my own wrestlings, I have come to the conclusion that people's specific questions always require specific answers, whenever they are possible, but a lack of specific answers is not most people's deepest problem. The real problem is that they have not thought through the challenge of evil on a foundational level, and therefore they have no framework out of which to answer specific questions when they arise.

Having thought things through for myself, and having often helped others to do the same, I have found it useful to survey the way anyone who desires to lead an examined life may begin to think about evil in the modern world. There are seven basic questions to explore in thinking through the challenges of evil and suffering:

1. *Where on earth does evil come from?* While none of us have a full answer to the ancient question *Unde malum?* (Whence evil?), which always remains a mystery, it is important to come to grips with the challenge by examining the everyday sources of evil and suffering as we are all liable to face them: in our bodies, in nature, and in other human beings.

2. *What's so right about a world so wrong?* A crucial step toward responding to the challenges of evil and suffering is to ponder the irrepressible and instinctive questions that they raise for us. "Why me?" "Where's God?" "And how can I stand it?"

3. *Are we really worse or just modern?* As with many other areas of life, the human experience of evil and suffering has been transformed out of all recognition by the power and pervasiveness of the modern world. These major changes are crucial to understanding and resisting evil today, especially the way in which the modern world has simultaneously minimized pain, magnified destructiveness, and marginalized traditional resources for responding to evil and suffering.

4. *Do the differences make a difference?* The measure of the supreme challenge of evil is that much of the greatest human thinking is an answer to the questions it raises—and these different explanations are very different. By setting out the main families of answers, through their own spokespeople rather than through critics, we can evaluate their ability to answer the deepest questions each of us has and choose those we believe to be true and most helpful.

5. *Isn't there something we can do?* Adequate answers to evil must always include appropriate action to express sympathy, alleviate pain, or resist evil. In a world of AIDS, genocide, and massacres, words alone are never enough, but practical responses are also costly and have to go beyond what is merely instinctive and easy.

6. *Why can't I know what I need to know?* All human answers to evil are partial, and yet nothing is more characteristically human than the drive to supply answers even when we do not have any—attempts that often have cruel and insensitive consequences.

7. *Isn't there any good in all this bad?* There is usually at least some positive side to evil and suffering, and it is healthy to recognize it—though finding the good in evil and suffering must never be

misused as an explanation for why the evil occurred in the first place.

As far as possible, our exploration together should honor two principles. One is the importance of *reason and thinking* in wrestling with the issues and choices. Limited though the reach of reason may be, this is the heart of coming to terms with evil and making sense of it. The very outline of these seven questions represents an invitation to explore with open minds and indicates the points at which each of us must make choices and decisions.

The other is the principle of *respect* in dealing with the diverse opinions and conclusions of others. One of the plainest lessons of today's multisplendored diversity is that it is a cardinal error to believe that if we are nice enough to each other, and keep talking to each other long enough, we will reach the common core of all our beliefs. No one has ever found the common core—except as an article of their own particular belief. In contrast, I unashamedly make three arguments throughout this book: that there are important differences between the various answers to evil; that these differences make a difference; and that the differences make a difference not only for individuals but for societies.

At the same time we must never lose sight of the fact that how we live with our deepest differences is a mark of our humanity and civility. To put my own cards on the table from the beginning, I understand myself and my life as a follower of Jesus of Nazareth, so I stand openly in the broad tradition of "the old faiths," the Jewish and Christian beliefs that are the single strongest set of ideas that have shaped Western civilization, including Western ideas of evil and suffering. But I am no extremist or fanatic, and my own friends and discussions include many people from a wide variety of other faiths and philosophies, some of whom are believers, some seekers, and some skeptics.

Unquestionably, for all who seek to live the examined life, it is our responsibility as well as our right to come to our own conclusions and to form our own convictions, based on freedom of conscience and our own independent thinking.

At the same time reason and respect both have their limits when we come to the subject of evil and suffering. On the one hand, there are limits to reason. There are things we simply do not know and cannot understand. Evil defies definition. It is rightly called a mystery and at some points is literally unspeakable. Evil can torture human minds just as it tortures human bodies because there are questions about evil to which none of us have the answer because there is no human answer.

On the other hand, in a day of careless tolerance, there must also be limits to respect. The right to believe anything does not mean that anything anyone believes is right. The former is freedom of conscience and must always be respected unconditionally; the latter idea is nonsense and must often be opposed, for it can be a license for evil itself. Many an evil would have done none of its terrible damage downstream if it had been challenged upstream at its source.

A Major Rethink?

Are we likely to see a major rethinking of evil and suffering today? I would hope so, but no one should hold their breath. After the revelations of the death camps in 1945, the philosopher Hannah Arendt famously predicted: "The problem of evil will be the fundamental question of post-war intellectual life in Europe." She was right, but only for a few and only for a while. Postwar prosperity quickly lulled such seriousness to sleep, and the signs are that the same has happened since September 11—except for the thoughtful and the few.

The fact is that we should not need a September 11—or a Lisbon earthquake, or death camps, or cancer, or a disaster of any kind—to make us think about evil and suffering. Understanding, identifying, and resisting evil should be central to the challenge of the examined life. "Why do bad things happen to good people?" we ask. But do not forget the second question that comes hard on the heels of the first: "What does it say of us as human beings that the people who do these things are the same species as we are?" These are the deepest questions we humans ever ask, and these are the questions we explore here. They are also the questions to which we all owe ourselves an answer.

Always Ready to Help

Facing up to human evil—and especially the magnitude and malevolence of contemporary evil—is disturbing. Some forms of evil, such as terrorism, are expressly designed to strike us dumb with fear; others, such as the vicious abuse of power or our human pleasure in cruelty, leave us speechless before their horror. No words of explanation can ever be easy, no written response can be adequate in itself, and no book about evil can ever be a casual read or an idle discussion.

Nor is a book on evil easy to write. A close look at evil is troubling for any of us, not least because it explodes the comforting conceit by which we see ourselves as good even as we are discussing evil and pronouncing others bad. I am not just writing to you about evil. I, who am writing to you, am aware of evil in myself and have never been more aware of it than in this writing.

Finding the words to come to terms with the unspeakable is crucial to facing up to it and to overcoming the fear that is so widespread in today's world, but exploring the challenge of evil need not be depressing; indeed, it may be bracing, even inspiring. For one thing, we examine here the strongest answers to evil that have been proffered down the centuries. For another, we encounter what has finally made the difference for countless people weighed down by evil: the contrasting mystery of goodness, which outweighs even the mystery of evil.

Yet another encouragement lies in the fact that we can each respond constructively in our own way. The full horror and magnitude of modern evil is unimaginable and overwhelming, and an unforeseen consequence of globalization has been the manufacture of added conspiracies, enemies, and monsters. But we are not each responsible for the entire world; we are accountable only for ourselves and our own spheres of influence. Certainly, evil could happen anywhere. Equally certainly, it does not happen everywhere. What we must each make certain is that it does not happen wherever we each call "here."

Expressed positively, in the words of the French Huguenots in the village of Le Chambon who rescued thousands of Jewish children from the Nazis during World War II, we should be "always ready to help." Expressed negatively, in the words of Alexander Solzhenitsyn's Nobel address, let the lie come into the world and even dominate the world—"but not through me."

"Always ready to help" . . . "but not through me" . . . could there be better mottoes for all who would take their stand for good and against evil in our world? Only through living by such truths can we raise up the just men and women whose lives will be the guarantee of a tomorrow better than the world has seen yesterday and today.

Where on Earth Does Evil Come From?

The first basic question explores the everyday sources from which we are likely to encounter evil and suffering in our lives. None of us know the ultimate origin of evil. "Where does evil come from?" (*Unde malum?*) is one of the oldest and deepest questions humans have wrestled with. But for all our exploration, discussion, and debate, we simply do not have a fully satisfactory answer to this question. The origin of evil remains an unfathomable mystery we can never finally plumb.

But we can begin our exploration at a level that our human minds can attain without overreaching. However we come to explain evil—an issue we look at in considering the different interpretations in the fourth question—a helpful approach is to explore the three everyday sources of evil and suffering: our bodies, nature, and other human beings.

This first question is a small and modest question, but it carries an important reminder. Evil and suffering are so nearly universal as to underscore how vulnerable we all are as humans and what it means that we are mortal. Those who have never experienced a real

crisis in their lives are fortunate and rare. The plain fact is that all
does not go well for all human beings. Most of us are well aware that
life is full of evil and suffering, that none of us is immune, and that
faith provides no exemption.

This first question is vital for finding answers grounded in realism
and compassion. We may not be experiencing evil today. But when
our minds are humbled and our hearts are touched by its
commonness, we find ourselves readier to reach out to those who
are suffering—and therefore we are more likely to know what it will
be for others to reach out to us if that experience is ever our lot.

CHAPTER 2

BRIEF AS A CANDLE, FRAGILE AS AN EGGSHELL

On a cold winter's night in December 1931, a European politician on a lecture tour in the United States took a cab from New York's Waldorf-Astoria Hotel and set out in search of Bernard Baruch's home a mile or so uptown for a late-night gathering of friends. After a fruitless hour spent searching for the house, he abandoned the hapless driver and attempted to cross Fifth Avenue on foot between Seventy-sixth and Seventy-seventh Streets. Believing he recognized the doorway of his host's house, he strode out but forgot that the traffic was on the right side, not the left, as in England. There was a sudden screech of brakes and squeal of tires. For an awful fraction of a second he was caught frozen and helpless in the headlights of a car, then knocked down like a rag doll and badly injured. Later, describing the moment, for which he acknowledged full responsibility, he reflected ruefully, "I do not understand why I was not broken like an eggshell or squashed like a gooseberry."

Winston Churchill's dramatic escape nine years before he became prime minister and led the free world against the tyranny of Hitler poses one of the big "what-ifs" of the twentieth century. It also takes us to the heart of the first of the three sources of evil and suffering in our everyday lives—our bodies.

The Unwalled City of Man

There is a marvel to the design of the human body, and in some cases a strength or beauty that takes the breath away. One need only think of the sculptures of Phidias, Michelangelo, and Rodin, of athletes we admire, or of the bodies of those we each have grown to love. At the same time the reach of the human mind is astonishing, and the accomplishments of the human imagination dazzle each succeeding generation. But even the strongest and most beautiful bodies do not remain so forever.

Menaced by abortion and genetic dysfunction before we are born, by sickness and accident at any moment of our lives, by old age and death at the end of our lives—the wonder is not that we realize we are fragile and vulnerable, but that at any time we ever fall for the conceit that we are not. Yet many people in their late teens and early twenties live as if they will live forever, and many of us who are older act, talk, and joke as if to perpetuate the illusion.

We are mortal, simply mortal, and to say so is not morbid but realistic. Set against the time span of our own creations, such as books and buildings, let alone the longevity of redwood trees, mountain ranges, and the universe itself, our little lives are as brief as a candle. Surely we do not need telling: we are small, we are weak, we are fragile and vulnerable. We are here only for a moment, and the thread of our lives can be snapped in the blink of an eye.

Blaise Pascal, the great French mathematician and philosopher whose own life was severed at the age of thirty-nine, was terribly aware of this fleeting smallness. "Man is but a reed," he wrote in his *Pensées,* "the most feeble thing in nature; but he is a thinking reed. The entire universe need not arm itself to crush him. A vapor, a drop of water suffices to kill him."

Pascal was not being pessimistic. He was arguing, from the perspective of his faith, that human fragility does not make human lives futile. "But, if the universe were to crush him, man would still be more noble than that which killed him, because he knows that he dies and the advantage which the universe has over him; the universe knows nothing of this." Still, the first half of his point remains true. Such is our basic human finiteness and our constant human fragility that no genetic luck or fitness program can halt the aging process forever, no surveillance system or weapon can ensure our complete safety, and no insurance scheme can protect us with a 100 percent guarantee. As humans, we are always and only mortals. The little power-packs that are our bodies eventually run down or are blasted or wasted into uselessness. The final lot for all of us is death.

"When it comes to death," the philosopher Epicurus wrote, "we all live in an unwalled city."

This realism can be expressed in a straightforward way, or with deepening shades of pessimism. The Spanish philosopher Unamuno took the former approach: "I am a man; all men are mortal; therefore I will die."

Examples of the latter are legion. David Hume, the Scottish skeptic and atheist, wrote: "The first entrance into life gives anguish to the new-born infant and to its wretched parent: weakness, impotence, distress attend each stage of that life, and it is, at last, finished in agony and horror."

Carl Sandburg wrote a poem—which he claimed was the shortest ever written in English—that underscores the same theme: "Born. Troubled. Died."

We cannot change this reality, though we can choose different reactions to it. One extreme is to trade on human vulnerability and exploit it. One of the terrible features of the mass murderers of modern times is their brutal assumption of the ease with which they can slaughter and dispose of the human body. The ghastly record of gas chambers, mass graves, killing fields, torture rooms, and suicide bombings attests to this simple fact. Central to the Rwanda massacre, for example, was the Hutus' repeated use of the word *cockroach*, both to demean their Tutsi enemies and to taunt them with their openness to extermination.

"You cockroaches must know you are made of flesh," a broadcaster ranted on "Hutu Power" radio RTLM in 1994. "We won't let you kill. We will kill you."

The effect is the same even when the intentions are better, as when civilian and military planners "look through" the human beings who are the "collateral damage" resulting from their decisions. As one of the survivors of Hiroshima said to his doctor, "A human being who has been roasted becomes quite small, doesn't he?"

At the other extreme, and far more respectably, it is equally possible to deny human vulnerability altogether. As the worlds of fitness and fashion show, entire industries in the Western world are dedicated to the illusion that the health, fitness, and beauty of our faces and bodies can be sustained forever. Writing from Los Angeles, Rabbi David Volpe comments: "In L.A. there is no autumn. People do not wish to age. They want to be young up to the day they die. Aging, with its insinuation of the end, is terrible to the city of illusions."

Sailing into the Darkness

We are now aware as never before of the possible breakdowns of the mind. As diseases such as schizophrenia and Alzheimer's show, our minds are just as vulnerable to decline and decay as our bodies.

To those who especially enjoy the life of the mind, or who live by their ideas, the challenge of Alzheimer's disease is particularly chilling. As the fate of President Reagan shows, Alzheimer's is no respecter of persons. *Elegy for Iris* by John Bayley draws back the veil and portrays the descent into darkness of one of the great creative minds of our day. Dame Iris Murdoch, portrayed in the film *Iris* by Dame Judi Dench, had been married to Bayley, a professor of English, for forty-three years. She was a distinguished Oxford philosopher who wrote twenty-six novels and a dozen works of philosophy, and she had received a long string of honorary doctorates from the world's major universities.

Yet none of this counted for anything when Alzheimer's clouded and then darkened Iris Murdoch's mind. Her legendary logic disappeared, as did her concentration, her ability to form coherent sentences, her knowledge of where she was and where she had been, and even her ability to remember who she was. What was the greatest loss? Was it her creativity, her memory, their relationship as husband and wife, or simply her sense of identity? All these qualities depended on her mind, and as her mind went her face took on more and more of a masklike quality. The face of the Alzheimer's patient, Bayley writes, is a "lion's face." It has a "leonine impassivity" that speaks only of "an absence."

Was Iris Murdoch aware of what was happening to her? Often there was no hint that she was, though sometimes she betrayed signs of fear, as if she knew. Twice she said to a friend that she felt she was "sailing into the darkness." And Bayley saw the steady diminishing of her clear remarks as social statements. "They have the air of last remarks before all the lights go out."

Hard to Bear

What does the vulnerability of our bodies mean for our exploration of the challenge of evil and suffering?

First, as with the other two sources of evil and suffering, it represents a blunt and inescapable lesson in realism. If this is who we are, no faith or philosophy that ignores this fact is worthy of the examined life. Some people, sadly, twist this lesson in realism to justify their contempt for human life; most see it as a spur to compassion. But the lesson remains.

This vulnerability is precisely the setting of Freud's famous comment in *Civilization and Its Discontents* that "life is hard to bear" (echoed in the opening words of Scott Peck's *The Road Less Traveled*: "Life is difficult"):

Unhappiness is much less difficult to experience. We are threatened with suffering from three directions: from our own body, which is doomed to decay and dissolution and which cannot even do without pain and anxiety as warning signals; from the external world, which may rage against us with overwhelming and merciless forces of destruction; and finally from our relations with other men.

Second, the vulnerability of our bodies reminds us that we need to make a more careful distinction between evil and suffering in our exploration. So far I have bracketed them together as if they were the same thing, but of course they are not. And how we see the distinctions depends on our interpretations of life and evil, which we examine later.

In the traditional Western view, evil—the intent to harm another—has been seen as more active than suffering and therefore as morally culpable and a source of suffering, whereas suffering has been viewed as more passive and not in itself evil. In a mugging, for example, the mugger is active, responsible, and evil, and the victim is innocent and passive, though the one who suffers.

Today, however, many people deny that evil has any objective reality at all. The only evil left, in this view, is the fact that human beings suffer. Put simply, evil was once the source of suffering, but for many people today, suffering—especially extreme and apparently senseless suffering—is the only source of evil.

Third, an appreciation of the vulnerability of our bodies points up questions that our later interpretations must answer. In this case, the challenge is to account for the extraordinary paradox at the heart of human nature: how can human beings be so great and so weak, so noble and so vile, so consequential in their deeds and so fleeting in their lives?

"What a piece of work is a man!" Shakespeare's Hamlet says to his friends. "How noble in reason! How infinite in faculty! In form, in moving, how express and admirable! In action how like an angel! In apprehension how like a god! The beauty of the world, the paragon of animals. And yet, to me, what is this quintessence of dust?"

I well remember the first time I saw a dead body. I was nine years old and walking on a golf course in Hong Kong. Earlier, I had often seen old Chinese men sitting contemplating their own coffins. And I had just escaped from Nanking, the former nationalist capital, so the memory of Mao's reign of terror was fresh in my mind. But both the quiet contemplation of death and the terror of the trials and executions were one thing, and what I saw in front of me was another: the body was lying under a gorse bush, and its decomposition was in grotesque contrast to the brilliance and beauty of the yellow flowers. The word *paradox* was not in my vocabulary at that age, but the reality most certainly was.

Since then I have been with many people in their moment of dying, but I have never forgotten the impression of that first encounter. There is a marvel, a beauty, and a belovedness about the human body, but that is only half of the paradox. Our little bodies are also as brief as a candle and as fragile as an eggshell, and the examined life must always remember it is so.

CHAPTER 3

WHAT A GAME OF CHANCE LIFE IS

One of my most treasured possessions is an old family Bible belonging to my grandfather, on a blank page of which he wrote—in the dark—what he thought were his last words as he was about to be butchered by a rampaging mob on July 10, 1900. Twenty-six years old, a Cambridge-educated doctor, and the great-grandson of Arthur Guinness, the Dublin brewer, he had left behind the world of Europe and gone to China to open up a hospital in Henan, China's most populous province, where the need for medicine was overwhelming.

On May 24, 1900, the British legation in Beijing had celebrated Queen Victoria's eighty-first and last birthday in an atmosphere of general calm and serenity. But within less than a month, the rebellion of the Boxers, or the "Society of the Righteous Fists," engulfed the capital, and a spasm of bloody violence convulsed China. In June a decree went out from the Empress Dowager herself: "Foreigners must be killed! Even if they retire, foreigners still are to be killed!"

By the time the Boxer Rebellion was over, 250 missionaries and more than 32,000 Chinese Christians had been slaughtered. Westerners were hacked to death, children were beheaded in front of their parents' eyes, and carts were driven backward and forward over the bodies of half-naked women until they were dead.

When the rebellion broke out, my grandfather, with only three years' experience in China, found himself in the old medieval capital of Kaifeng as the leader of a tiny band of Westerners, including a six-week-old baby. Taking refuge in a loft infested with cockroaches and rats, and also reputed to be haunted, they huddled in the stifling heat, with little drink and no food, for six long days. All around them they could hear the angry shouts of the murderous mob and the roar and crackle of flames as successive hospital buildings were set on fire. But the baby never cried, and the fear of the haunted building shielded them from a closer search.

At one stage the rioters with flaming torches were clambering over the roof above them, threatening to set the building on fire; from below, one of the ringleaders thrust up a sword into the trap-door on which my grandfather was sitting—fortunately missing him, and any hopes of a family future, by inches. Finally, under cover of darkness, my grandfather and his tiny band were able to slip out and begin the perilous thousand-mile journey through Boxer-infested country to the coast and safety.

A Famine for the History Books

My parents' stories from the thirties and early forties in China were equally hair raising, though they were not about incidents worthy of the world's headlines. Ten-mile runs with bandits in hot pursuit, friends beheaded by the rising tide of Communist insurgents, daily strategies to escape the assaults of Japanese bombers, survivors' seared memories from the horror of the Japanese massacre of Nanking—my mother and father were well acquainted with the dangers and devastation of being at the mercy of hard, cold, pitiless men. But none of these experiences, they said, prepared them for the unmitigated horror of the Henan famine in the winter of 1943.

Famines are unnecessary in today's world. Those that still occur are humanly induced, the result of callousness or political ideologies, such as Muslim fanaticism in Sudan. But in China in those days famines were a recurring feature of life, so common and so devastating that families marked their histories by them. The province of Henan was prone to famine, not because it was poor, backward, and crowded, but because its fertile yellow soil depended crucially on rain. When the rains came, the harvests were rich; when they did not, nothing at all could be grown and the peasants died. In 1942 there was no rain, and by 1943 people were dying by the thousands.

Theodore White, the famous *Time* correspondent and author of *The Making of the President*, was then a young reporter in China who sent back harrowing accounts of the Henan famine. By his estimate, five million people died in the space of a few months. The devastation of drought, aggravated by the ravages of war and the callousness and ineptitude of the distant, uncaring government of Chiang Kai-shek, made for a disaster beyond comprehension. What struck White first were the endless lines of people, strung-out families stumbling along in a hopeless search for food that was not there. Then people began dropping by the hundreds and thousands—exhausted, hungry, cold, despairing—and dying where they fell.

Food became the sole business of life and the one desperate obsession. Without it, death was sure. Lovers clutched each other in a long, farewell embrace out in the fields, intertwined to give themselves warmth until death released them. Speculators swarmed in to buy up land. Parents sold their children for food, and rumors of cannibalism were rife. "Fundamentally," White wrote later in his account *In Search of History*, "there was no idea that could embrace what was happening. . . . Compassion, kinship, customs, morals were swept away." It was no wonder, he said, that the Henan peasants went over to the Japanese the next year to help them defeat their own government—and then over to the conquering Communists to seek their help in turn.

"I know how cruel Chinese communists can be," White concluded, "but no cruelty was greater than the Henan famine."

My parents' stories were equally graphic, printed indelibly on their minds. My mother was a surgeon, but without food or medicine, she might as well have been a stockbroker or a ballet dancer for all the medical help she could bring to the sick and dying. And as isolated Westerners in an ocean of despair, they were besieged with impossible requests and burdened with hopes they could not fulfill. Babies were left on their doorstep, beggars clung to them in the streets, officials and heads of families groveled before them, pleading for food and medicine that they did not have—not even for themselves.

As the long, slow, silent nightmare unfolded, my two brothers died too. Weakened by malnutrition and racked by dysentery, one succumbed among the five million dead in the famine, and the other among the twenty million victims of the invasion. My younger brother was buried on the eve of our setting out on the long trek on foot to India and safety. I was on the verge of death too, several times, as was my mother. But somehow we survived, made it across China, over the Himalayas, and lived to tell a tale as awful as any my parents ever experienced.

Lunch with Friends, Dinner with Ancestors

The story of the Henan famine opens up the second of the three sources of evil and suffering in our lives—nature, or natural disasters. Not only are our little bodies fragile and vulnerable in themselves, but our vulnerability is magnified into pathetic helplessness when we are up against the monumental forces of the universe.

Yes, nature can attack us individually through disease or accident, but large natural disasters make clear our plight in the face of nature's unfriendly displays. With our science, technology, medicine, and insurance, we can keep the worst at bay and shelter ourselves from its most harmful effects. But this has not been the case for most people throughout history. Fires, floods, storms, hurricanes, tornadoes, earthquakes, tidal waves, avalanches, volcanoes, and, supremely, disease, epidemics, and plagues—all these can be added to famine in the long list of terrible reminders of the suddenness of disaster and the rag-doll helplessness of its victims.

We have our limited list of disasters in the Western world, and we tend to think of them almost in stereotypes—earthquakes for the Californians, tornadoes for the Kansans, hurricanes for the Floridians, storms for the Scots, floods for the Italians, and forest fires for the Australians—as if such hazards were as regional as cuisines, and as if the rest of us could reduce our experience of horror to a special genre of action film with computerized effects in plush, air-conditioned cinemas.

Three far rougher features, however, characterize real reactions to natural disaster, especially outside the modern world. The first is suddenness. Typically, such disasters come right out of the blue. They hit like a blow to the solar plexus, and there is little we can do to predict them, let alone prepare for them. The poet Boccaccio, writing on the Black Death that hit Italy in 1347, remarked that the victims often "ate lunch with their friends and dinner with their ancestors in paradise."

Part of the suddenness is objective and part is psychological. There are things we know but do not want to know, and one of them is death. In Albert Camus's wartime novel *The Plague*, in which he uses the plague as a metaphor for evil, he describes the citizens of Oran as going on living as usual despite the outbreak of the plague. "How should they have given a thought to anything like plague, which rules out any future, cancels journeys, silences the exchange of views. They fancied themselves free, and no one will ever be free so long as there are pestilences."

The second feature of natural disasters is the sense of helplessness they induce. There is no more heartwarming sight than a fire in the hearth, but the roar of a forest ablaze is terrifying. As normal life becomes more routine and boring, extreme sports have come into vogue; it is one thing, however, to ski a Himalayan glacier or surf in a Hawaiian green cathedral, and another to be caught in an avalanche or in the path of a killer wave. We set off our nuclear explosions and pity the poor people below them, but woe betide those who lie in the path of a twister or are hit by the wall of a hurricane. In the face of such disasters, the strongest and most resourceful of us are like toddlers before a raging bull or like matchsticks in a white-hot furnace.

The third feature of natural disasters is the chaos and havoc they create. As humans, we love freedom, but we need order and security to enjoy freedom. The devastation of disaster is a primal havoc that strikes not only at our homes and our worlds but at our very sense of being. And all too often, as Shakespeare says in *Hamlet* and as the story of Job shows as well, "When sorrows come, they come not single spies, but in battalions." In his *History of the Peloponnesian Wars*, Thucydides reports on the plague that struck Athens in 430 B.C. "The nature of the distemper was such as to baffle all description, and its attacks almost too grievous for human nature to bear." As a result, "men now coolly ventured on what they had normally done in a corner. . . . Fear of gods or of man there was none to restrain them."

To be sure, disasters often bring out the best in people. They can rise to the occasion with acts of exceptional heroism and compassion. But a fourteenth-century proverb demonstrates the cowardice—or canniness—of many others: "The best means against plague is a pair of new boots used till they break."

Was Lisbon Worse Than London?

Just as we did with the first source of evil and suffering, our bodies, so we must ask with the second: what does the appreciation of natural disasters mean for our exploration of the challenge of evil and suffering?

First, it again underscores the lesson of realism, but this time in the direction of complete helplessness rather than potential vulnerability. Natural disasters strike terror into human hearts because there is so little we can do to prevent them and often no way we can escape them. Indeed, we might call them "nature's terrorists," for they seem as mindless as they are merciless. They make us feel "jumpy at home" because they remind us that our universe home is not a place in which we can rest with final order and security.

Second, an appreciation of our human helplessness in the face of natural disasters points up further questions for our later interpretations. Most obviously, natural disasters raise searching questions for all who believe in a personal God and his providence or those who take refuge in stock phrases such as "an act of God." How can God be just, let alone benevolent, if such disasters fall on the innocent and the guilty alike?

That was exactly Voltaire's line of attack after the Lisbon earthquake in 1755. "Will you say," he wrote in a famous poem: "This is the result of eternal laws / Directing the acts of a free and good God?"

> *Did Lisbon, which is no more, have more vices*
> *Than London or Paris immersed in their pleasures?*
> *Lisbon is destroyed and they dance in Paris!*

Later, writing to his doctor in Lyons, Monsieur Tronchin, Voltaire waxed more angry still. "This is indeed a cruel piece of natural philosophy! We shall find it difficult to discover how the laws of movement operate in such fearful disasters . . . where a hundred thousand ants, our neighbors, are crushed in a second on our ant-heaps, dying undoubtedly in inexpressible agonies, beneath debris from which it was impossible to extricate them." Voltaire's conclusion? "What a game of chance human life is!"

Less obviously, natural disasters also raise questions for secularists—because of the catastrophe to end all catastrophes that, according to scientists, will finally end the universe. A philosophy of life must engage not only the short-term scale of human history but the long-term scale of cosmic history. If, as secularists believe, everything in the universe comes from chance and moves toward ultimate extinction, a hope based on human progress in history alone amounts to short-term whistling in the dark set against final futility—even if what one physicist calls "the stay of execution" extends well beyond our tiny lives.

Is the universe ultimately cosmos or chaos? If the immediate evidence for human progress is debatable, natural disasters show us the face of an inhospitable universe here and now, and the final prospect for the human race is extinction, then the grounds for secularist optimism amid the chaos of a chance universe become thinner and thinner. As we shall see, the austere courage of Bertrand Russell's variety of secularism has its own nobility, but it is a far cry from the sunny optimism of ungrounded suburban atheism.

Plainly, Jews, Christians, and secularists all have questions to carry forward in the light of natural disasters. Ours is a generation in which scientists and filmmakers routinely imagine scenarios of the end of the world, with the oxygen burnt up and the sun swelling into a gigantic red ball that burns all life on the earth to a cinder—quite literally, a catastrophe to end all catastrophes. But ours is also a generation that is seeing the slow, wasting scourge of AIDS become the most destructive plague in history—now projected to take more than 100 million lives. Even in the modern world—especially in the modern world—we dare not shut our eyes to the place of natural disaster. Accounting for the disastrous is a surprisingly central part of living the examined life.

CHAPTER 4

OUR GREATEST ENEMY

Some of the world's greatest thinking has been prompted by some extremely varied settings, only rarely a classroom or a lecture hall. For Heraclitus, it was a river. For the Buddha, a tree. For Archimedes, a bathtub. For Socrates, a marketplace and a dinner party. For Aristotle, two royal palaces. For Descartes, a heating stove. For Isaac Newton, an apple tree. For Ludwig Wittgenstein, a don's room, with a fire and a poker. The eminent contemporary philosopher Eleonore Stump needed no more than the headlines in her daily newspaper.

In her moving essay "The Mirror of Evil," Stump writes simply, "Contemplation of human suffering tends to raise the problem of evil." She then takes examples of human suffering from her morning newspaper in the early 1990s.

> Although the marines are in Somalia, some armed Somalis are stealing food from their starving neighbors, who are dying by the thousands. Muslim women and girls, some as young as ten years old, are being raped and tortured by Serb soldiers. In India, Hindus went on a rampage that razed a mosque and killed over 1,000 people. In Afghanistan gunmen fired into a crowded bazaar and shot ten people, including two children.

Her circle of examples sweeps closer and closer to her own home-town, and she finishes with the story of a man tried for murder in the death of a nine-year-old boy he used as a shield in a gunfight. "I could go on," Stump says, "racism, rape, assault, murder, greed and exploitation, war and genocide—but this is enough." We could fill in the stories from our own newspapers today. Which leads to her central theme: "There is no time, no part of the globe, free from evil. The crust of the earth is soaked with the tears of the suffering."

Stump points out that we all respond differently to such evils. Some look away. Like cheerful hobbits, they go about their business not unduly worried by what they have seen. Others look at the evil and cannot get it out of their minds. Others again work hard at forgetting, drinking or throwing themselves into work. Still others set out to eliminate evil, Good Samaritans and reformers on a global scale. And some react with loathing to what they have seen—loathing the world or loathing themselves. To all of us, however, the central thrust of the evidence is plain. "This evil is a mirror for us. It shows us our world; it also shows us ourselves."

Stump then fires her questions point-blank:

> How could anyone steal at gunpoint food meant for starving children? How could anyone rape a ten-year-old girl? How could anyone bear to steal money from disabled workers or get rich by selling a product he knows will damage the health of thousands? But people do these things, and much worse things as well. We ourselves—you and I, that is—are members of the species that does such things.

To sharpen her point against those who say they live in a night in which all cats are gray, Stump distinguishes between "ordinary wrongdoing and real wickedness." She argues that, for all our sophisticated views, we know the difference intuitively. "A young Muslim mother," she recounts from her newspaper's coverage of the Bosnian war, "was repeatedly raped in front of her husband and father, with her baby screaming on the floor beside her. When her tormentors seemed finally tired of her, she begged permission to nurse the child.

In response, one of the rapists swiftly decapitated the baby and threw the head in the mother's lap."

"The taste of real wickedness," Stump declares, "is sharply different from the garden-variety moral evil, and we discern it directly, with pain."

The Same Species We Are

Eleonore Stump's account, of which this is only the beginning, is distinctly different from the treatment of most philosophers. And it introduces us directly to the third and last of the three sources of evil and suffering in our everyday worlds—our fellow human beings.

The point is not new, of course, though it runs directly counter to the Enlightenment strain of utopianism that until recently proved so stubbornly resistant to reality. Far from being essentially good—and improving all the time, with occasional lapses on the upward evolutionary path to perfection—our human nature is blatantly contradictory. Its nobility and evident goodness are offset by an equally evident propensity to plan and carry out acts of the most malevolent and destructive kind—whether brazenly monstrous, devilishly subtle, or yawningly routine. Quite apart from the gruesome record of the last century, the evidence of history and our own hearts is clear: we are capable of the very best and the very worst.

And to be blunt, when we speak of "our fellow human beings" as a source of evil and suffering, we are not just talking of other people. We are talking of ourselves. We have to include ourselves, for not only are we the "others" to others, we often do the worst and most foolish things to ourselves.

We do not usually take the one drink too many at the point of a gun. We do not typically help ourselves to the extra-extra helping of ice cream under a torturer's pressure. We do not normally smoke a pack of cigarettes with a sword hanging over our heads. We rarely have to believe the destructive things people say to us because we have no alternative. If we do these things and get caught for driving under the influence, or suffer problems from being overweight, or succumb to cancer from too much nicotine, or develop an inferiority complex, it is because we choose to do these things, and often we choose to do them knowing the consequences full well.

Needless to say, the dark side of human nature is no more the full story than the bright side. But it must be taken into account as the warranted conclusion of the open-eyed and the honest, not simply dismissed as the grumpy pessimism of certain misanthropes or reactionary Neanderthals.

"What region of the earth is not full of our calamities?" Virgil wrote in the *Aeneid*.

"Man," Thomas Hobbes wrote in *De Homine*, is "the most cunning, the strongest, and most dangerous animal."

"I pity the Portuguese, like you," Voltaire wrote to a Protestant pastor after the Lisbon earthquake, "but men do still more harm to each other on their little molehill than nature does to them. Our wars massacre more men than are swallowed up by earthquakes."

"Man," Rousseau wrote in *Émile*, "seek the author of evil no longer. It is yourself."

"Man is the greatest enemy of man," Hume wrote in his *Dialogues Concerning Natural Religion*.

"The defining feature of humanity is inhumanity," Ambrose Bierce wrote in *The Devil's Dictionary* after the carnage of the American Civil War—a paradox that Elie Wiesel echoed eerily in a comment in an interview: "Man is not human."

"We talk of wild animals," G. K. Chesterton wrote in *Orthodoxy*, "but man is the only wild animal. It is man that has broken out."

Man, Ernest Becker wrote in *Escape from Evil*, is "the most devastating animal that ever stuck its neck up into the sky."

"There are no categories to express such horror," U.S. ambassador Robert Seiple wrote after returning from Rwanda following the massacre in 1994. "Someone used the word 'bestiality'—no, that dishonors the beasts. Animals kill for food, not for pleasure. They kill one or two prey at a time, not a million for no reason at all."

Most of us would pride ourselves on our honesty and our realism.

As thinking people, few of us knowingly choose to be ostriches with our heads in the sand when it comes to human nature. But a recurring feature of the worst evils is their capacity to shock and sober the most realistic and hardened.

Elie Wiesel encountered Auschwitz as a sheltered teenager, and his soul-shuddering shock was understandable as he turned to his father and said, "The world, Father, the civilized world would not allow such things to happen." But his postwar comment in *Night* was written from the other side of such innocence. "And yet the civilized did know, and remained silent. Where was man in all this? And culture, how did it reach this nadir?"

"We knew man was evil," said one of the American soldiers who liberated Auschwitz, "but hadn't suspected he was *that* evil."

In his searing book on the Rwanda massacre, *We Wish to Inform You That Tomorrow We Will Be Killed with Our Families*, Philip Gourevitch tells of a visit to a church with one of those who gave him firsthand accounts of the horror. "We stood in silence in the empty chapel with its cement pews. On the floor below the altar stood four memorial coffins, draped in white sheets, painted with black crosses. 'The people who did this,' Arcene said, 'didn't understand the idea of a country. What is a country? What is a human being? They had no understanding.'"

The Woeful Century

Toward the end of the nineteenth century, A. R. Wallace, a scientific rival to Charles Darwin, wrote a book titled *The Wonderful Century*. After almost complete peace in Europe for the best part of a hundred years, following the Treaty of Vienna in 1815, and in the wake of what were probably the greatest scientific advances and social changes in all history, his late-Victorian euphoria was understandable.

For Europeans, however, that little idyll and all its illusions went down forever in the mud and carnage of battles such as the Somme in World War I. And now, just over one hundred years later, in the after-

math of a century of wars, revolutions, totalitarian tyrannies, and nuclear and environmental crises, utopian dreams seem quaint; apocalyptic fears have replaced them in private imaginations, on cinema
screens, and in the angry shouts of protesters around the world.

Our recent black record need not, however, be a reason for pessimism—the twenty-first century may be as different from the twentieth as the twentieth was from the nineteenth, especially if we learn
the lessons taught by the sorrows of the last century. But there is no
doubt about the last century. What Solzhenitsyn called "the cave-
man's century" could equally be called the woeful century. And at the
heart of the twentieth century is the black fact that it was the most
murderous century in history and a lamentable witness to the sorry
state of human development at the high noon of the modern world.

How can we begin to take in the scale and scope of recent evil? "A
single death is a tragedy, a million deaths is a statistic." Joseph Stalin's
well-known remark pivots not only on the brutal cynicism that allowed
him to brush aside his atrocities but on the psychological defenses with
which we all shield ourselves from appreciating their horror. Or as
Stalin said to Churchill at Yalta, "It's only one generation."

Mass murderers can count on our incomprehension. As Hitler said
in urging his SS troops to enter Poland and kill without pity, "Who
now remembers the massacre of the Armenians?" It is literally
unimaginable to take in the full moral and emotional weight of millions and millions of slaughtered human beings. It would be too
much for us. Yet that is the story of our times, and it must become
part of the moral realism of its legacy.

"In the twentieth century," says a report of the International Association of Genocide Scholars, "genocides have killed more people than
all wars." And wars have taken more than one hundred million lives.

"Between 1914 and 1990, the population of the world tripled,"
writes Philip Bobbit in *The Shield of Achilles*, his monumental study of
war in history, "but an estimated 187 million persons—about ten percent of the population of 1900—were killed or fated to die by human
agency."

Is Religion to Blame?

We can argue over the estimates and debate the precise evidence, but we must never lose sight of the undeniable fact mentioned in chapter 1: more people were killed by secularist regimes in the twentieth century than in all the religious persecutions in Western history, and perhaps in all history.

Let me elaborate, for the issue is more than factual; it bears on the quality of our democratic debates. It is a widely held and largely unquestioned belief in educated circles today that religion is the main cause of repression and violence in our world and an essentially divisive and explosive force in public life that we would be wise to exclude from the public square altogether. For example, one *New York Times* reporter argued after September 11 that our main problem is not terrorism but "religious totalitarianism" and that the danger of religious totalitarianism was represented not just by Islam but by Judaism and the Christian faith as well—in fact, by all faiths that have "absolute" or "exclusive" claims. Only faiths that are relativistic—faiths that are "true for their believers" rather than true independently of any believers—are safe in the public square.

Another recent book warning about the evils of religion opens (and closes) with a similar point: "It is somewhat trite, but nevertheless sadly true, to say that more wars have been waged, more people killed, and these days more evil perpetrated in the name of religion than by any other institutional force in human history."

Whatever our personal views of religion, this statement is simply and factually wrong, and its lazy repetition seriously distorts public debate and endangers democratic freedom. Its root is an unexamined Enlightenment prejudice that simultaneously reduces faith to its functions and recognizes only the worst contributions of faith, not the best—such as the rise of the universities, the development of modern science, the abolition of slavery, and the promotion of human rights.

Obviously, there have been egregious religious massacres and persecutions in history, each one as vile as it was real. Among the most notorious Christian evils in the Western story are the slaughter of the

Albigensians (killing around 60,000), the massacre of St. Bartholomew (another 30,000), the Sicilian Vespers (8,000), the Spanish Inquisition (10,000), and the expulsion of the Jews from Spain (160,000 uprooted from their homes).

Obviously, too, the prejudice against religion gains its head-nodding acceptance today from the fact that atrocities such as September 11 were committed in the name of Allah and by Islamic extremists. But when the argument then jumps to the position that religion should have no place in public life because it is private at best and pathological at worst, it does more than distort the truth: it impoverishes public life and undercuts the sustainability of democracy itself.

I have long been a proponent of the "civil public square," set off clearly from the extremes of the "sacred public square" on one side and the "naked public square" on the other. The full arguments for genuine democratic diversity would take us too far afield to be in-cluded here, but two straightforward facts contradict today's widely accepted myth.

First—and more theoretically—secularist philosophies such as athe-ism are just as "totalitarian" as the three "religions of the Book." What secularists believe is so total, or all-encompassing, that it excludes what the religious believer believes. No atheist I know says, "I don't believe God exists, but I believe he is *there for you*." On the contrary, every athe-ist I have ever encountered—and they would include such eminent atheists as the philosophers Bertrand Russell and A. J. Ayer—says that there is no such thing as God and that anyone who persists in believing in God is putting his faith in an illusion, a figment of the imagination, and a projection.

Secularists would, of course, reply, "Yes, that is true, but it does not prevent atheists from respecting the right of religious believers to believe what they want, however false it may be."

Exactly. In other words, the totality of the intellectual coherence of atheism need not translate into totalitarian political coercion. And that is precisely the position of all but a tiny handful of Jews and Christians today toward people of other faiths, including secularist faiths—despite their absolute and exclusive claims. Historically, the great advance of freedom of conscience in the seventeenth and eighteenth centuries owed more to religious believers than to secularist skeptics.

Thus, contrary to what is commonly argued, our problem in the public square is not "religious totalitarianism," and the solution is not a "multilingual relativism" that bans all absolute and exclusive claims. In a day of exploding diversity, the real question is: how do we live with our deepest differences when many of those differences are absolute, including those of secularism? This question, which is vital for the future of democracy, would take us beyond our present topic. But raising it properly frees us from the distortions of the current public debate.

The second, and more practical, fact is that more than one hundred million human beings were killed by secularist regimes and ideologies in the last century. Secularists, and particularly secularist intellectuals and opinion-makers in the press and media, owe the public debate a larger dose of humility as well as candor.

Hitler and the Nazis are something of a special case. Hitler was implacably hostile to the Christian faith, but not an advocate of atheism. With good reason, he and his extermination camps are often taken as the epitome of twentieth-century evil; no comparisons will ever mitigate their evil. But to blame the Christian faith or the Catholic Church for Hitler and his henchmen is a travesty of truth.

Almost to a person, as the history of Nazism and the record of the Nuremberg trials attest, the Nazi leaders were ex-Christians and ex-Catholics. Those, including Hitler, who had Christian backgrounds vehemently rejected them. "I shall never come to terms with the Christian lie," he declared. "Our epoch will certainly see the end of the disease of Christianity. It will last another hundred years, two hundred years perhaps. My regret will have been that I couldn't, like whoever the prophet was, behold the promised land from afar." Eichmann too was clear beyond doubt. As Arendt reported, he declared in his trial in Jerusalem that he was no *Gottgläubiger* "to express in common Nazi fashion that he was no Christian and did not believe in life after death."

There is no such ambivalence when it comes to communism. The full story of the evils of Stalin and Mao is yet to be unearthed and told with anything like the completeness accorded to Hitler and the Nazis, but the secularist commitments are clear beyond dispute. Communism, the most dangerous delusion in history so far, has been accurately described as an atheistic millennialism. Our most damning evidence to date is *The Black Book of Communism*. A huge and exactingly meticulous eight-hundred-page compendium written by scholars who are ex-Communists or former fellow travelers, the book reads as if the recording angel of history had written the greatest indictment ever brought against a human crime—the Communist crimes against world civilization, against national cultures, and, above all, against multitudes and multitudes of human beings too numerous to name and even to count.

What does it mean to say that Cambodia's Pol Pot slaughtered two million people—a quarter of his nation's population? Or that Stalin murdered thirty million and Mao sixty-five million? Does the staggering "relative weight" of the first equal the equally staggering "numerical weight" of the other two? The mind boggles at such questions, and the heart becomes numb at the mention of such figures. We have no calculus to measure them, and our emotions are not strong enough to embrace them. The historian Will Durant once estimated that in all history there have been only twenty-nine years in which there was no war under way somewhere, but does this say something overwhelming about us as humans or is it only a tasty morsel for dinner party conversation?

In his magisterial moral history of the twentieth century, *Humanity*, Jonathan Glover points out that even those who do not believe in a religious moral law should be troubled by its fading. "It is striking how many protests against and acts of resistance to atrocity have also come from principled religious commitment." Among others, he mentions Bishop George Bell confronting the bombing of civilians in World War II, the philosopher Elizabeth Anscombe's protest against Oxford University's honoring of President Harry Truman after Hiroshima, André and Magda Trocme's stand against the Nazis in Le Chambon, and the bishops in Denmark rescuing thousands of Jews.

Dietrich Bonhoeffer and Helmut James von Moltke are still others whose stands were the direct result of their faith.

Genocidal statistics such as those just cited are from the Communist atrocities, but the secularist dimension—as the U.S. ambassador Henry Morgenthau witnessed in World War I—goes right back to the Young Turk leadership of the Armenian massacre. And when we go wider still and recall the full twentieth-century story by adding the numbers from non-Marxist countries and nonsecularist massacres—from the one and a half million Armenians massacred through to the two million Christians and animists slaughtered in the Sudan in the 1990s to the three or four million victims of the current civil war in the Congo—the counter ticks at an insane speed.

And of course, humanly perpetrated evil covers the little and local abuses of power too. It includes not only the tortured and the slain who were massacred by the millions but also the neglected child, the abused teenager, the battered wife, the cheated employee, and the robbed pensioner.

Both morally and emotionally, the fact of modern evil is simply too much—far, far too much. Yet sadly, it is also true.

Tears for Humanity

What does this third source mean for our exploration of evil?

First, as with the two previous sources—nature and our bodies—our exploration of our fellow human beings as a source of evil underscores the element of realism—but this time with such force that we are either moved to compassion and action or else hardened beyond caring. In his 1893 essay "The Tragic," Ralph Waldo Emerson wrote: "He has seen but half the universe who has never been shown the house of Pain. As the salt sea covers more than two-thirds of the surface of the globe, so sorrow encroaches in man on felicity." In today's world the fellowship of human suffering includes more members, in more countries, and with greater reasons, than ever before in history.

Second, the scale of suffering because of human inhumanity in the modern world raises titanic questions about our practical responses, whether as private citizens or as leaders at the highest levels of our nations. One of the effects of globalization today is that our eyes vastly outreach our hands and our pockets. We always see more evil and suffering than we can possibly respond to. So we have to make sure that we have reasons, not excuses, when we do not respond, and that our reasons reflect true limitations, not rationalizations for walking by on the other side of the street. "Ignorance," "limited resources," "national sovereignty," "compassion fatigue," being "peacekeeping'd out," as the United Nations puts it—all these can be genuine or bogus reasons to turn away from evil. "In the end, does it really matter?" some say. "Finally, God only knows."

But it matters to the victims.

Romeo Dallaire, the Canadian general who commanded the UN forces in Rwanda during the massacre, suffered an emotional breakdown afterward. He was haunted by the thought that, given the green light by his superiors, "he could have stopped it." His comments on the later visit to Kigali by President Clinton were scathing: "Kept the engines on Air Force One running, spent a couple of hours in the airport terminal, and said he was sorry, he didn't know."

"Didn't know?" said Dallaire. "I saw the NATO electronic aircraft overhead. I've spent my life in NATO. I know what they do."

For himself, the general said later, he was still haunted in his dreams by the eyes—thousands and thousands of them, disembodied, staring out of the African darkness. "You can't just walk away from something like that saying you did what you could. . . . You can't just Pontius Pilate 800,000 people."

Third, this appreciation of the evil in human nature adds its own sharp questions to our later exploration of the interpretations. On the one hand, evil of the malevolence and magnitude of the last century exposes many of our modern explanations as shallow and inadequate. A generation ago, Ernest Becker, in his book *The Denial of Death*, argued that psychological categories are fundamentally inadequate to explain virulent evil. "Thus the plight of modern man: a sinner with no word for it, or, worse, who looks for the word for it in a dictionary of psychology and thus only aggravates the problem."

Becker's point was placarded for the world after the shootings at Columbine High School in Littleton, Colorado, in 1999. "Littleton Shootings Are Symptomatic of Male Identity Crisis," one headline ran, as "grief counselors" by the score flew in from all around America.

Reactions to such psychobabble were rightly indignant. "When we need Reinhold Niebuhr, we get fifty Dr. Joyce Brothers," the political theorist Jean Bethke Elshstain declared. "Part of the evil is all these experts coming out with their shrinky comments," said the psychiatrist Robert Coles. "The problem," said the historian Jackson Lears, "is that it leads to a stupefied response in the face of palpable instances of evil."

On the other hand, radical evil requires radical explanations, and the questions for our interpretations mount with increased urgency. Above all, we cannot avoid the fact that the present record of evil flies directly in the face of progressive and utopian views of human evolution. As I have stressed, the deepest questions about God are once again inseparably tied to the deepest questions about humanity.

A story from Auschwitz puts it simply. One prisoner turns to another and asks: "Where is God?"

A second prisoner replies, "Where is man?"

In our world today, neither question can be raised without the other.

QUESTION TWO

What's So Right
About a World So Wrong?

The second basic question explores the instinctive and irrepressible questions raised by the challenge of evil and suffering as it hits us. Whatever our eventual response to evil, it will be shaped by the questions that evil and suffering raise for us, and we need to listen to these with care.

Suffering is irreducibly individual. It never affects two people in exactly the same way. But experience shows that there is a widely shared response to the nub of suffering. The pain may be slight and fleeting, such as when stubbing a toe against a chair. Or it may be excruciating and life-changing, such as after the loss of a child. But in each case, what happens is that we expect one thing and encounter another. We desire something and discover something else. Expecting to find that life goes on unchanging and unsurprising, we are suddenly hit in the face by disruption and irrationality.

The deepest cases of pain and suffering cause the most savage rupture and create a sense of the most monstrous irrationality. The reaction goes far beyond loss of trust in the world. The mismatch between what we expect and what we encounter is so outrageous, and the experience so senseless, that it strikes us as flagrantly unfair. In a blind, raw reaction, we feel that such pain and suffering are somehow contrary to our very contract with life. These experiences violate our sense of the ground rules of human existence itself.

This raw reaction to the outrageous and the unfair is the breeding ground of the questions that evil and suffering raise—questions that are instinctive, irrepressible, and emphatically insistent on being answered. Three questions stand out among all the others:

1. *Why me?* This question about fairness probes our own personal responsibility as well as the responsibility of the universe.

2. *Where's God?* This question moves from the immediate to the ultimate, and from the experience to the explanation, and asks where the ultimate responsibility lies. The evil is so awful and so obvious that the buck must stop somewhere.

3. *How can I stand it?* Or in its more traditional form, "How long, O Lord?" This question is the most down-to-earth of the three. Suffering afflicts not only our bodies but our minds— and therefore our courage, our patience, and our endurance. Sometimes the pain is such that the challenge is just to get through the day, hanging on to the thought that the sun will rise tomorrow.

These three questions often overlap. Together they constitute one gigantic, concentrated protest thrown down like a gauntlet before the seeming unfairness of the universe. Life is outrageous and unfair. It hurts and we want to know why.

Notice that we are not yet examining answers, only questions. The focus here is on clarifying the questions before considering the answers. For answers we must wait until the fourth exploratory question. The issues are hard enough without complicating them further or leaping to premature answers.

Our task here is to examine the questions, to make sure we are looking for the right answers.

CHAPTER 5

WHY ME?

"It's much easier to be a terrorist than a policeman," an Irish Republican Army leader once boasted. "One split-second of violence spells success for a terrorist, whereas a lifetime of vigilance and one split-second of violence is failure for a policeman. Defensive forces can't afford to nod even once, but attackers need only be effective one time and they win."

In other words, not all moments in life are equal. Is it any surprise that few moments in life are more equal than those of supreme joy— or those in which evil and suffering crash into us and change the landscape of our existence forever?

So it was for Gerald Sittser, a college professor and his family in the Northwest of the United States. Nothing could have been more normal than the day on which all six of them packed themselves and their grandmother into a minivan and set off for an Indian reservation in Idaho. The Sittsers were home-schooling their children, and since the lesson was on Native American culture, they decided to take a field trip and introduce their children to a powwow at a Native American reservation. With Gerald's mother visiting and eager to join the excursion, their excitement was palpable, and the prospects for a vivid teaching experience were strong.

All went well. Dinner that evening provided the opportunity to talk with the tribal leaders about their project and about problems facing the tribe, such as alcoholism. When dinner was over, the family strolled to the gymnasium where the powwow had started and sat next to a tribal leader, who explained the dances the tribe was performing and the dress the dancers were wearing. After a long, full day, the moment came when the Sittser children had had enough, and so they all returned to the minivan and set off for home, tired but happy.

Ten minutes later their world changed forever. A drunken local, driving at eighty-five miles an hour with his pregnant wife next to him, also drunk, jumped his lane and smashed head-on into the minivan in the darkness. When Gerald, dazed, breathless, and in pain, was able to look back at the rest of his family, he was faced with terror on the faces of his surviving children and horror all around him. His wife, four-year-old daughter, and mother were dying, and his surviving children were panicking in the mayhem and chaos. Helpless, the father watched his wife, daughter, and mother all die before him—three generations of his family in a few terrible minutes.

Those moments are etched in Gerald Sittser's mind forever. Carnage, pandemonium, and panic, with lights flashing, orders barking, emergency vehicles circling, helicopters whirring overhead, and his children crying and groaning. But already there was the choking grip of anguish, the vicelike realization that darkness had descended and life would never be the same. His family as he had known it had been obliterated. Sixty seconds had changed the world.

Sixty seconds? Time to start munching into a hamburger, to listen to the opening bars of a symphony, to read the first page of a book, or to get an initial impression of a stranger—but time too to shatter a family's world forever. Moments heavy with pain and suffering far outweigh moments light with casual happiness.

Trust in Life

Such is the grand tale of human suffering that stories like this one, so shattering and sharply individual to those involved, could be multiplied endlessly to outside observers like the rest of us. For all the happy thoughtlessness of most of our lives, a single moment can change them forever, and that is why such experiences open up the first of the three instinctive questions squeezed out of us by pain and suffering: why me?

First responses to disasters are often nagged by the thought, *If only. . . .* Tugging at their minds, torturing their imaginations, and dominating the macabre replays of their memories, the survivors of the lethal crash were haunted by the thought that it had not been necessary, and even that it might not have been true. Three years later the Sittsers were still playing out the possibilities endlessly. "Dad," said a surviving son, "if I had only gone to the bathroom after the powwow, Mom would still be alive. If you had been busier that day, Mom would still be alive."

The hunt for a satisfying "if only" was endless. If only they had watched two more minutes of the powwow. If only they had pumped gas a little more slowly. If only the other driver had drunk one beer less or lingered to drink two beers more. The lines of possible thoughts shoot off in all directions because our minds are as restless as our hearts are inconsolable. But the harried search always comes back to the same brute fact of what actually happened—which is when the first of our three instinctive questions erupts: why me?

As modern, democratic people, we pride ourselves on our commitment to freedom. But a moment's thought shows us that our need for order is even more basic than our need for freedom—which is why human beings often submit to tyranny rather than feel the terror of their hands shaking in the face of chaos. Without order, even repressive order, life would be literally intolerable. We need order to make sense of our world and find security in our lives. We need order in our individual lives, order in our societies, and order in the very universe itself.

This trust in life, or trust in the world, is essential to everyday living. As the great social scientist Peter Berger points out, the child who cries out in the night and is reassured by its mother that "everything is all right" is invoking the mother as "a high priestess of protective order." It is she who has "the power to banish the chaos and restore the benign shape of the world." To be a parent, let alone a king or president, is to play the role of world-builder and world-protector. This trust may be grounded in truth or it may be an illusion and a projection. The mother may be a Christian, a Jew, a Muslim, a Buddhist, or an atheist, and she may explain it later in different ways. But as Berger says, the message is essentially the same right across the human experience: *"Everything* is in order, *everything* is all right," which essentially means, "Have trust in being."

But this sense of order is precisely what evil assaults. One moment we trust in the order of reality, and the next it is gone. Tragedy strikes, and solid ground shudders to reveal a yawning abyss and life's expected friendly welcome turns into a punch in the face. Jean Améry, a survivor of Auschwitz, described that first reaction in his book *At the Mind's Limits*: "I don't know whether the person beaten by the police loses human dignity. Yet I am certain that with the very first blow that descends on him he loses something that we'll temporarily call 'trust in the world.'"

Why me? Why did this happen to me? What did I do to deserve this? Such questions may be raised in anger or laced with self-pity or even murmured in depression. But every such question is the heart's protest against the disruption and disorder in evil and suffering. Like a corkscrew, the question "Why me?" bores down through deepening levels of our betrayed trust in life.

At the first level, it protests our loss of control. At the heart of the promise of the modern world are control and choice. Our birth, death, and genes are beyond our control. But much of the rest of our lives—our education, our job, our spouse, our friends, our home, our vacations, our cars, our entertainments, our retirement—are a matter of our own choice and come under our own control, or so at least we imagine.

Then disasters, sickness, or death blow such pretense to smithereens. Most of life is simply beyond our control.

At a deeper level, the question "Why me?" protests the unfairness of life. We are not claiming that we have no flaws, let alone that we are perfect. Most of us know our hearts too well to demand that life judge us according to our deserts. But the question is not really about us at all; it is about life and the world, and our trust in both.

From an aggrieved child cheated in a game to an angry claimant in a lawsuit to a vehement protester in a cause, the claim is the same and instinctive: we want justice, and we demand fairness. And the point is the same here. Argue any way you want about the grounds of justice—in God, in tradition, in economic interest, or in raw power—but the outcome is the same. If life is fair, some things require rewarding and some things require punishing. And if life is unfair—wildly and grotesquely unfair—we feel violated and terribly wronged.

There has to be redress. We may not be perfect, and we are not out for revenge, but we have our rights. Whatever the cause, no one and nothing can convince us that we deserved this. "Why me?" may be uttered with indignation or with a whine, but it represents the heart's notice of a legal complaint served against the universe itself. Of course we know that the innocent suffer every day, the wicked prosper all the time, and there is no end to the good dying young, but that is abstract. When life is unfair to us, it is different. We know the math of our own lives, and we do not need anyone else to add it up and tell us the sum is wrong.

The Terror of Randomness

At the deepest level of all, the question "Why me?" probes the frightening thought of ultimate chaos and the terror of randomness. Perhaps the universe is not our home. Perhaps it is finally absurd, not only deaf to our cries but menacing to our safety. Perhaps life is really a roulette wheel of death. Describing his feelings after the crash in which he lost the heart of his family, Gerald Sittser kept using the words *nervousness* and *terror*. He remembered an earlier conversation with his wife about an accident reported in their local newspaper. It haunted him now. A station wagon driven by a mother had skidded off the road, killing three of her six children. "We shivered with fear," he recalled of the conversation with his wife, "before the disorderliness of tragedy."

It was not just that something bad had happened to innocent people, "but that something bad had happened so randomly." The accident was not predictable, and the victims were not prepared. Life is not just difficult. Life turns out to be unfair, and cosmically unfair in a way that is terrifying. After that, the ground no longer seems so firm.

Soldiers and war veterans know this terror. One comrade on the battlefield is killed, another is seriously wounded, and a third walks off scot-free—apart from the haunting dreams. When General Leopoldo Galtieri was leader of Argentina's oppressive military regime, he visited a prison and spoke to a woman prisoner who had been tortured for months. "If I say you live, you live," he said, "and if I say you die, you die. As it happens, you have the same Christian name as my daughter, so you live."

Citizens of a city under sniper assault know this randomness. Today he strikes here, tomorrow there, and who knows where he will strike next? So the victims are truly victims. Their only fault is to be in the wrong place at the wrong time. It is certainly no fault of their own that they met with disaster—no more so than it was for those who happened to be visiting the World Trade Center on September 11, 2001, for those who found themselves in Hiroshima on August 6, 1945, for those whose parents gave birth to them as Jews in Nazi-occupied Europe, or for those whose travels took them to Lisbon rather than Paris or Madrid in November 1755.

Children often blame inanimate things for hurting them. "Naughty chair!" they say, for instance. As adults, by contrast, we have come to know that not everything that happens to us in life says something about us. But however mature we are, we often bracket that knowledge when suffering hits us. If something that bad has happened, we want to know why the universe has picked on us in life's great lottery of possibilities. There are so many in our world whose only fault is to have been born of the wrong parents, to be walking around in the wrong skin, and to be living in the wrong country at the wrong time.

Why Not Me?

For some of us, of course, the harrowing question is the reverse: why not me? I survived the Henan famine when my two brothers died; my friend made it down from the 104th floor of the Twin Towers when nearly seventy of his colleagues perished; Alexander Solzhenitsyn escaped the Gulag and recovered from inoperable cancer when millions died around him; and some Jews happened to get out of the Auschwitz trains on the right-hand side and entered the camp and lived, whereas others got out on the left-hand side and went to the gas chamber.

"Every survivor wonders why he is alive," said Abbé Modeste, a priest, after the Rwanda massacre.

Or as the psychiatrist Robert Jay Lifton wrote about the survivors of Hiroshima: "Whatever his sense of good or bad fortune, whatever his claimed virtue or inner sense of the opposite, the survivor's concerns about the accidents of survival reflect his profound feeling that he was saved by an unknowable destiny or fate."

"Why are you alive today while others are not?" Elie Wiesel and Philippe-Michäel de Saint Cheron ask in *Evil and Exile*. "In other words, what accounts for your survival? Do you think it was providence, predestination, miracle, or simply chance and dumb luck?"

Is it selfish and shameful to survive when others did not? Should we feel guilty? Or is it a matter of grace and gratitude? I have felt the latter all my life, and for Churchill it was a key component of his sense of destiny. "Why have I always been kept safe within a hair breadth of death," he asked, "except to do something like this?"

In contrast, Primo Levi, in *Survival in Auschwitz*, tells of an old Jew in his hut who thanked God when he survived the day's selection for the gas chamber. "Didn't he understand?" Levi retorted in anger. What had happened was an abomination, and no cause for gratitude by anyone to anyone. "If I was God, I would spit at Kuhn's prayer."

So it all goes, apparently. "Why me?" or "Why not me?" Does it matter which? For in our pain at being hit—or our relief at missing the blow—such experiences seem to turn life into a cosmic lottery, fabulous for the lucky winners but hellishly unfair for those with the short straws dealt out by sickness, tragedy, and evil.

Life Goes On

The final pressure in the question "Why me?" comes from the dull, obvious fact that for the rest of the world life just goes on. That is not how we feel it should be. What has hit us is like a hurt that throbs and throbs and allows us to think of nothing else. Just as we smash a hammer on a thumb and become all thumb, or stub a toe and become all toe, so the hurts in our lives shout for attention—and the bigger the hurt, the more it screams to be the center of the universe. We are hurting, and it is so painful that everyone should care. Anyone who does not surely has a deficiency of humanity.

But most people do not even notice. It is not that they do not care, but that they simply do not know and cannot be expected to care. W. H. Auden captured this haunting fact in his poem "Musée des Beaux Arts," written after viewing Pieter Brueghel's sixteenth-century canvas *Landscape with the Fall of Icarus*. The Old Masters were never wrong about suffering, he says. They well understood its position in human life—"how it takes place / While someone else is eating or opening a window or just walking dully along."

So a family loses its young mother to breast cancer while, a block away, neighbors are rolling with laughter at a television comedy. A middle-aged man despondently leaves his office for the last time, retired early with blank indifference, while outside on the street people are just strolling by. Or a torturer's victim spits out the blood from his battered mouth while in the café next door to the police station two lovers are gazing into each other's eyes over a glass of wine. Life just goes on. The cries of our hearts are unheard, and the loneliness adds to the pain.

For the philosopher Simone Weil, this aloneness is the very heart of the pain as well as what makes it true affliction. "Affliction," she wrote in an essay, "is anonymous . . . it deprives its victims of their personality and makes them into things. It is indifferent; and it is the coldness of this indifference—a metallic coldness—that freezes all those it touches right to the depth of their souls. They will never find warmth again. They will never believe any more that they are anyone."

All this and more is in the plea "Why me?" For none of us is safe. Life is not safe. The world is not safe, and we ourselves are not fully safe for the world and for others. Any of us may suffer, and all of us will die, but "Why me?" will still be a universal cry.

CHAPTER 6

WHERE'S GOD?

On the wall of my study, behind me as I write, are signed portraits and photographs of many of my heroes, including the great reformer William Wilberforce, the scintillating and prolific writer G. K. Chesterton, and Prime Minister Winston Churchill flashing his signature V sign. One of the most arresting is a photo of Elie Wiesel, next to which is a signed page from his searing essay on Auschwitz, *Night*. The photo was taken in his study in Manhattan when I interviewed him for a documentary, and almost invariably it sparks comments from friends, even from those who do not know who he is or do not recognize him from his photo.

With his slightly craggy features and his half-disheveled hair, it is easy to see Elie Wiesel in the photo as the prophet of the death camp survivors and a leading witness to twentieth-century evil. But it is his eyes that make people pause. Dark, intense, and visionary, they are looking into the distance, indifferent to the customary niceties of smiling vacantly for the photographer. Yet they draw you in, as if challenging you to see what he has seen and to see through the surface of things to their depth.

The signed page next to his photograph is one that has long riveted me. I remember sitting in silence for nearly an hour when I first read it many years ago. Wiesel's description of his first moments in Auschwitz is appalling enough. A mere slip of a fifteen-year-old, he gets off the train and is separated abruptly and forever from his mother and sister, then goes forward with his father to his fate in the men's camp. His illusions, he says, were left behind him in the carriage, along with his last, cherished possessions. But plainly there is deeper disillusioning to come with every step he takes.

"What have you come here for, you sons of bitches? What are doing here, eh?" a voice shouts. Young Elie's introduction to Dante's inner circle of hell is brutal, and if there are any in his group who have not yet abandoned hope, those already there stamp savagely upon their naïveté. "You'd have done better to have hanged yourselves where you were than to have come here. Didn't you know what was in store for you in Auschwitz? Haven't you heard about it? In 1944?"

And then, as if to bludgeon their faces into the grim prospect: "Over there—that's where you're going to be taken. That's your grave, over there. Haven't you realized it yet? You dumb bastards, don't you understand anything? You are going to be burned. Frizzled away. Turned into ashes."

Utterly appalled but still disbelieving, Elie and his father trudge toward their hut; the road takes them past the crematory and past an informal crematory where flames are leaping up from a ditch as babies and little children are burned alive. At one point, someone in their group begins to recite the Kaddish, the traditional Jewish prayer for the dead. Surely, Wiesel comments, it is the first time that people ever recited the prayer for the dead for themselves.

But then, when his father instinctively joins in—"May His Name be blessed and magnified"—Elie chokes and equally instinctively reacts the other way: "For the first time, I felt revolt rise up within me. Why should I bless his name? The Eternal, Lord of the Universe, the All-Powerful and Terrible, was silent. What had I to thank him for?"

Summoning up his strength, and only just resisting the temptation to end it all and throw himself on the electric fence, Wiesel makes it to the end of the day when he entered the inferno and sums up his first full encounter with the Angel of Death.

Never shall I forget that night, the first night in camp, which turned my life into one long night, seven times cursed and seven times sealed. Never shall I forget that smoke. Never shall I forget the little faces of the children, whose bodies I saw turned into wreaths of smoke beneath a silent blue sky.

Never shall I forget those flames which consumed my faith forever.

Never shall I forget that nocturnal silence which deprived me, for all eternity, of the desire to live. Never shall I forget those moments which murdered my God and my soul and turned my dreams to dust. Never shall I forget these things, even if I am condemned to live as long as God Himself. Never.

"Where is God? Where is He?" another inmate asks later, when the SS forces the entire camp to watch the public hanging of a child. "Where is He now?" And all the fifteen-year-old Elie can answer is through a voice within him saying, "Where is He? Here He is—He is hanging here on this gallows."

The Question with Three Horns

Is Elie Wiesel an atheist? Did he lose his faith at Auschwitz? Many people who read *Night* come to that conclusion, but they are wrong. Wiesel is a deeply observant Jew who believes that trusting God is quite compatible with arguing, and even quarreling, with God. As he wrote later in *A Jew Today*, "Only the Jew knows that he may oppose God as long as he does so in defense of his creation."

It is a stunning fact that the two strongest and most anguished outcries against believing in God in light of evil in modern literature were written, not by atheists, but by believers. One, by a Jew, is Elie Wiesel's damning description in *Night*, and the other, by a Christian, is Fyodor Dostoyevsky's impassioned argument by Ivan in *The Brothers Karamazov* that the world's justice and harmony are not worth the tears of one single child.

What does this striking fact show? At the very least, it calls into question the facile pretense that evil is simply "the rock of atheism," in the words of the German playwright George Büchner. It certainly can be. For some people, evil is the rock against which their faith stumbles, never to rise again. But for others, and probably for the majority, it simply is not. The stumbling block becomes the stepping-stone to real and deeper faith, and the difference between the two responses can be traced to differences between the answers to evil that we examine later.

Equally importantly, this fact highlights the irrationality of the prejudice that treats faith as a way of avoiding reality—for instance, the charge that faith is a projection or form of wish fulfillment that plasters its sunny optimism over the grim realities of the human condition. The truth is that the last holdouts clinging to the utopian illusion that the world is getting better and better are usually secularists, not religious believers.

As the examples of Dostoyevsky and Wiesel underscore, true faith is far from unrealistic and bent on avoiding reality. Nineteenth-century Siberian labor camps and twentieth-century Nazi death camps were hardly schools for Polyannas. Faith, of course, is never authenticated by what spurs it, but there is surely some integrity to faith if it is entered, as Dostoyevsky said of his journey, through "the hell fire of doubt" in the teeth of the world's ferocious evil.

But most importantly, the stunning fact introduces us to the heart of the second of the three universal questions spurred by evil and suffering: where's God? This question is one of the deepest we ever raise. If the horror of evil or the pain of suffering is so awful, someone somewhere in the universe must be held accountable. The buck must stop somewhere, and who else is the last resort of all?

When we are hit hard and hurt by evil, our experience demands an explanation. So our minds set out, searching everywhere, from the immediate to the ultimate, and asking ceaselessly where the ultimate responsibility lies. Everything inside us knows that what has happened is not fair and cannot be right. There has to be a reason for the senselessness. There has to be an indictment to clear up the injustice. Someone has to hear our case and put right the wrong. But where do we have an ear? And who will judge on our behalf? If there is to be final order in the universe, as day-to-day life assumes and requires, there must be some explanation for the *dis*order. So the very passion of our intuition of order becomes the vehemence of our protest against the disorder. But who will listen and who cares?

In the end the universe is cold and silent, so all eyes look to heaven and all fingers point to the one believed to be the final author and arbiter of it all—God. As Simone Weil points out, "One can only excuse men for evil by accusing God of it." So even those who do not believe in God often blame God for their suffering.

Start thinking about what is behind the cry "Where's God?" and you see that if it is natural for skeptics, it is urgent for believers. "Where's God?" is urgent for faith because the question that for the skeptic is an attack on someone else's faith is anguish for the believer because it is an assault on his own.

But the fact that many turn to God in times of evil is not an unmixed argument for faith. On the contrary, for where the eyes look naturally, the questions follow necessarily. Where the buck stops, there surely the blame lies too. This is exactly where the much-discussed trilemma comes in—the famous three-horned question on which faith seems to be impaled. In the early version of the Greek philosopher Epicurus, "Is God willing to prevent evil, but not able? Then he is impotent. Is he able but not willing? Then he is malevolent. Is he both able and willing? Whence then is evil?"

Or as the Scottish skeptic David Hume expressed it in his *Dialogues Concerning Natural Religion*, "Why is there any misery in the world? Not by chance, surely. From some cause then. Is it then from the intention of the deity? But he is perfectly benevolent. Is it contrary to his intention? But he is almighty. Nothing can shake the solidity of this reasoning. So short, so clear, so decisive."

Is evil truly evil? Is God truly all-good? And is God truly all-powerful? There is no deeper objection to faith in God. The three-pronged challenge of the trilemma is a mortal contest that faith dare not duck.

When Faith Hurts

Skeptical ways of asking, "Where's God?" are so well known that many people forget that people of faith can ask the question even more passionately. The strongest example is that of Jesus of Nazareth himself, in his loud, anguished cry during his crucifixion: naked, bloody, beaten, falsely accused and unjustly condemned, hideously tortured, racked by excruciating pain, betrayed by a follower, and abandoned by his friends, he takes up the opening words of Psalm 22 to utter the depths of his desolation: *"Eloi, Eloi, lama sabachthani?"* ("My God, my God, why have you forsaken me?").

Similar cries ring out down the centuries, varying in their occasion and their intensity, but all arising from the commitment of faith. Sometimes the question raised is mild. The story is told of Teresa of Avila, the sixteenth-century saint who, when thrown from her carriage and deposited in the mud, challenged God, only to hear the response, "This is how I treat all my friends." To which she replied tartly, "Then, Lord, it's not surprising that you have so few."

Usually, the question was far stronger, squeezed out in grief, complaint, or anger. Gerard Manley Hopkins expresses the grief in *Last Sonnets*, "And my lament / is cries countless, cries like dead letters sent / To dearest him that lives alas! away."

Simone Weil, reflecting on affliction in light of her own suffering in war-torn France, raises the question more cosmically, but still from the vantage point of faith: "Affliction makes God appear to be absent for a time, more absent than a dead man, more absent than light in the utter darkness of a cell. A kind of horror submerges the whole soul."

C. S. Lewis felt desolating hurt and experienced waves of anger after the death of his wife, Joy Davidman, from cancer. He writes in *A Grief Observed*:

> Meanwhile, where is God? This is one of the most disquieting symptoms. When you are happy, so happy that you have no sense of needing him, if you turn to him with praise, you will be welcomed with open arms. But go to him when your need is desperate, when all

other help is vain and what do you find? A door slammed in your face, and a sound of bolting and double-bolting on the inside. After that, silence. You may as well turn away.

Rabbi Harold Kushner's variation on the same question in *When Bad Things Happen to Good People* is pained perplexity. After his son Aaron is diagnosed with a rapid-aging disease and becomes like an old man of eighty, Kushner asks:

> I believed that I was following God's ways and doing his work. How could this be happening to my family? If God existed, if he was minimally fair, let alone loving and forgiving, how could he do this to me? And even if I could persuade myself that I deserved this punishment for some sin of neglect or pride that I was not aware of, what grounds did Aaron have to suffer?

When Skepticism Hurts

The cries from the skeptical side are just as strong; only the motive is different. For the common intention of the skeptic is to query God, not in order to find him but to escape him or to justify an earlier rejection.

"The only excuse for God," the French writer Stendhal wrote, "is that he doesn't exist."

"If there's a God," said the French poet Charles Baudelaire, "he's the devil."

"If he created me, who asked him to?" the composer Richard Wagner wrote. "And if I am made in his image, the question remains whether I am pleased by that."

"If a god has made this world," the philosopher Arthur Schopenhauer wrote, "then I would not like to be the god; its misery and distress would break my heart."

"In fact, the problem of the origin of evil haunted me as a thirteen-year-old lad," Friedrich Nietzsche wrote in *On the Genealogy of*

Morals. "At an age when one has 'half child's play, half God in one's heart,' I devoted my first literary child's play to it, my first philosophical writing exercise—and as to my 'solution' to the problem back then, well, I gave the honor to God, as fitting, and made him the *father* of evil."

Sometimes the skeptic's confusion is quite apparent. "I can't understand how all this can happen," Hitler's mistress Eva Braun is reputed to have written to a friend from Hitler's bunker during the bombing of Berlin. "It's enough to make one lose faith in God."

Sometimes the motivation is not to dismiss God but only to understand why, in our anger, we want to blame someone or something for the wrongs of the world. "When I am furious about something," the philosopher Ludwig Wittgenstein reflected, "I sometimes hit the ground or a tree with my stick, and the like. But I certainly don't think the ground is to blame or that this hitting can help at all. I give vent to my anger."

Sometimes the skeptic's motive is surely propaganda or the advocacy of long-held views. For instance, in his play *The Devil and the Good Lord*, Jean-Paul Sartre set out an attack on belief that he had held for years. "I prayed, I demanded a sign," the protagonist says with more melodrama than personal anguish.

> I sent messages to heaven, no reply. Heaven ignored my very name. Each minute I wondered what I could be in the eyes of God. Now I know the answer: nothing. God does not see me, God does not hear me, God does not know me. You see this emptiness over our heads? That is God? You see that hole in the ground? That is God again. Silence is God. Absence is God. God is the loneliness of man.

The Ledger of Life

After the death of his son in 1860, T. H. Huxley wrote back to Reverend Charles Kingsley, who had written to console him. Known as "Darwin's bulldog" and as the man who had coined the term *agnostic*, Huxley put an assured face on his grief.

The ledger of the Almighty is strictly kept, and every one of us has the balance of his operations paid over to him at the end of every minute of his existence. Life cannot exist without a certain conformity to the surrounding universe—that conformity involves a certain amount of happiness in excess of pain. In short, as we live we are paid for living. . . . The absolute justice of the system of things is as clear to me as any scientific fact.

"As we live we are paid for living"? Absolute justice is "as clear to me as any scientific fact"? Tell that to Job. Tell it to the innocent millions slaughtered in the twentieth century and all the countless victims of sickness and disease down the centuries. For all the nobility and the religious-sounding sentiment, this statement says more about Huxley's Victorian agnosticism and stoicism than it does about faith. He certainly does not speak for the Jewish and Christian faiths or for the blood that cries out from modern atrocities.

Contrary to Huxley, the ledger of life often does not add up in this life. What of those to whom life doles out more pain than happiness? What of those who face evil or suffering that is monstrously irrational, totally unfair, and so utterly lacking in any conceivable purpose that someone somewhere must be held accountable for it? In the face of such experiences, our hearts know beyond any question that ultimate silence and inaction are a monumental insult to add to the injury. "Where's God?" is not a request for information but a protest and an accusation or a cry for reassurance and help.

Whatever the motive, whatever the intensity, and however ugly or regrettable the form of the expression, the question "Where's God?" is almost irrepressible to people in pain. We should never be ashamed to acknowledge the full force of the question, and we should never be slow to seek to answer it. "Where's God?" is written in blood in the human story. If life is to make sense and be tolerable, let alone fulfilling, it is a cry from the heart that has to be answered.

CHAPTER 7

HOW CAN I STAND IT?

Prisoner 174517 was thirsty. Seeing a fat icicle hanging just outside his hut in the Auschwitz extermination camp, he reached out of the window to break it off and quench his thirst. But before he could reach it, a guard thrust out his fist and dashed it to pieces on the filthy ground.

"*Warum?*" the prisoner burst out instinctively—"Why?"

"*Hier ist kein warum,*" the guard answered with brutal finality—"Here there is no why."

That, for Primo Levi, the Italian Jewish scientist and writer, was the essence of the death camps—places not only of unchallengeable, arbitrary authority but of absolute evil that defied all explanation. In the face of such wickedness, explanations born of psychology, sociology, economics, or politics were pathetically inadequate. But what could not be understood still had to be survived, and when the Allied liberation ensured physical survival, it became clear that bare survival was not enough. The survivors of the death camps began their second—perhaps greater, certainly different—struggle for survival in postwar freedom.

Yet despite the horror, Levi gave the impression that he was one who had survived the deadly poison of Auschwitz and come to terms

with his nightmarish experience. One of only three returning survivors of the 650 Italian Jews transported to Poland in 1944, he eventually married, had children, wrote books, won literary prizes, lived a
full life, and became one of the world's most famous witnesses to the
Holocaust.

So it came as a terrible shock and sadness for many when on April
11, 1987, more than forty years after his release from Auschwitz,
Primo Levi plunged to his death down the stairwell of his home in
Torino, Italy. His mounting depression in the last weeks of his life was
known to his family and friends, but not to his many admirers and
readers around the world. Other direct or indirect victims of the
Nazis had committed suicide, but Levi had always argued sternly
against that act. Now he too had succumbed. In the end he had no
"why" strong enough to sustain his life after the terrible evil for which
there was no "why."

In retrospect, Levi's long, painful battle is all too clear. Writing
about his deportation to Poland, he stated: "Auschwitz left its mark
on me, but it did not remove my desire to live. On the contrary, that
experience increased my desire. It gave my life a purpose, to bear witness, so that such a thing could never happen again." That desire was
on one side of the scales, and its weight gave solidity to his life. He
wrote to a fellow survivor, Jean Samuel, "Whether we like it or not,
we are witnesses and we carry the weight of that fact." So he lived for
truth and justice, but as he fought for them he found that it gave him
another reason to live. The struggle itself was liberating and invigor-
ating—"he found himself becoming a man like other men again."

But the factors on the other arm of the scales proved heavier still.
For a start, the eyewitnesses' task is next to impossible. A survivor of
the Armenian massacre wrote: "You can never really write what happened anyway. It is still ghoulish. I still fight with myself to remember
it as it was. You write because you have to. It all wells up inside of
you. It is like a hole that fills constantly with water and no amount of
bailing will empty it." In Levi's case, there were too few witnesses to
the Holocaust, their ranks were thinning all the time, and as the years
went by he found that he was losing his own memory. "There are not

many of us in this world to bear this witness," he wrote in *The Drowned and the Saved* a year before he died, and "little by little the remaining witnesses disappeared."

Worse still, it seemed that after all his efforts, nobody and nothing had changed. The weight of his firsthand witness to truth meant little to the revisionists and deniers of the Holocaust, who were always given a sympathetic hearing by some. It was painfully obvious too that many in the general public did not listen and did not want to understand. For some, their moral deafness was due to the media-induced sense of unreality. For others, it went deeper. As Itzhak Schipper, murdered at Majdanek in 1943, had said to a fellow inmate, "Who will believe us? No one will want to believe us because our disaster is the disaster of the entire civilized world."

Worst of all for Levi, his philosophical convictions crumbled and gave way the year before he died, plunging him into a pit of desolation. On the one hand, he was tortured by a sense of guilt for having survived. He even wrote that those who had come out of the camps alive had something to reproach themselves for. Obviously, the "best all died." On the other hand, he was gnawed by thoughts of despair. He had entered and left the camp as an intellectual and an atheist, with a staunch belief in the superiority of reason and the Enlightenment. But this sustaining hope had collapsed under the weight of evil. As one biographer wrote, "Once this bad world, inexplicably bad, was no longer accessible to the light of reason, he had no recourse left but to despair."

At 10:20 A.M. on the day he died, Levi had phoned Elio Toaff, the chief rabbi of Rome, and told him: "I don't know how to go on. I can't stand this life any longer. My mother has cancer and each time I look at her face I remember the faces of the men lying dead on the planks of the bunks in Auschwitz." Sadly, an experience of evil that was impossible to forget and impossible to communicate became impossible to survive. Levi could not stand it and he did not.

The Sun Rises Tomorrow

No suicide ever returns to speak after his or her death, and Primo Levi left no note. But Levi's long struggles and his last interviews and writings take us straight to the heart of the third of the three universal questions spurred by evil and suffering: how can I stand it? Or in its traditional form, "How long, O Lord?"

This is obviously the most practical of the three questions, but it is no less deep because it goes to the very core of our lives.

There is a world of difference between the sufferings of an Auschwitz survivor, a terminal cancer patient, a parent grieving the loss of a child, and someone with an agile mind trapped in a badly disabled body. Physical pain is not the same as emotional pain and mental pain. But what links all sufferers is as profound as what separates them. In one form or another, life has thrust them into the fire, and in the agonizing pain that will not be soothed, they need to know how they can stand it and survive.

Anyone who thinks about this third question notices something odd. It triggers two apparently contradictory responses. On the one hand, "How can I stand it?" raises an unabashedly practical question that is usually given a straightforward answer. We can stand the pain if we live moment by moment and day to day. On the other hand, as we shall see, though the question is truly practical, it is also highly philosophical.

When Iris Murdoch showed signs of slipping into Alzheimer's disease, her husband, John Bayley, used to divide their days into simple discrete units—posting a letter, walking around the block, and so on. These at least could be handled, but it was useless to think too far ahead. As a precedent, he would cite Jane Austen's benevolent clergyman Reverend Sydney Smith, who would counsel parishioners in the grip of depression to "take short views of human life—never further than dinner or tea."

I have often found that when people are really hurting, it is the simplest deep truths that make a difference and help them through the day.

"This too shall pass," "The sun rises tomorrow," "Sufficient unto the day is the evil thereof," and (for those who believe in God) "Father, I do not understand you, but I trust you." In other settings these truths might sound like truisms or even clichés, but they become lifelines to cling to when a sea of troubles threatens to wash us away.

Those Who Have a Why

The other half of the response to "How can I stand it?" is not so simple, for behind the practical answer lies a philosophical question that must be answered first. Very close to our hurting hearts and the desperate twisting of our minds in pain is the beautiful saying of Nietzsche: "He who has a why to live for can bear almost any how." Or, as he wrote another time, "It is not so much the suffering as the senselessness of it that is unendurable." However bad our suffering may be, there is always one thing worse: suffering and not knowing why.

At one level, Nietzsche's point is obvious. Soldiers will pay the supreme sacrifice for the country they love, just as martyrs will die in a thousand excruciating ways for the faith by which they live. To be sure, soldiers have often died pointlessly for false glory and pointless tracts of real estate. And purported martyrs can be inspired by fanaticism to become suicide bombers rather than witnesses to any spiritual truth. But Nietzsche's point still stands. A single why, whether true or illusory, will see us through the fire and rain of a thousand desperate whats.

But at another level, the helpfulness of having a why comes up short precisely because, as we have seen all along, the experience of evil undermines our why. The Spartan prince Leonidas may have known that he was dying in order to defend the pass at Thermopylae against the Persians, as did young Allied soldiers on the beaches of Normandy on D-day. But when Mrs. Jones hears she has inoperable cancer, Mr. Smith loses his only son to a drunken driver, and the in-

habitants of Town X and City Y find themselves in the path of a tor-
nado or the sights of a terrorist, we simply do not know why—yet
they still have to face the what.

There is the rub. Not having reasons when we most need them is
what stokes the anguish of "How can I stand it?" It also creates a
spawning ground for contrived reasons. Not surprisingly, the story of
the human response to suffering is rich with proffered answers that
are heartless and entirely off the mark. The most famous is that of
Job's "comforters," who, out of a desire to comfort, felt the need to
explain his suffering and went far beyond the evidence and ended up
making moralistic judgments that were ignorant and cruel—only to
find themselves roundly rebuked by God, whom they thought they
were defending.

Dying for What You Live For

This third question, "How can I stand it?," must be distinguished
from modern notions of pursuing risk and extremes and "seeing how
much I can stand." One of the ironies of the modern world is that
our passion for order, predictability, comfort, convenience, and insurance has bred a countervailing passion for taking risks, going to extremes, and testing boundary situations. "Better barbarism than
boredom," Baudelaire cried in the nineteenth century. "The closer
you are to death, the more alive you feel," we say today, so flirting
with risk and courting danger become the avenue to a life that is alive
and authentic.

At a more popular level, this translates as "better white-knuckle
fear than couch-potato boredom," so we ski down Mount Everest,
dive over Niagara Falls, and leap from bridges at the end of an elastic
rope. But whether in extreme sports or on reality television shows,
the actual risk is usually limited, and most people are happy to remain
spectators—in essence, voyeurs of the risks and ordeals of others.

People who truly live all their lives at the edge and revel in it, people
who risk everything to see what they can take, are few and far be-

tween. Max Weber, arguably the greatest of all social scientists, was such a man who lived at the frontier of the realm of ideas. One day late in his life he was asked by a friend why he pressed on with his research despite the pessimism of his conclusions and an earlier breakdown in his career. He replied fiercely, "I want to see how much I can stand."

But even this is not the same as the setting that pushes up our third question. Evil and suffering are quite different from extreme sports and reality shows. Disasters do not ask our permission. Accidents do not give us advance notice. Oppression does not come with warnings and ingredients spelled out for its victims. Terminal disease has no opt-out clause if we cannot cope with the initial experience. Whatever the source of the evil or suffering, it is the ultimate extreme reality. It plunges us into an experience that rips the skin off our normal feelings, presses the ice-cold barrel of a gun into our reeling minds, and brutally blocks out any prospect of rescue or relief.

At such moments, evil and suffering pose the supreme challenge to whatever faith we have and offer the supreme temptation to despair. The latter is easy to see and to sympathize with. When we experience real pain, the devastation can be so total, the senseless irrationality so complete, the impossibility of a way out so bleak, and the combined tensions of all the conflicts so unbearable, that it seems the only way out is to quit, and the only relief is to give up. Some people at that point seek relief for their bodies, others for their minds. But for both it is the weary hopelessness and burden of the pain that leads them to despair.

What makes the temptation so seductive is that the alternative—to stand and fight, whatever the cost—may appear even more painful than the suffering. Despair at least brings relief, for there is a certain numbness that is the reward of no longer caring, even if we do not take the next step and end it all. A French nihilist wrote in the 1930s, "Life is not even worth the trouble of leaving it."

But refusing to give up requires faith, and faith requires endurance, and endurance requires courage. In short, the stake for which we find ourselves playing in this third question is our very selves—our faith, our character, and our virtue staked out in our willingness to endure whatever the cost. Only such courage expresses our character. Only such courage keeps us spiritually and morally intact in the core of our being in the heat of the crucible.

An English survivor of Dachau was asked how he endured the brutality and slavery of the camp. At first he said did not know, but then added: "It was important to [me] never to do anything in order to survive that would mean [I] couldn't sleep at night, would not be able to have a tranquil heart. You had to remain a human being. That was how you won. They wanted to make us into beasts. Behaving like men, not letting them destroy the human being in us, was how we won."

Courage in suffering, then, is not a matter of casual bravado or weekend recklessness. Courage is our bravery issuing from a passionate desire to live called into question by a powerful threat of death, then countered with our equal readiness to die—but only on terms that are true to the faith that makes us who we are and by which we live. Thus, only what is worth living for is worth dying for, so we should never sell our souls to save our lives. But neither should we ever take our lives to ease our minds or relieve our bodies. As G. K. Chesterton put it, "Courage is almost a contradiction in terms. It means a strong desire to live taking the form of a readiness to die."

The Sole Philosophical Problem

In sum, we see that our three questions—"Why me?" "Where's God?" and "How can I stand it?"—all point beyond themselves toward the need for a higher answer in some worldview or moral vision of life. But do we need to be able to figure all this out to be able to display such courage in suffering? Of course not. We all know people whose indomitable spirit has triumphed over the most appalling odds with supreme courage and grace. Not only have many such people never thought things through like this, but many of those who have done so came up short when real life brought their theories into play.

Jean Améry, who wrote *At the Mind's Limits* and then took his own life after Auschwitz, had this to say in his study of intellectuals in the camp: "Once the intellectual's first resistance had flagged, with all his knowledge and analyses he had less with which to oppose his destroyers than the unintellectual."

These three elemental questions are as profound as they are simple and as unavoidable as they are irrepressible. Together they demand answers that we explore through the fourth essential question: do different explanations of evil make a difference? They also raise the question that Albert Camus addressed in the famous opening words of *The Myth of Sisyphus*:

> There is but one truly philosophical problem, and that is suicide. Judging whether life is worth living amounts to answering the fundamental question of philosophy. . . . I see many people die because they judge life is not worth living. I see others paradoxically getting killed for the ideas or illusions that give them a reason for living (what is called a reason for living is an excellent reason for dying). I therefore conclude that the meaning of life is the most urgent of questions

Are We Really Worse
or Just Modern?

How have evil and suffering been transformed by the modern world? This is the third basic question in exploring the challenge of evil and suffering. As with many other areas of life, our human experience of evil has been transformed out of all recognition by the power and pervasiveness of modernity. These changes are crucial to understanding and resisting evil today.

What is meant by *modernity*? We all know the word *maternity*. It stands simply for motherhood and everything that belongs to it. *Modernity* is no less straightforward. It stands for the entire spirit and system of the modern world and is simply shorthand for the world created by the rise of modern science in the seventeenth century and by the industrial revolution that began in England in the eighteenth century and is now continued by what we call globalization. Importantly, modernity is more than simply ideas. It includes all that we understand as the consequences of such great revolutions as industrialization, science, technology, capitalism, urbanization, bureaucracy, and telecommunications.

Each of these great revolutions has been driven in part by ideas, but they have also become institutional forces. We cannot simply change our minds about them and expect them to disappear or be whisked away. We have created them, for better or worse, and they animate the world in which we now live—a world that in many ways constrains and shapes us, especially if we are not aware of its molding power. One of these forces, market capitalism, has been described as the most revolutionary force in all history. Another, telecommunications, has brought us to the stage of instantaneous, simultaneous, and globally interconnected communication. As a result, we can conduct our human affairs around the world regardless of space, time, and governments. This capacity is the core of what we call globalization.

Not surprisingly, modernity has transformed our human experience of evil and suffering just as it has touched and changed almost every other part of life. We must understand these transformations clearly if we are to find adequate answers when we explore the fourth essential question. Three great transformations stand out above the others.

First, modernity has minimized pain. Through a combination of the discovery of anesthesia in 1846 and the commercial production of aspirin in 1893, pain was banished in a way that drugs and alcohol had never managed to do. Soon after the start of the twentieth century, historians have said, it was possible for the first time in history for adults in the West to live most of their lives without serious pain.

This astonishing advance does not mean, of course, that pain has completely disappeared. In some ways it has just shifted and changed shape. And a largely pain-free existence may make us more vulnerable to pain when we do meet it, because we have become less realistic about its presence in the world. Apart from this last point, freedom from pain is predominantly a positive advance and we do not examine it further here.

Second, modernity has magnified destructiveness. In the very obvious sense, modern science and technology have allowed us to create weapons of mass destruction that can kill horrifying numbers of innocent people, seriously damage our planet home, and for the first time ever raise the possibility of utterly destroying the earth.

But the deepest reinforcement of evil comes from a less obvious source. Through the very rationality of modern processes such as management and bureaucracy, more people become unwitting accomplices to evil—so that even monstrous evil assumes, in Hannah Arendt's famous term, a certain "banality." And millions of ordinary people become careless bystanders to human suffering through modern forms of powerfully induced indifference. Seen this way, the Holocaust was a monstrous, horrendous, and aberrant evil and yet also a natural culmination of some of the central forces of modernity—which are still with us.

Third, modernity has marginalized traditional ways of understanding and resisting evil. On the one hand, the steady secularization of modern life has undermined the authority of traditional religious and moral categories, just as the rise of modern therapeutic experts, such as the psychologist, has replaced traditional players, such as pastors and priests. On the other hand, the crisis of ethics and the celebration of both permissiveness and transgression have led to what Solzhenitsyn warned of as "the tilt of freedom toward evil"—and in particular toward the idea that "evil is cool."

The net effect of these three major transformations has been to create the appalling situation we face. We have lived through the five most murderous decades in history, yet our moral categories and responsibility are pathetically inadequate for facing up to this fact— let alone a future, in Churchill's words, "made more sinister, and perhaps more protracted, by the lights of perverted science."

The point is not that modern people are more evil than those in previous generations, but that modern destructiveness is infinitely greater because of the mismatch between the weakness of morality and the power of modernity.

As we explore these modern transformations, we encounter new questions that we must add to those raised in the earlier chapters.

The deepest question is simply: After Auschwitz, what? After Auschwitz, what does it mean to believe in God, and what does it mean to believe in humanity? Only when we have probed such questions thoroughly can we turn to the next essential question and the all-important issue of explanations and answers.

CHAPTER 8

ORDINARY PEOPLE, EXTRAORDINARY EVIL

He was so tense that he hardly seemed to be breathing. All the concerted energies of some of the world's most brilliant minds had finally come to fruition, and it had come down to this. What happened next could be as heavy with promise and peril for the future of the world as any moment in history. As the last seconds ticked away, he found all eyes trained on him, just as all the decisions, burdens, and inspiration had looked to him throughout the entire project. He was, after all, the director, and as he told a reporter later, he dreaded failure but he also dreaded success. "Lord," he exclaimed to a colleague, "these affairs are hard on the heart." Steadying himself, he held on to a post and stared ahead of him out across the desert called the Journey of Death.

"Now!" the announcer shouted at last. A stunning burst of light flashed across the sky, followed by the rumbling roar of an explosion; a cloud rose to a height of 33,000 feet and took the shape of a mushroom. He relaxed, the tension draining from his face. It had worked. The experiment was a stupendous success. It was 5:30 A.M. on July 16, 1945, at Trinity Site Zero in New Mexico, and he was Dr. J. Robert Oppenheimer, director of the Manhattan Project. A few weeks later, "Little Boy" and "Fat Man," the children of what he called "Gadget," rained down on Hiroshima and Nagasaki. When two hundred thousand Japanese were incinerated in seconds, and more than one-third of a million were killed in an unimaginable hell, the world was changed forever. He and his dedicated band of scientists had given birth to the nuclear age.

Awesome, unprecedented, magnificent, beautiful, shattering, searing, terrifying—the eyewitness responses of those at ground zero in New Mexico that day were understandably awestruck.

"Should we have the chaplain down here?" the supervisor wrote the night before.

"No man-made phenomenon of such tremendous power had ever occurred before," a brigadier general said. "The lightning effects beggared description. The whole country was lighted by a searing light with the intensity many times that of the midday sun."

"Now we are all sons of bitches," said the director of the site itself.

"My God! What have we done?" the captain of the *Enola Gay* wrote in the logbook of his B-29 after Hiroshima.

"This is the greatest thing in history," President Truman said to the sailors at his table on board ship when he heard the news of Hiroshima.

Fifty years later Oppenheimer's own responses have become legendary. As he recounted the moment to a friend the day after, when the ball of fire rose majestically into the sky, a passage from the Bhagavad Gita, the Hindu sacred text, flashed into his mind:

> *If the radiance of a thousand suns*
> *were to burst into the sky,*
> *that would be like*
> *the splendor of the Mighty One—*

Then, a few seconds later, as the colossal cloud rose to dominate the horizon with its full sinister significance, another line from the Gita came to him:

I am become Death, the shatterer of worlds.

What a brilliant image, successive generations of schoolchildren have been told. Western references to Armageddon, the Four Horsemen, and the Apocalypse had become hackneyed and worn out. So what more dramatic way for an American to conjure up the black potential for nuclear destructiveness than to associate it with the frightening Indian deity Shiva, "the destroyer of worlds"?

Detachment

Evil in the modern world has been magnified devastatingly, not so much because of the lethal power of modern weaponry as because of the destructiveness of modern attitudes and processes, which have proved as lethal as the nuclear devices and high-tech weaponry. These modern attitudes, though not Eastern in source, are uncannily close to Oppenheimer's.

Take Oppenheimer's quoting of the Gita. He was not just reaching for a dramatic metaphor to convey the unprecedented potency of the bomb. In the sternest crisis of his life, he was looking to the Gita for encouragement to help him do his duty with unswerving devotion through detachment. The Bhagavad Gita is perhaps the supreme text of Hinduism, and at its core is the idea, taught by Lord Krishna to the warrior Arjuna, that detachment is the key to discharging one's duties as a way to salvation.

Like Arjuna, who was troubled about going into battle against his own relatives, Oppenheimer had reasons to be reluctant about the bomb. A Jew, he had been brought up in Felix Adler's Society for Ethical Culture, whose stress on secular humanitarianism his father hoped would replace Judaism and the Christian faith. While studying at Cambridge University, Oppenheimer had attended a meeting of pacifists. Soon after the bombings of Hiroshima and Nagasaki, he became a leading critic of nuclear weapons, saying that they were tools of "of aggression, of surprise, and of terror," and even that they were "the devil's work." The bomb represented "the inhumanity and evil of modern war," he said, conceding that he himself had "blood on his hands." Two years after the bomb, he wrote, "in some sort of crude sense . . . the physicists have known sin."

At the same time, Oppenheimer built the bomb with no apparent agony of conscience, and for the rest of his life he steadfastly maintained that he had been right to do it. At one level he was plainly bowing to the momentum of scientific curiosity. "When you see something that is technically sweet," he said, "you go ahead and do it and you argue about what to do about it only after you have had your technical success."

But at a deeper level Oppenheimer found in his decades-long study of Hinduism the grounds for a detached dedication to duty that overrode any consideration of the consequences. Just as Arjuna's *dharma*, or duty, was to be a warrior, Oppenheimer's was to be a scientist. Krishna's "new philosophy" of duty-with-detachment replaced his parents' "old morality" of personal responsibility for human welfare. According to this new philosophy, we are each responsible only for our duty, not for what the Gita calls "the fruits of his work." Or as Oppenheimer told *Newsweek* in 1965, "There was uncertainty of achievement but not of duty."

At a still deeper level, Oppenheimer's understanding of Hinduism allowed him to achieve a personal freedom that transcended the morality and moral scruples of others. The teaching of the Gita, echoed by Nietzsche's celebration of the Superman, is that once you have achieved a pure heart, you are beyond good and evil and therefore permitted to act in ways that may appear wicked to others.

"Do not grieve," Krishna counseled. Oppenheimer had only one comment on the bomb before a television audience in 1965: "When you play a meaningful part in bringing about the death of over 100,000 people and the injury of a comparable number, you naturally don't think of that as—with ease." All he would own up to was having had "qualms."

Blame It on the Monsters

Robert Oppenheimer's state of mind as he masterminded the of the nuclear age leads us to the first great transformation of evil in the modern world: *the stupendous magnifying of its destructiveness*, owing not so much to technology alone as to the attitudes and processes that are the fruit of modernity along with technology.

This claim runs squarely counter to widespread opinion. Most people would blame the power of modern weapons, and above all of weapons of mass destruction. What the club, knife, sling, sword, arrow, gun, and Molotov cocktail could never do, even in the hands of the most calculating and ferocious, the nuclear device can do with precision and devastation in a second—and all at the touch of a tyrant's button or a terrorist's finger. Technology and inhumanity are a fatal combination.

But weapons themselves are obviously not the real culprit. Hundreds of millions of humans have been slaughtered in the last century even though none of the purported monsters of recent history did their killing with weapons of mass destruction. The only nation to have used the atom bomb—which Dwight Eisenhower opposed and called "that awful thing"—is the leader of the world's free democracies.

The picture would certainly change if monsters were able to lay their hands on nuclear weapons. But behind that argument is the notion that evil is simply the result of monsters—malevolently evil people with greater or lesser weapons in their hands or on their shopping lists. This focus on malignant and malevolent evil is a major reason why the searchlight has been shone so relentlessly on the Nazis, for no one can deny the malevolence and malignancy of Hitler, Heinrich Himmler, Rudolf Höss, and their grizzly gang, especially in their virulent hatred of the Jews.

Stalin killed far more people than Hitler, but he has been relatively shielded from scrutiny. On the one hand, his fellow Russians have not investigated their leader's crimes as the Germans have Hitler's. On the other hand, the image of "Uncle Joe," the jovial, bearlike leader and staunch wartime ally, has softened his portrait in a way that never happened with the portrait of Hitler as a monster.

But the monster view of evil is dangerous because it simultaneously seduces and distances us. Often we have a strange fascination with wicked people, but through them we can also push evil away because "we are not like them." Equally importantly, the monster view of evil does not come close to doing justice to the full horror of modern evil. Hitler, Stalin, Mao, and Pol Pot were unquestionably monsters—as were Saddam Hussein, Idi Amin, and a long line of tyrants stretching back to Nero, Caligula, and beyond. But to restrict evil to such men is to slip into the error of seeing it as an aberration, a rarity, an exception, as something well distanced from ourselves and perhaps also as a thing of the past. To think like that is to miss the real menace of evil here and now. It may seem so from the comfortable enlightenment of our Western vantage point, but evil is never something long ago and far away.

In his magisterial book *Modernity and the Holocaust*, Zygmunt Bauman, the eminent Polish social scientist who is himself Jewish and married to an Auschwitz survivor, confronts this complacency bluntly. The Holocaust, he argues, was not an aberration: it grew from processes at the heart of the modern world. It cannot be dismissed with relief as a thing of the past: the same processes are with us today. It must not be attributed solely to extraordinary people: it was carried out by millions of ordinary people. And it is not just a Jewish or a German tragedy: it is a disaster for the entire modern civilized world whose lessons and challenges remain with us still.

From the Heart of Civilization

Bauman's point is widely echoed among those who have pondered the relationship between twentieth-century evil and civilization, whether pessimists or optimists, secularists or people of faith—especially in a day when advances in technology are accompanied by retreats in morality.

In 1903 the novelist George Robert Gissing wrote:

I hate and fear "science" because of my conviction that for long to come, if not for ever, it will be the remorseless enemy of mankind. I see it destroying all simplicity and gentleness of life, all the beauty of the world; I see it restoring barbarism under a mask of civilization; I see it darkening men's minds and hardening their hearts; I see it bringing a time of vast conflicts, which will pale into insignificance "the thousand wars of old," and as likely as not, will whelm all the laborious advances of mankind in blood-drenched chaos.

"Our common enemy is the fearful master, the spirit of technology," the historian Johan Huizinga wrote in 1933. "We must not underestimate its power."

"The latest refinements of science are linked with the cruelties of the stone age," wrote Winston Churchill at the beginning of World War II.

The possibility that murder is logical and rational, Camus wrote in *The Rebel*, is "the question put to us by the blood and strife of our century."

"Civilization means slavery, wars, exploitation, and death camps," Richard Rubenstein wrote in *After Auschwitz* in 1966.

It also means medical hygiene, elevated religious ideas, beautiful art, and exquisite music. It is an error to imagine that civilization and savage cruelty are an antithesis. . . . In our times the cruelties, like most other aspects of our world, have become far more effectively administered than ever before. They have and will not cease to exist. Both creation and destruction are inseparable aspects of what we call civilization.

Robert Kaplan wrote in *Warrior Politics* in 2002, after the century had ended: "For that is another lesson of the twentieth century: the link—when we are not vigilant—between technological acceleration and barbarism."

Far from diminished today, such apprehensions have been reinforced by our so-called risk society—a world that seems to be out of control because of the unforeseen and uncontrollable consequences of all our innovations in atomic energy, genetic technology, nanotechnology, and computer science. What was designed to produce control has produced uncontrollability, and the result is a "culture of fear" in which people are likely to see ever more conspiracies, darker enemies, and the production of a wider range of new monsters.

Thoroughly Modern Evil

There are three levels at which modern attitudes and processes are closely linked to modern evil.

At the most obvious level, modern evil represents a diabolical union of industrialization and killing that has produced "industrial-strength killing," or the mass production of dead men. The Nazi extermination camps are the most obvious example. From the chimneys that epitomized the modern factory to the acid pellets produced by the most advanced German chemists to the railway grid that was planned and run to the highest levels of modern management brilliance, the death camps were as much a triumph of German industrial engineering as the autobahns and Volkswagens of the same era. As one historian wrote, Auschwitz was "a mundane extension of the modern factory system. Rather than producing goods, the raw material was human beings and the end-product was death, so many units per day marked carefully on the manager's production charts."

September 11 is another example. That deliberate, cold-blooded plot to wreak as much havoc as possible on as many people as possible is a clear-cut case of the old definition of evil as the intent to harm with "malice aforethought." But other aspects of the terrorist strike were stunningly modern. The meticulous Internet planning and co-ordination, the use of fuel-laden airplanes as tools, the soaring sky-scraper target, the media-amplified global audience—all would have been impossible without the aid of modern means of production. The Al Qaeda attacks were literally modernity turned against itself. The author Wendell Berry even claimed that September 11 will go down as the day when unquestioned technological optimism came to an end.

At a deeper level, modern evil proceeds with all the smooth running of modern management and bureaucracy—including such key features as the division of labor, the diffusion of responsibility, the distancing of objects, and the detached and submissive attitudes they engender. Hannah Arendt's celebrated analysis of the "banality of evil" applies here. SS Lieutenant Colonel Adolf Eichmann, she found at his trial, was not the monster the prosecution portrayed him to be. Instead, he was a functionary, a very ordinary man, and almost a clown. His remark that he "was just following orders" was widely quoted, but among her penetrating observations was her insight into Eichmann's language: he used a bureaucratic jargon that he himself described as "officialese" and that rarely rose above the level of cliché. "The longer one listened to him," Arendt observed, "the more obvious it became that his inability to speak was closely connected with an inability to *think*, namely to think from the standpoint of somebody else."

Was Arendt arguing that evil itself is banal? Was she denying that evil is monstrous at some levels? In her posthumously published *Life of the Mind*, she wrote: "The deeds were monstrous, but the doer—at least the very effective one now on trial—was quite ordinary, commonplace, and neither demonic nor monstrous."

In other words, the banality of evil supports the monstrosity of evil—routine evil reinforces radical evil. Arendt's point was that the processes that make evil possible are often trivial and banal, and these cannot be understood by those who see only "the legend of the greatness of evil, of the demonic force." The term *banal* came from a letter in 1946 from Arendt's friend the philosopher Karl Jaspers ("We have to see these things in their total banality, in their prosaic triviality, because that's what truly characterizes them"), though the concept may well have come from her study of Saint Augustine and his view of evil as privation—a radical depletion of good.

At the deepest level of all, modern evil that is part fantasy and part fanaticism grows from the heart of the modernist worldview: the drive of secularist intellectuals to create and control a better world, purged of all defects and based only on reason, science, management, and our human understanding of them all. Bauman underscores that, from the Enlightenment on, the modern world has been distinguished by its "activist, engineering attitude toward nature and toward itself." Science becomes the tool of secular utopianism that allows its proponents "to improve on reality, to reshape it according to human plans and designs, and to assist it in its drive to self-perfection." Hitler's language, he notes, was replete with references to gardening and medicine and therefore to the battle with weeds, disease, and infection.

In sum, Bauman says, the entire Nazi approach—including the calls for eugenics and euthanasia and the whole paraphernalia of the gas chambers—was "an exercise in the rational management of society. And a systematic attempt to deploy in its service the stance, the philosophy, and the precepts of applied science." Yes, the Holocaust was a Jewish tragedy, but it was also far more. "The Holocaust was born and executed in our modern rational society, at the high stage of our civilization and at the peak of human cultural achievement, and for this reason it is a problem of that society, civilization, and culture."

When Common Folk Become Dangerous

Several sobering lessons stand out from this analysis of the modern transformations of evil:

First, *modern processes make it possible for extraordinary evil to be carried out by millions of very ordinary people.* "Only a tiny proportion of this century's massive killings," wrote Fred Emil Katz, "are attributable to the actions of those people we call criminals, or crazy people, or socially alienated people, or even people we identify as evil people. The vast majority of killings were carried out by plain folk in the population—ordinary people, like you and me."

"By conventional criteria," two visiting American psychiatrists wrote, "no more than 10 percent of the SS could be considered 'abnormal.'" The overwhelming majority "would have easily passed all the psychiatric tests ordinarily given to American army recruits or Kansas City policemen."

"Monsters exist," Primo Levi wrote in *Survival in Auschwitz*, "but they are too few in number to be truly dangerous. More dangerous are the common men, the functionaries ready to believe and to act without asking questions."

Second, *modern processes come with a specious neutrality that disengages ethics and discourages personal virtue as irrelevant*. On the one hand, this leads to a distancing and dehumanization: decisionmakers are able to "look through" people and ignore the consequences of their policies. The Allies' slide into the deliberate killing of civilians in World War II is a case in point. Always justifying it as retaliation, and in defiance of "just war" theory, Western democracies for the first time deliberately slaughtered hundreds of thousands of innocent civilians. What began unofficially and then became official policy was rooted in the blockade of Germany in World War I, which led to the deaths of more than three-quarters of a million Germans. The next step was the Allied "area bombing" of Hamburg, Dresden, and Cologne, then the American firebombing of Tokyo and other Japanese cities, and eventually Hiroshima and Nagasaki. In the documentary *Fog of War*, Robert McNamara, later secretary of defense during the Vietnam War, admits that if the United States had lost the war, he and General Curtis LeMay would have been prosecuted as war criminals.

On the other hand, by neutralizing ethics and virtue, modern processes actually reinforce a downward swing toward vice, so that under modern conditions even the highest virtues can be debased until they become vicious. Trust and obedience, for example, are vital to the ordering of any good society. But divorce them from personal responsibility and they become a form of submission and compliance from which evil grows—the so-called crimes of obedience. Thus, from Auschwitz to Abu Ghraib in Iraq, prison guards are always merely "following orders."

"Show me one Nazi," a cabaret joke ran in the 1930s. "What do you mean? Here is a whole room full of Nazis." "Yes, but show me one Nazi."

"I surrendered my moral conscience to the fact that I was a soldier," said Otto Ohlendorf, the commander of a Nazi death squad, "and therefore a cog in a relatively low position of a great machine."

"As I write, highly civilized human beings are flying overhead, trying to kill me," George Orwell wrote during the Second World War.

> They do not feel any enmity against me as an individual, nor I against them. They are only "doing their duty" as the saying goes. Most of them, I have no doubt, are kind-hearted law-abiding men who would never dream of committing murder in private life. On the other hand, if one of them succeeds in blowing me to pieces with a well-placed bomb, he will never sleep any the worse for it.

"Nothing is more dangerous to human survival," wrote Stanley Milgram after his celebrated "Eichmann Experiment" in New Haven, "than malevolent authority combined with the dehumanizing effects of buffers. . . . As for the man who sits in front of a button that will release Armageddon, depressing it has about the same emotional force as calling for an elevator."

The shattering lesson of modern evil, Dwight Macdonald observed in 1945, is that we must now fear the person who obeys the law as much as the one who breaks it.

Third, *modern processes have complicated traditional understandings of evil, changing them out of all recognition, so that it is rare today to be able to define evil adequately.* Earlier, the essence of evil was linked to the will and captured in the straightforward notion of "intent to harm" (or "malice aforethought" in law). Some modern thinkers shy away from this notion out of fear that it points back to the idea of sin. But those who have studied the Holocaust have a far more honest reason for this reluctance: they have learned that much of the Holocaust's malignance came from people who wreaked horrendous evil *without ever willing it.*

To be sure, the Nazi ranks included brutal sadists, perverts, and vicious Jew-haters, at the highest levels and all the way down. But the cooperation of most Germans was enlisted by such petty notions as "following orders," "the desire to get ahead," "getting along," and "respect for the Great Leader." As Susan Neiman argues, Auschwitz contradicted two centuries of modern assumptions about intention and evil: "At every level, the Nazis produced more evil, with less malice, than civilizations had previously known."

Intention is still a powerful part of some forms of evil, such as terrorism, but to limit evil to cases where the intent is clear is to simplify evil and miss the many cases in which the evil is profound but less clear-cut and more elusive. Intent to do wrong may be necessary for a crime, but not for doing evil. Villains are evil by definition, but many who do the worst evil could be described as good citizens rather than villains. The mismatch between otherwise good citizens and the monumental evils for which they become responsible is a sobering feature of our modern understanding of evil. Evil may be done by people with no evil intentions; indeed, evil may be done by people with good intentions. Personal virtue is no longer a sufficient barrier to evil.

In sum, we see once again that the heart of darkness is a mystery. But more than being merely inexplicable and elusive, the horror of evil is also surprising and mercurial. Just when we think we understand it and have it pegged, it disappears and reemerges in a different guise. With its myriad forms, its infinite capacity to morph between them, and its talent for breaking out where we least expect it, evil never allows us to declare ourselves safe and free. We can all agree that Hitler was malevolently and malignantly evil. But if we relax after analyzing Nazi evil and thanking God it was so long ago and far away, we will be unprepared for a different form of evil—perhaps democratic, perhaps liberal, perhaps American, perhaps British, certainly surprising, and perhaps close to home.

As modern people, we have to face the fact that modernity has made evil as modern as we are, and in doing so it holds a mirror to our thinking and our ways of life. As Einstein warned, "It is easier to denature plutonium than to denature the evil spirit of man."

CHAPTER 9

FREEDOM'S TILT TOWARD EVIL

Soldier, hunter, woodsman, storyteller, marksman, backwoods states-man—he was a man who had become a legend in his own lifetime, long before he became a legend all over again through his Hollywood revival in the 1950s. From his signature coonskin cap to the tall tales told around a thousand fires to his martyr's death at the Alamo, he was the epitome of his world—the great, wild, exuberant American frontier in a single person. Said to have been born a gigantic child, "half horse, half alligator, with a little touch o' snapping turtle," it was also said that he "could whip ten times his weight in wildcats and drink the Mississippi dry," that he had ridden up the Niagara Falls on an alligator, that he could snuff a candle with a bullet, and that he was hated by every bear in the state of Tennessee.

But Davy Crockett was also a congressman with a conscience: his stand against the removal of the Cherokee Indians in 1830 was no tall tale and as courageous as his fight with any bear or his last stand against Santa Anna's army. "Be sure you're right, then go ahead," had always been his motto. But never had he more needed to know he was right than when he faced the entrenched opposition of President

Andrew Jackson and many of his constituents and fellow representatives in one of the darkest incidents in American history.

The status of the Native American peoples had been a troubling issue ever since the arrival of the first Europeans in North America, and in many ways it was made worse after twenty slaves from West Africa were landed from a Dutch man-of-war in Virginia in 1619. But the general pattern of the relationship was clear. Slowly and methodically, the Indian people were being pushed off their ancestral lands and relentlessly driven west. By the early nineteenth century there was a sharp division in white people's attitudes toward what they were doing.

Among some, rank prejudice and hatred flourished still: they viewed the Indians as "the barbaric savage" who blocked the path toward progress and civilization—or less idealistically, toward America's new "manifest destiny" of continental expansion. But for many others, two movements were casting the Indians in a new light. On the one hand, the reform movements growing out of the Second Great Awakening were stirring a new passion for justice for oppressed peoples. On the other hand, the Romantic movement in art and literature, with its renewed stress on the natural and the spiritual, called into question the costs of civilization and fueled nostalgia for the vanishing world of "the noble savage."

To most people, then, the Cherokee question was neither sudden nor simple. It was a long-festering sore. The Georgia Cherokees were the last fifteen thousand Indians in the settled part of the nation who were still living on their own ancestral lands, so their removal represented either the completion of a nasty but necessary task or a human tragedy and outrage of monumental proportions. Not only had the Georgia Cherokees fought with General Jackson on the side of the Union against the Creek Indians, but they had created their own alphabet, founded their own republic in 1827, and written their own constitution. In short, they were making huge strides in "civilizing" themselves, as they had been urged to do.

Besides, the interests of the half-million European Americans who wanted to settle the Indian land for speculation and profit were brazen. To make their motives plainer still, gold had been discovered where the Cherokee lived, and the would-be settlers were hungry to get their hands on it.

Above all there were the broken promises and treaties and, as with chattel slavery, the glaring contradiction with the Declaration of Independence: "We hold these truths to be self-evident, that all men are created equal, that they are endowed by their creator with certain inalienable rights, that among these are life, liberty, and the pursuit of happiness."

To complicate matters further, many people on both sides shared the assumption that there were only two options for the Indians: "civilization or extinction." The removal was therefore justified in humane and benevolent terms, as a way of preserving their heritage, as well as in openly rapacious terms. Many of the greatest voices in the country—among them Thomas Jefferson, James Monroe, President Jackson, and John C. Calhoun—were either openly in favor of Indian removal or could be quoted favorably by those who were.

There were certainly powerful voices raised against the removal, especially national leaders such as Chief Justice John Marshall and Daniel Webster, writers such as Ralph Waldo Emerson ("A crime is being projected that confounds our understandings by its magnitude . . ."), and foreign visitors such as Frances Trollope. Visiting Washington as the debate was raging over the Removal Act of 1830, she commented sharply that "if the American character may be judged by their conduct in this matter, they are most lamentably deficient in every feeling of honor and integrity."

In the U.S. Congress the loudest voice in opposition to the president from Tennessee was that of the congressman from Tennessee—Davy Crockett. The pressure on him was intense. As he described it later, when Jackson's Indian bill was brought forward, his colleagues in the House gathered around, told him that they loved him, but warned him that he was ruining himself. "They said this was a favorite measure of the president, and I ought to go for it."

But Crockett told his colleagues that "I believed it was a wicked, unjust measure, and I should go against it, let the cost to myself be what it might; that I was willing to go with General Jackson in everything I believed was honest and right; but further than this I wouldn't go for any other man in the whole of creation. I voted against this Indian bill," he concluded, "and my conscience yet tells me that I gave a good honest vote, and that I believe will not make me ashamed in the day of judgment."

The outcome was brutal. Crockett lost his seat after three terms, the Cherokee Nation lost its land after a thousand years, and many Cherokees lost their lives. In May 1838, General Winfield Scott and seven thousand U.S. soldiers invaded the Cherokee Nation, forcibly rounded up all the men, women, and children, and drove them out on a thousand-mile march with too little food and shelter. By the time they arrived in Oklahoma that winter, four thousand had died on the way, and the journey itself became known as the Trail of Tears.

Once Far More Than a Cliché

Nearly two centuries after Davy Crockett's stand, the Cherokee rose is the official flower of Georgia, but many Cherokees would rather carry two ten-dollar bills than carry a single twenty-dollar bill bearing the face of President Jackson. For many Native Americans, Jackson is the worst president ever and Davy Crockett is the hero who stood up for them at the cost of his political career. But the principle for which he stood—living and acting "under God" and therefore not being "ashamed in the day of judgment"—has become a cliché and a controversy in America today.

Davy Crockett's stand, the ground on which he took it, and its disappearance today lead to the heart of the second great modern transformation of evil. *The modern world has marginalized traditional responses to evil—by dismissing traditional categories and sidelining traditional ways of responding.*

The general way in which this has happened is plain and needs little comment. As we saw earlier, the categories in which we speak about evil have been transformed: "sin" became "crime," which in turn became "sickness," which in its turn became "dysfunction."

What is true of categories is true of institutions too. Professionalism, most people would agree, is infinitely better than being unprofessional, amateurish, and mediocre. But professionals, experts, and specialists not only enable but all too often disable—by removing traditional ways of handling human responses to problems and creating dependency on a layer of experts, such as the "grief counselors" who descend on communities after catastrophes such as the Columbine School murders. As Dostoyevsky noted in *Crime and Punishment* of the early stages of the trend, "Compassion has been outlawed by science."

Such broad ways of marginalizing traditional responses to evil and suffering can be seen throughout the modern world. But what matters even more are the specific ways in which this sidelining affects each nation's capacity to recognize and resist evil. When none dare call it evil, evil does not disappear—it is all the freer to surprise us and do its deadly work.

The result of this careless erosion of barriers is what Solzhenitsyn has called "the tilt of freedom toward evil," and the greatest example today is not found among the Germans, Russians, Chinese, Cambodians, or Rwandans, or in any nation with vast atrocities in its recent past. The worst example is the vast carelessness of the citizens of the world's lead society, "the land of the brave and the free," who pride themselves on being in the forefront of fighting environmental erosion and pollution but care little about their even deadlier cultural erosion and pollution.

Under God

Take three grand erosions of traditional barriers to evil that Americans have allowed to happen in the last generation.

First, the notion of "under God" has been neutered in American life, becoming little more than an amiable cliché in private life and a topic for controversy and litigation in public life. It was not always so. There was a time when the concept of "under God" was as radical in America as the radical monotheism behind not only the notion but the West itself. It spoke of a sovereign providence above all human affairs and a decisive moral accountability for all that humans do, seen or unseen.

Before the time of Mount Sinai and the voice that spoke to Moses out of the fire, the pagan earth was crowded with small deities. Fearsome or favorable, such gods were pliable and portable. Humans made them, so humans could manipulate them. At Sinai everything changed, as George Steiner wrote: "The Jew emptied the world by setting his God apart, immeasurably apart from man's senses. No image. No concrete embodiment. No imagining even. A blank emptier than the desert. Yet with a terrible nearness. Spying on our every misdeed, searching out the heart of our heart for motive." Invisible, unimaginable, unmanipulable—the God of Sinai is the One before whom all hearts lie open and no secrets are hidden, the One before whom all other authorities, loyalties, allegiances, and accountabilities rapidly recede into a distant second place.

It was this understanding of "under God" that led John Cotton to declare in the early New England days about both church and state, "It is necessary, therefore, that all power that is on earth be limited."

It was this understanding that inspired Davy Crockett to vote his conscience in light of the day of judgment at the cost of his career.

It was this understanding that moved Congressman Henry Storrs of New York to stand with Crockett in opposing the Cherokee removal. "Your history, your treaties, and your statutes," he told the president's supporters, "will confront you. The human heart will be consulted—the moral sense of all mankind will speak out fearlessly, and you will stand condemned by the law of God. . . . You may not live to hear it, but there will be no refuge for you in the grave."

It was this understanding that earlier led Benjamin Franklin to propose as the national seal of the United States "Rebellion to Tyrants Is Obedience to God."

It was this understanding that caused Thomas Jefferson to declare in the face of slavery, "I tremble for my country when I reflect that God is just, that his justice cannot sleep forever," though we might add that the great deist did not tremble enough to do something about it.

Do our brave new activists appreciate what "under God" once meant and did? With their lust for lawsuits and their vigilante noses sniffing out every discoverable reference to God, whether engraved in marble, cast in bronze, or written on parchment or paper, they are pressing an extremist separation of church and state that the framers would never have recognized. In the process they are removing the one reference higher than all human power and higher even than the state—the one transcendent authority in history capable of producing the constitutional monarchy and capable today of restraining its equally miraculous modern counterpart, the constitutional republic.

Are they ignoramuses or fools? After centuries of toil and blood, have monarchy and aristocracy been finally bounded only for democracy now to declare itself unbounded? History alone will show what happens to American freedom when this bulwark is removed and the ultimate appeal against human power and its abuse is taken away from public discourse.

The Framers' Forgotten Issue

The second grand erosion concerns the contemporary dismissal of the American framers' solution for the problem of freedom. For the brilliant generation that devised what George Washington called the "great experiment," the hardest problem to solve was the transience of freedom. Not only is it harder to be free than not to be free, but freedom never lasts. In politics, as in all spheres of human endeavor, no success is forever. Success finally fails. The challenge therefore is not just to win freedom (the achievement of the revolution in 1776), or even to order freedom (the achievement of the Constitution in 1787); the challenge is to sustain freedom—an achievement that is never finished because it is the challenge not of years or even decades but of centuries.

The framers' realism in tackling this task was born of their knowledge of history, and in particular their intimate knowledge of the classical understanding of why freedom never lasts. They used history to defy history, and the roots of their wisdom are the key to understanding the revolution of their solutions.

For such writers as the Roman statesman Cicero and the Greek historian Polybius, there were three menaces to sustaining freedom: external menaces from other powers and two internal menaces—the corruption of customs and the passing of time. The American experiment was designed to counteract all three.

If asked today what the framers' solution was, most Americans cite the distinctive separation of powers in the Constitution, and this is indeed a crucial part of the solution. But in fact, the ingenious American system of checks and balances is only half of the framers' solution, and in the framers' view, it would be inadequate without the other part. The forgotten part of the framers' solution may be called the enduring triangle of freedom: freedom requires virtue, virtue requires faith of some sort, and faith requires freedom. Only so can a free republic hope to remain free.

"Only a virtuous people are capable of freedom," Benjamin Franklin said in support of the first assumption, and the framers' unanimity on this point is a powerful chorus in his support. At the same time they were equally clear that law alone is not enough to restrain evil and sustain freedom. As John Adams put it—and the support was again overwhelming—"We have no government armed with powers capable of contending with human passions unbridled by morality and religion. Avarice, ambition, revenge, or gallantry would break the strongest cords of our Constitution as a whale goes through a net. Our Constitution was made only for a moral and religious people. It is wholly inadequate to the government of any other."

The force of the framers' declaration of this triangle of freedom is undeniable. But it is equally undeniable that many American leaders dismiss or overlook it today. On the one hand, the majority of believers in America have a faith so privatized that it has become "privately engaging and publicly irrelevant"—too amiably innocuous to serve the strenuous cause of freedom. On the other hand, the educated elites have espoused a different vision of public life, one in which faith, character, and virtue are to be inviolably private and the public square—a neutral arena of competing interests—is to be inviolably secular.

The framers' arguments can be dismissed in one of several ways. Some argue that their views were only a matter of rhetoric and cant, though they themselves denied this. Others argue that they were children of their times, but a study of other republicans of their day shows this was not so. Finally, still others argue, we moderns have discovered some sustaining power for freedom that does what the framers thought the triangle of freedom was needed to do.

This last possibility is the most plausible, though people who make this claim should openly declare what the substitute is. Most people have nothing convincing to say at this point and fall back lamely on the answers of law and technology. A moment's thought, however, would show that reliance on law without faith and virtue only produces more laws and greater regulations, just as reliance on technology without faith and virtue produces tighter and tighter systems of surveillance. In either case, freedom is steadily undermined.

It is also possible that the framers were not indulging in high-flying rhetoric better suited for the Fourth of July but were in fact correct—soundly, solidly correct with all the realism and wisdom of history and political theory on their side. For America to "work," Americans must cultivate the virtues necessary for freedom and ensure that they are passed from generation to generation. This is the political challenge of our times. Without this triangle of freedom, freedom cannot and will not last. If we celebrate freedom but remove from it all virtue until no good remains, we will not only lose freedom but ensure that what is left is evil. Thus, if the framers were correct, the contemporary adulation of their genius that ignores the heart of their realism and brilliance is a fateful neglect that tips the scales toward some future evil that no checks and balances will be able to stop.

When Evil Is Cool

The third grand erosion is the most startling. It comes from the unbridled passion to transgress, the drive to destroy traditions, flout standards, and defy conventions. This passion has become the hallmark of many contemporary intellectuals and creators of popular culture, and it has the effect of turning evil from a latent into an aggressive force. "Forbid us thing, and that desire we," Chaucer wrote in the "Wife of Bath's Tale," putting his finger on a perverse trait of human nature. But that curiosity-turned-lust-to-experience traditionally had its limits. As Roger Shattuck points out in *Forbidden Knowledge*, every society has its forbidden knowledge, its social taboos, its moral boundaries, and its spiritual barriers against blasphemy. But at the heart of the modern world is a refusal to accept any limits and therefore a drive to cross lines, to break taboos, to open the seals of forbidden knowledge, and so to celebrate a culture of transgression— as an assertion of heroic greatness.

Much of the modern passion to transgress is a form of childish exhibitionism and is relatively harmless. "Madonna told me to break every rule I could think of," her choreographer said after a world tour with the rock star, "and then when I was done to make up some new ones and break them." The destructiveness of the passion to transgress grows exponentially, however, when blended with factors such as unrestrained artistic license, greed for commercial profit, a rage for free-speech-and-be-damned, a ravening hunger for celebrity power, a wild desire to abolish the lines between fantasy and reality, a crazy belief that lives lived closest to death are those that are most alive, and an abysmal lack of history that allows us to lounge in a fool's paradise of deeds without consequences.

But the real heart of the passion to transgress is the grand Prometheanism that the modern secular world has resurrected and made available to a wider number of people than ever before. Riches, power, fame, and sexual adventures, Shattuck observes, have always been available as goals for the enterprising. And there have always been individuals, such as Alcibiades, Caligula, Tamerlane, and Napoleon, who "can experience no lasting satisfaction, who must reach beyond to a higher tier of drives and rewards, of attractions and repulsions."

In our case today, the excesses of the great ones and the fascination of the general public come together in an unholy package. The "splendidly wicked ones," whether presidents, sports heroes, or rock stars, are unstoppable, and we are unable to avoid admiring, envying, and excusing them. So they range free in the higher altitudes of our society, while our ethics are disarmed, evil as transgression is made heroic, and the siren lure of real evil grows ever more irresistible.

Thus, radical idea by radical idea, violent film by violent film, explicit song by explicit song, brutal video game by brutal video game, edgy cable show by edgy cable show, and shameless scandal by shameless scandal, the momentum grows and the binding forces concentrate. What was once unimaginable becomes thinkable and then fashionable. What used to be abnormal is now normal. Where we were shocked, we are now indifferent. What started as soft-core ends as hard-core. Where before the definition of deviancy slowly became more limited, now, in the mad scramble for ratings and market share, there is an all-out race for the bottom in the name of the "daring" and the "edgy"—which always turns out to be the violent, the vulgar, the explicit, and the tasteless.

Each transgression builds on the last one and binds us to the next one. To break off at any point is to cast everything up to that point in a bad light, so each transgression serves as the permission and the dare to press on to the next. The result is an entire society following the addict's piecemeal slide into bondage and a civilization's descent into decay.

In this process the "great corrupters" are always the great ones, and their passion to transgress always begins in the mind—"For there is no crime to the intellect," as Emerson wrote dangerously.

Common or garden-variety evil is easy, Pascal wrote, and its forms are infinite. "But there is a kind of evil as difficult to identify as what is called good, and often this particular evil passes for good because of this trait. Indeed, one needs an extraordinary greatness of soul to attain it as much as to attain good."

"There have been men, indeed splendidly wicked, whose endowments threw a brightness on their crime," wrote Samuel Johnson, "and whom scarce any villainy made perfectly detestable, because they could never be divested of their excellencies; but such have been in all ages the great corrupters of the world."

"Laws," wrote the Marquis de Sade in *La Nouvelle Justine*, "are made only for the common people; being both weaker and more numerous, they need restraints that have nothing to do with the powerful man and that do not concern him."

"There is a mode of being I call 'the Demonic,'" Goethe wrote. "They are not always the most excellent people . . . but a terrible force comes out of them. From such considerations arises that strange and striking proverb: 'No one can rival God except God himself.'"

"The best and highest that men can acquire," Nietzsche wrote in *The Birth of Tragedy*, "they must obtain by a crime." Or as he wrote in *The Will to Power*, there is "the seduction that everything extreme exercises; we immoralists, we are the most extreme."

In key parts of our Western culture today we have demolished a shared moral universe, evacuated heaven to create room for our thrusting pretensions, celebrated rebellion in the name of absolute freedom to do whatever is forbidden, and encouraged "great corrupters" to emerge from among our politicians, business leaders, sports heroes, rock stars, and film directors. In the process we have devoured every morsel dropped from their celebrity scandals and trials, winked at their transgressions, mitigated their evil, and excused in them what we would not tolerate in our children for a second.

In our "cool complicity," Shattuck concludes, we have reached the dangerous point where evil itself is cool. "Let us beware of applying our intellects to condoning evil or to making ourselves into 'splendidly wicked' people. Twice this century has spawned overwhelming state terrorism—in communism and fascism. We cannot afford such blindness to history and such naïveté as to embrace the morality of the cool."

Thought Before Deed as Lightning Before Thunder

How long will we continue to confuse evil with freedom? At what point will freedom's tilt reach the tipping point and collapse into more and more blatant examples of evil? What will it take to shock us into realizing the links between what we have done and the disasters we have sown for our children? Time will tell, but the tilt is pronounced, the slipway is greased, and the preparatory work of careless leaders, breathless celebrities, and ravenous, money-driven creators of culture is well advanced. Unquestionably this warning will be dismissed as the product of fevered alarmism. After all, Pisa's leaning tower is still standing and, for all the warnings, the floodwaters have not drowned Venice.

Those who are nonchalant about what we have allowed to slip should ponder how our popular culture is viewed as sewage by much of the world—or more pointedly, they should be asked to consider earlier warnings about the erosions of Western heritage. In his story "Earth's Holocaust," written in 1844, Nathaniel Hawthorne tells of a moment in time when the wide world has become so overburdened with the accumulated treasures of the past that the citizens decide to burn them all on one of the broadest prairies of the West. A huge cheer and joyous shout goes up as the flames from the conflagration mount. The past is gone. The future is freer. But suddenly a gray-haired man rushes toward the flames.

> "People," cried he, gazing at the ruin of what was dearest to his eyes with grief and wonder, but nevertheless with a degree of stateliness; "People, what have you done! This fire is consuming all that marked your advance from barbarism, or that could have prevented your relapse thither."

More sobering still is the poet Heinrich Heine's warning about Germany written more than a century before the Nazi death camps. It is to the great merit of the Christian faith, he writes, that it has softened "the brutal German lust for battle." But it cannot destroy it entirely. "And should that taming talisman break—the Cross—then will come roaring back the wild madness of the ancient warriors. . . . That talisman is now already crumbling, and the day is not far off when it shall break apart entirely." At that point, Heine predicts, the old stone gods will rise from their thousand-year sleep and crush the hollow remains of Western civilization.

> And laugh not at my forebodings, the advice of a dreamer who warns you away from the Kants and Fichtes of the world, and from our philosophers of nature. No, laugh not at the visionary who knows that in the realm of phenomena comes soon the revolution that has already taken place in the realm of spirit. For thought goes before deed as lightning before thunder. There will be played in Germany a play compared to which the French revolution was but an innocent idyll.

The idea that our moral and social progress will be as effortless as our scientific and technological progress and that we no longer need the boundaries and restraints of faith, ethics, and the past is one of the pernicious follies of the twentieth century. To see the idea still continuing defies belief. History underscores the opposite. The great peaks of civilization are rare, scaled only with strenuous dedication and enjoyed only briefly. It is therefore no small thing to marginalize traditional responses to evil, for any tilt toward evil is an act of hostility toward civilization and a vote for barbarism. Only the time and manner of the decadence are to be decided.

QUESTION FOUR

Do the Differences
Make a Difference?

In asking the fourth basic question involved in exploring the
challenge of evil, we look at the different explanations for evil—
explanations that take us as close as we can get to knowing why evil
is evil, where it comes from, and how we are to respond to it—and
then choose the explanation we believe to be true and adequate for
our lives.

This is the hardest and most difficult question of all, a question
that goes far beyond the reflection and discussion that we have time
for here. Not surprisingly, much of the greatest human thinking is
about evil and suffering. And many of the greatest philosophies and
religions—supremely Buddhism and Stoicism—were born
specifically as answers to the challenge of evil and suffering. For
example, when we say someone is "philosophical" in the face of
suffering, we are not referring to his gifts in logic or analysis but to
his similarity to the Stoics in his use of thinking to provide a helpful
detachment from his suffering.

Many people today believe—or at least act as if they believe—that
all the answers they need in life come from science. But as brilliant
and helpful as the natural sciences are, they are not competent to

speak of evil, for evil cannot be seen, touched, weighed, or measured with any of the senses. Only a fool, for instance, would ask the color or weight or height of evil. Others resort instead to the soft sciences and to such disciplines as sociology and psychology to discover the dynamics of evil.

Such analysis is immensely valuable, yet it scratches only the surface of the questions we need to probe. The range of questions we need to ask must go wider and deeper than the sciences. Human life is unique among living species because we are aware of ourselves, yet we find ourselves in a world that does not explain itself. So we are compelled to ask why things are as they are and how we fit in. What gives life to life? Why is there something rather than nothing? And what is evil?

Deep inside us we know the facts of the matter are not the end of the matter. So we seek a final explanation, a source of meaning that goes as far back as we can go, an ultimate answer before which all questions cease. Such an explanation goes far beyond science. Even science is understood within the framework of such a larger answer. In George Steiner's memorable words: "More than *homo sapiens,* we are *homo quaerens*, the animal that asks and asks."

At this point many people are derailed by one of two objections. Some are told that exploring different answers is unnecessary because all the answers are the same at their core. Others are told the opposite: there are too many answers to look into, so the search is futile.

The response to the first objection is that no one has ever found the supposed common core. The closer we look, the plainer it is that there are differences between the answers and that the differences make a difference. Moreover, as I have stressed repeatedly, the differences make a difference not only for individuals but for whole societies and civilizations. In short, contrast is the mother of clarity. What Leon Battista Alberti said about Renaissance painting is true too of the contrast between faiths and the cultures to which they give rise. "All things are known by comparison, for comparison contains within itself a power which immediately demonstrates."

The response to the second objection is that, while there are countless beliefs in the world, there are only so many "families of faiths"—in the sense that different faiths have a common family resemblance because they go back to the same ultimate source of reality. Here is the real divide in discussing evil today. It is not between "pre-Lisbon" and "post-Lisbon" thinking or between "pre-Auschwitz" and "post-Auschwitz" thinking—Lisbon being the symbol for the rise of Enlightenment optimism after the earthquake, and Auschwitz the symbol for the death of Enlightenment optimism after the death camps. Lisbon and Auschwitz are truly gigantic milestones in the story of the discussion of evil, but they are both European events and relatively recent, whereas some of the deepest answers are far older and more truly global.

In our discussion of evil, the real divide is between the three leading families of faiths in the modern world. They all have very different views of the challenge of evil and its place in the meaning of life. In part 4, we examine each of them in turn.

The first is the Eastern family of faiths, which includes Hinduism, Buddhism, and varieties of New Age thought. Their common view of ultimate reality could be termed the impersonal ground of being, or "the undifferentiated impersonal," and their response to evil and suffering flows from this view. The main focus here is on Buddhism, which I believe will be the main contender among the Eastern religions to capture the mind of the global world of tomorrow.

The second is the secularist family of faiths, which includes atheism, naturalism, and secular humanism. Their common view of ultimate reality is "chance plus matter plus time." The significance of secularism here is paramount because it represents the leading faith of the educated elites in the Western world and throughout much of the entire world.

The third is the biblical family of faiths, which includes the three monotheistic or "Abrahamic" religions—Judaism, the Christian faith, and Islam. Despite important differences, their shared view of ultimate reality is an "infinite, personal God." The resurgence of Islam makes it extremely important again, though its main task is still to negotiate its responses to modernity constructively. Thus, my focus here is on the first two biblical faiths, which are crucially important because they are the primary shapers of Western civilization and today's world as we know it.

Bear in mind two things as we explore this fourth question. First, each faith should speak for itself rather than being understood through the words of outsiders or critics. This is partly a matter of elementary fairness and partly a response to some evident unfairness—some faiths are notorious for spending more time attacking the supposed inadequacies of their rivals' views than in setting out their own.

Plainly I am not fulfilling this ideal here myself, as I have stated openly that I am writing as a Christian. So I set out all the positions here as fairly as I can, while feeling free to comment on them without pretending to be more objective than I am. Those who take different positions are welcome to respond, and I trust with the same civility.

Second, each faith and philosophy should be understood in its best form rather than its worst. "One should not judge a doctrine through its by-products but through its peaks," Albert Camus wrote. It is important for a searcher to examine the link between beliefs and behavior, but when we see what we consider to be bad behavior by practitioners of a belief, we need to remember that some behavior accurately reflects the faith, while other behavior is such a contradiction that it is no reflection at all. As the novelist Herman Wouk said with an insider's sympathy, "If a way of life should be judged by its misinterpreters, which way will stand?"

In 1995, on the fiftieth anniversary of the liberation of Auschwitz, Arnost Lustig, a survivor and literary scholar, put forward a challenge that captures the spirit of this fourth question. It was his wish that sometime during the time when the death camp rather than the tourist museum was in operation, "all men and women, wherever they live on earth, would have to visit Auschwitz-Birkenau for a day, an hour or even a single second."

This visit would be a test of maturity before they could receive a driver's license or be allowed to vote or get married, with a guarantee, of course, that nothing would happen to them. I believe that this peek into hell would ripen their image of the world, for only those who have seen how little is needed to peel what is human from us—to turn us again into animals—can understand the world into which we are born.

Would this be a fair "test of maturity"? What would count as passing? Would you be prepared to submit your own views to this scrutiny? At the very least, I would argue, an examined life should be able to give an account of evil that is realistic in its diagnosis, hopeful in its remedy, and practical in offering solid grounds for both courage and comfort in facing evil. These are the sort of challenges that we should consider as we explore the fourth essential question.

CHAPTER 10

NIRVANA IS NOT FOR EGOS

It was one of the most poignant moments in Asian history, a turning point expressed in a look. He had made up his mind after a long period of thought and indecision. But there was still the cost to consider. As far as riches, honor, and his position were concerned, the price was cheap; these things were baubles to him. His wife and son were another matter. They were his passion and delight, and the choice here cut deep. So deep, in fact, that even after making the decision, he had promised himself one last moment alone with them, but only if they were asleep and he was unseen.

So it was that he slipped into the bedroom where his wife lay sleeping with the child of their love in her arms. Desire swelled in his heart. He longed to take the infant into his arms once more and leave a parting kiss that would print a father's love on him forever. He longed to take his wife in his arms and love her with a wild, sweet passion that would nourish them both in the long, lonely miles ahead.

But it could not be. He stood in the shadows gazing at them, and his heart grieved. The pain of parting overcame him powerfully. Although his mind was determined—nothing, either good or evil, could shake his resolution—the tears flowed freely from his eyes.

Finally he suppressed his feelings, tore himself from the scene, and walked swiftly to where his horse and servant stood waiting at the gate.

"Do not leave now, my lord," a woman's voice cried out in the darkness. "In seven days' time you will be ruler over four continents and two thousand islands. This is no time to leave."

"Well do I know it," he replied without stopping. "But it is not sovereignty I desire. I will become a Buddha and make all the world shout for joy."

The Only Dead Man?

Thus, the young Indian prince Siddhartha Gautama, known later to the world as the Buddha, or the Enlightened One, rode out into the night and into history. He "renounced power and worldly pleasures," according to one account, "gave up his kingdom, severed all ties, and went into homelessness. He rode out into the silent night, accompanied only by his faithful charioteer Channa. Darkness lay upon the earth, but the stars shone brightly in the heavens."

Brought up the son of a rajah of the Sakya tribe in Nepal, Siddhartha had led a life that was not only privileged but pampered. His father surrounded him with every conceivable pleasure and shielded him from all sorrow and suffering, with the intention "that no troubles should come nigh him; he should not know that there was evil in the world."

Three things, however, tore holes in the naïveté woven so assiduously by his father and made Siddhartha a seeker with questions about suffering. The first and deepest experience grew from the knowledge of his mother's death upon giving him birth. She had died that he might live—this left a heartache he could not escape.

The second experience occurred when he was nine. Siddhartha was taken out to watch the annual Sakya plowing festival, where his father made the first ceremonial cut into the ground. Instead of admiring his father's regal splendor, the sensitive young prince saw only the ground gashed open, insects hurtled from their habitat, worms cut in pieces, and birds descending to eat the squirming creatures on the broken soil. He was appalled and felt the suffering in his soul.

The third experience came years later when Prince Siddhartha, now grown, set out to see the world in a jewel-fronted chariot, on a route carefully decorated and arrayed by his father so as to show him only the beauties and pleasures of life. Along the way, however, he encountered first an old man, then a sick man, and finally a corpse. On seeing the corpse, Siddhartha is said to have asked, "Is this the only dead man, or does the world contain other instances?"

"All over the world it is the same," his charioteer replied with a heavy heart. "He who begins life must end it. There is no escape from death."

"Oh, worldly men!" Siddhartha exclaimed, as if addressing his father and all others who were caught up in diversions. "How fatal is your delusion! Inevitably your body will crumble to dust, yet carelessly, unheedingly, ye live on." From then on, the son he left behind became *Rahula* ("the fetter"), and Siddhartha himself became "the stream enterer," whose goal was to have no self and become the *Tathagata* (the one who had quite simply "gone").

The Great Deathless Lake

The story of Siddhartha Gautama's journey from privilege to disillusionment, to asceticism, and finally to enlightenment under the bodhi tree in Buddh Gaya, Bihar, is prototypical of the response to evil and suffering in the Eastern family of faiths—detachment. In both Hinduism and Buddhism, evil and suffering are seen as basic to human life. Many Hindus, probably the majority, choose to pursue salvation through sacrifices, but the more thoughtful Hindu minority and the majority of Buddhists reject the sacrificial tradition and pursue the goal of *Nirvana*—the blowing out of the fires of all desires and the absorption of the individual self into the infinite, "the great deathless lake of Nirvana."

The clearest expression of this approach to evil and suffering is

Buddha's first sermon, "Setting in Motion the Wheel of Dharma," in which he introduces the Four Noble Truths. He delivered this to his first five followers at the Isipatana Deer Park, near Benares, soon after his enlightenment. For 2,500 years, Buddhists have revered it as the heart of his message and the defining moment in his mission.

Buddha begins by highlighting two ways of life that do not work. On the one hand, self-indulgence—whether through drugs, alcohol, overeating, or sexual promiscuity—causes more problems than it solves. On the other hand, self-mortification—through such practices as fasting, solitude, and going without sleep—is not an effective path to happiness. "Avoiding these two extremes," Buddha says, "I have realized the Middle Path."

This Middle Path is the way of right view, right thought, right speech, right action, right livelihood, right effort, right mindfulness, and right *samadhi* (or concentration). And the four essentials behind these eight steps are the Four Noble Truths: *dukkha* (affliction), *samudaya* (cravings), *nirodha* (containment), and *marga* (the right track).

Clearly, attitudes toward evil and suffering are more than just a part of Buddhism; Buddhism itself is one grand response to evil and suffering. The First Noble Truth is the reality of affliction. "This is the Noble Truth about *dukkha*. Birth is *dukkha*. Aging is *dukkha*. Sickness is *dukkha*. Death is *dukkha*. Sorrow, pain, grief, and despair are *dukkha*. Not getting what one wants is *dukkha*. In short, the whole process of attachment is *dukkha*." In other words, bad things happen, they happen to us all in some measure, and they are part and parcel of reality as we know it.

Most people would give Buddhism the highest possible marks for realism—a realism to satisfy the requirements of the most stringent seeker. In the Buddhist view, evil, suffering, and affliction (*dukkha*) are in the very warp and woof of life. They cannot be ducked, imagined away by the most positive thinking, or escaped in any way in this world.

How does this view allow us to live with hope, both *in* this world and *for* this world? Here opinions differ sharply, even among Buddhists. For as they themselves admit, their answer to evil and suffering is radical, even drastic. There is no remedy for evil either in this world or for this world; there is only renunciation of this world. In the words of an American Buddhist, "Buddhism is not a superficial palliative."

As the majority of Buddhists see it, the First Noble Truth establishes the human problem—affliction and suffering. The Second Noble Truth points to its cause—craving, desire, or attachment. The Third Noble Truth then highlights the way to overcome suffering through containment, or extinguishing desire. And the Fourth Noble Truth describes the path to the end of desire, which in turn brings about the end of suffering. Thus, "disease" is followed by "diagnosis," which is followed by "prescription," which is followed by "treatment," until suffering is overcome. Or in the words of a sacred Buddhist text:

On the cessation of sensation ceases desire;
On the cessation of desire ceases attachment;
On the cessation of attachment ceases existence;
On the cessation of existence ceases birth;
On the cessation of birth ceases old age and death,
sorrow, lamentation, grief, and despair.

Thus does this entire aggregation of misery cease.

A Collision Course

The Buddhist remedy for suffering is stern, even drastic. If "the great deathless lake of Nirvana" is a state of extinguishedness, what is extinguished is not only suffering but attachment, desire, and—finally—the individual who desires. It is significant, Buddhists say, that in the moment the Buddha achieved enlightenment under the bodhi tree, Gautama did not cry, "I am liberated," but, "It is liberated." He had transcended himself and become the "not-self." Or as the philosopher Ninian Smart concluded bluntly, "There is Nirvana, but no person who enters it."

To say it again, in the Buddhist view there is quite simply no remedy for suffering in this world. Nor is there any prospect of a coming world without suffering. There is not even the hope that you and I will ever live free of suffering. And finally, there is no "you" or "I" at all. As Buddhagosa said of his state of enlightenment, "I am nowhere a somewhatness for anyone." There is only the nobility of the compassion of the enlightened on their road to the "liberation" of extinction.

As I see it, the modern, global era raises a titanic challenge for the Eastern family of faiths at this point. These faiths are essentially and explicitly world-denying, whereas the modern world is essentially and explicitly world-affirming. The inescapable contradiction need not mean the East is wrong, but it does put it on a collision course with the force and flow of the modern world. Thus, modern people tend to respond to the Eastern faiths in one of two ways: either they admire and maintain the tough world-denying character of the East, but use it as a "refugee ideology" by which to escape the unwanted pressures of modern life, or they maintain the world-affirming character of the modern world and tailor Eastern ideas and practices to fit the Western framework, losing in the process the more radical traditional features of the East.

An example of the first response is the fact that many Westerners espouse Eastern ideas and practices but are markedly clearer about what they reject in the West than about what they embrace in the East. They dislike the rush and noise of the West, for example, but keep their yoga to the level of a workout in the gym rather than a decisive step on the path to extinguishing the self.

As an example of the second response, baby boom Buddhism is increasingly touted in the West as a "religion of hope" and offered as a "spirituality for activists," whereas traditional Buddhism has no vision whatever of a world entirely just and affliction-free. Or again, the Four Noble Truths are reduced to "an authentic way of living life as it really is" or an "optimum way of mental health free of self-defeating views"—as if Buddha were an Asian Marcus Aurelius, his "right-mindedness" a handy precursor to psychotherapy and the positive thinking of Norman Vincent Peale, and Buddhism were a new market image for humanism.

As a Hindu yoga enthusiast, the actress Julia Roberts expressed this boomer consumerism perfectly: "I don't want it to change my life, just my butt."

Is Buddhism's offer of enlightenment a satisfactory remedy for evil and suffering, both theoretically and practically, both for individuals and for societies? Or is the cure worse than the disease? Where, if anywhere, is the place of hope for lives or a world free of affliction? What are the Buddhist answers to the instinctive questions raised by evil and suffering that we examined earlier? In my judgment, Buddhism falls short in answers to such questions, but each of us must make up our own mind about questions like these.

Excarnation, Not Incarnation

The grand challenge of a world-denying faith in a world-affirming age is more strenuous still for the dominant tradition of Hinduism, such as the thought of the great ninth century Hindu philosopher Shankara. Take the implications of its view of ultimate reality for the concept of individual human dignity that is at the heart of the modern world.

If the final reality in the universe is the "undifferentiated impersonal," or ground of being (God or Brahman), what are we humans? Who are you? Who am I? Why does an individual matter? The answer of the great ninth-century Hindu philosopher Shankara is straightforward: the relationship of God to the world is that of a dreamer to his dream. The dreamer alone is real; the world is unreal. The world of our experience is therefore *maya*, a world of illusion, ignorance, and shadow—a world where individuality and diversity are thought to be real but are not. God as the ultimate reality plays hide-and-seek with himself, "freaks out" at the end of the cosmic dance, or simply forgets himself. "This is the magic power of God by which he himself is deluded," says Shankara. In other words, the world is considered real only because of our ignorance. "Brahman alone is real; the phenomenal world is unreal, or mere illusion."

This version of Hinduism obviously has radical implications for science, and many have argued that modern science could not have risen from the Hindu worldview. But it has equally radical implications for individuality and human dignity. Are there grounds in Hinduism for notions such as human rights and the inalienable dignity of each individual? Shankara's answer is simple: "Who are you? Who am I? Whence have I come? Who is my mother? Who is my father? Think of all this as having no substance; leave it all as the stuff of dreams."

What are we? We are the extension of God's essence into the world of diversity in the sense of the dream, the dance, the hide-and-seek. Humans are "God's temporary self-forgetfulness," says Radakrishnan, the former president of India. Alan Watts explains, "God entranced himself and forgot the way back, so that now he feels himself to be man, playing—guiltily—at being God." The true self is God, and the "I" that each of us considers himself or herself to be is really the "not-self" caught in the world of illusion, bondage, and ignorance.

It follows then that freedom is liberation from illusion—the "not-self" assimilated into the "true self" of the ground of being. As the Upanishads explain, just as pollen merges with honey, just as salt dissolves in seawater, just as the Ganges flows into the Bay of Bengal, so the divine spark in humanity is freed by its merging with the Absolute.

In short, if God alone is the "true self" and individuality is never more than the mistaken "not-self," then individuality and freedom are contradictory. Freedom within Hinduism can never be freedom to be an individual. Freedom is always freedom *from* individuality. As Lord Krishna says in the Bhagavad Gita, humanity must be cut from "the dark forest of delusion." Or as D. T. Suzuki, the Zen teacher, said, the goal of Zen is not incarnation but "excarnation."

Lewis Carroll expressed this position playfully in *Through the Looking Glass*. Speaking of the dreaming King, Tweedledee says, "And if he left off dreaming about you, where do you suppose you'd be?"

"Where I am now, of course," says Alice.

"Not you!" Tweedledee retorts contemptuously. "You'd be nowhere. Why, you're only a sort of thing in his dream."

And Tweedledum adds, "If that there King was to wake, you'd go out—bang! Just like a candle!"

Our Problem Is Existence

This view of ultimate reality means that neither traditional Hinduism nor traditional Buddhism shows the slightest concern about human rights—which, of course, is a problem only for those who care about such rights. Entirely logical within their own frames of thinking, Hinduism and Buddhism regard the Western passion for human rights as a form of narcissism as well as delusion. R. C. Zaehner, who followed Radakrishnan in the Spaulding Chair of Eastern Religions and Ethics at Oxford University, underscored their logic bluntly: "In practice it means that neither religion in its classical formulation pays the slightest attention to what goes on in the world today."

Once again, my point here is not to argue that Hinduism and Buddhism need be wrong because of this view. Each seeker must decide that for himself. My concern with the contrasts is twofold.

First, the contrasts provide an opportunity to underscore again how differences make a difference—and for whole societies, not just individuals. Certainly, if the Eastern family of faiths is right, both the Western secularist family and the biblical family are wrong. Human rights are an illusion. Inalienable dignity is a conceit. The Eastern family contradicts the other two families sharply. Both sides cannot be right, and the consequences of their differences are plain.

Second, the contrasts highlight the difference between examining the Eastern religions on their own terms and diluting the Eastern religions to make them palatable for Western consumption. If the superficiality of much New Age thinking is an indication, our Western tendency is to trivialize the Eastern religions and turn them into a Disney ride to the Orient.

The same taming tendency happens to sternly pessimistic thinking of all kinds. It can always be turned into a consumer fashion. Samuel Beckett's pessimism, for example, was virtually Eastern in its content and severity even though he was an atheist. "The major sin is the sin of being born," he asserted, echoing the Eastern view. Our real problem is existence itself. It is not what we do but who we are.

But who in the West would swallow such pessimism, unless sweetened? So over the years Beckett's plays were slowly sentimentalized. Eventually, as one of his loyal drama critics pointed out, audiences began to delude themselves into thinking that at bottom his plays were jolly good fun. "Well, they are not jolly good fun," wrote Harold Hobson, theater critic for the London *Times*. "They are among the most frightening prophecies of, and longing for, doom ever written."

In the same way it is time to protest the Western trivializing of the Eastern religions—their tailoring for a New York magazine article or a California hot tub as if they were simply a dash of curry to flavor the chicken soup for the Western soul. Eastern religions are one of the modern world's three great families of faith—time-honored in their age and history, rigorous in their thought and practice, and powerful in their cultural influence. The way lies open for the seeker to explore but not to cheat. Checking out answers means following their logic to the very end.

CHAPTER 11

I DO IT MY WAY

The author of the essay called it his "gospel," but few readers have found any good news in it. It was written in Florence, but by a writer with an embarrassing lack of appreciation for the arts. Its setting is the gracious home of his hospitable hosts, but its tone is characterized by the bleak loneliness of the author's own heart, and he later said the essay was "only for people in great unhappiness."

In short, Bertrand Russell's "A Free Man's Worship" had unlikely beginnings. But when it was published in 1910, it was immediately hailed as a tour de force—a powerful, lyrical, impassioned statement of life without God on planet earth. Soon it was being quoted as if the author were Pericles or Shakespeare. Eventually it was celebrated as the leading manifesto of humanism in the twentieth century.

Russell wrote the essay in 1902 at i Tatti, the beautiful villa above Florence owned by his brother-in-law, Bernard Berenson, the legendary art historian and critic. Russell's loneliness was made all the bleaker by observing Berenson's devotion to his wife Mary (the sister of Russell's wife Alys). Berenson had married her after a passionate affair. By contrast, Russell found himself locked in a loveless marriage that was tearing him apart.

Russell described Alys as an "intellectual ball and chain" and their relationship as "long years in prison." Meanwhile, he experienced what he called his "first conversion," which brought him a profound new abhorrence of violence and a sudden new love for humanity, especially children. The transformation grew not from any spiritual experience, however, but from a relationship with the wife of Alfred North Whitehead, his collaborator in writing *Principia Mathematica*.

In his friendship with Evelyn Whitehead, Russell became acutely aware of her "utter loneliness, filled with intense tragedy and pain." With the secret of her suffering locked inside him, Russell endured a year of emotional warfare that drove his wife close to suicide and himself toward the edge of insanity. "Strange, the isolation in which we all live," he wrote to Gilbert Murray. "What we call friendship is really the discovery of an isolation like our own, a secret worship of the same gods."

Russell's repeated use of religious language in describing his love life—conversion, gods, and so on—points to the fact that his search for love was closely linked to his loss of faith. He was appalled by the overpowering piety of his elderly grandmother, who had raised him after the death of his parents. Her faith was not only claustrophobic but anti-intellectual. She squashed all hints of her brilliant grandson's budding philosophical interests with her favorite put-down: "What is mind? No matter. What is matter? Never mind." Not surprisingly, Russell declared himself a devout agnostic two days after his sixteenth birthday. But he never lost a sense of mysticism, and in his relationship with Evelyn Whitehead he gained a new passion for love as the only force capable of filling his empty heart.

So Russell arrived in Florence to spend Christmas in 1902. His near-desperation was in savage contrast to the beautiful villa, with its cypress-covered hillsides echoing the deep-toned Italian bells, and to the honeymoonlike love of the Berensons. Nor did the cultural richness of Florence bring any solace. "I am a good British philistine," he confessed to Berenson, whose dazzling tour of the Uffizi left Russell unmoved. "I've looked at everything you wanted me to look at; I've listened to all you've said; but the pictures still don't give me the funny feeling in the stomach they give you."

Indeed, Russell confided in a letter that, though the Berenson house was exquisitely furnished, "the business of existing beautifully, except when it is hereditary, always slightly shocks my Puritan soul."

Such was the setting for Bertrand Russell's great tract on humanism—the misery of his marriage, the trauma of his discovery of Evelyn Whitehead's lonely suffering, the ecstatic happiness of his hosts, and the idyllic beauty of his environment. "The human surroundings were ideally the worst," he remembered later, "but I spent long days alone on the hillsides & in the groves of olive and cypress, with the Arno below & the austere barren country above."

The essay, Russell admitted, was his way of working out the shock that had made him "suddenly and vividly aware of the loneliness in which most people live, and passionately desirous of finding ways of diminishing this tragic isolation." He began with Mephistopheles' account of the world to Dr. Faust. Having set down the human problem as he saw it, he gave his celebrated answer. Man, he wrote, "is the product of causes which had no prevision of the end they were achieving." Man's "origin, his growth, his hopes and fears, his loves and his beliefs, are but the outcome of accidental collocations of atoms," and therefore "no fire, no heroism, no intensity of thought and feeling, can preserve an individual life beyond the grave."

He saw that "all the labours of the ages, all the devotion, all the inspiration, all the noonday brightness of human genius are destined to extinction in the vast death of the solar system, and that the whole temple of Man's achievement must inevitably be buried beneath the debris of a universe in ruins." He concluded that "all these things, if not quite beyond dispute, are yet so nearly certain, that no philosophy which rejects them can hope to stand. Only within the scaffolding of these truths, only on the firm foundation of unyielding despair can the soul's habitation henceforth be safely built."

Thus I Willed It

"A Free Man's Worship" and Russell's life behind the words take us straight to the heart of the second great family of faiths, Western secularism (or humanism, or naturalism), and its response to evil and suffering. In certain circles the word *humanism* has become pejorative rather than descriptive, but there is no doubt that a secular form of humanism is one of the most powerful faiths in the modern world.

There are different accounts of the rise of humanism—from the religious humanism of the Renaissance through the Enlightenment to today—but there is no question that secular humanism became prominent in the nineteenth century and has been dominant in educated circles since then.

At the same time the central place of God in the world has been taken over by humanity. "Man is the measure of all things," Protagoras had said in the fifth century B.C. "A man can do all things if he will," Leon Battista Alberti had said during the Renaissance. In the nineteenth century this confidence matured and climaxed in a belligerent, all-out anti-God campaign, as typified by Algernon Swinburne's "Hymn of Man": "Glory to Man in the highest! For Man is the Master of Things."

Usually, however, the tone of secular humanism was more urbane and assured. Count Saint-Simon instructed his valet to wake him every morning with the words, "Arise, your highness, great deeds are to be done."

"Man makes himself," said the archaeologist Gordon Childe.

"We see the future of man as one of his own making," said the geneticist H. J. Muller.

"Today, in twentieth-century man," Sir Julian Huxley remarked, "the evolutionary process is at last becoming conscious of itself. . . . Human knowledge worked over by human imagination is seen as the basis to human understanding and belief, and the ultimate guide to human progress."

"All man's problems were created by man and can be solved by man," John F. Kennedy declared in his inaugural address.

Humanism's all-decisive claim is that, since there is no God, there is no revealed meaning and no intrinsic meaning in the universe at all. Therefore meaning is not disclosed or even discovered. It has to be created. Human beings are both the source and standard of their own meaning, so it is up to each of us to create our own meaning and impose it on the world. And if we cannot impose our meaning on the world as a whole, we can impose it in our own small lives as an act of self-creation.

As Nietzsche asserted in *Ecce Homo*, instead of settling for a passive life summed up in the words "it was," we must so live that we can say, "Thus I willed it."

In the words of his Russian-American disciple, the philosopher and novelist Ayn Rand, "My personal life is a postscript to my novels; it consists of the sentence: *'And I mean it.'*"

In Russell's picture, each of us is Atlas carrying the world of our own meaning on our own shoulders.

Or as Frank Sinatra put it simply, "I did it my way."

The World as We Find It

What does this view of life mean for humanist responses to suffering and evil? What are the salient features of such a response?

There is no orthodoxy in secular humanism and therefore no end to the possible variations that may claim the name. But across the prominent examples of the philosophy, two features of its response to suffering stand out.

The first feature is the frank acknowledgment that suffering and evil are part and parcel of the inhospitable universe in which humans find themselves. In Russell's vision, not only are we the product of blind chance, but we are moving toward an end that contradicts and cancels out purpose—the "extinction" that he saw as the destiny of "all the labours of the ages, all the devotion, all the inspiration, all the noonday brightness of human genius."

The same point can be expressed less bleakly, but it remains the same point. I well remember as a university student meeting and listening to Bertrand Russell, then in his early nineties. Sometimes I admired the grandeur of his courage in describing such bleak realities; more often I was chilled by the arctic quality of his conclusions.

At the time I found Albert Camus, with his philosophy of the rebel, far more appealing. Camus's call to fight the "plague" heroically, one patient at a time, struck chords with our passion in those days. It excited our sympathy for victims of evil. It appealed to our outrage at the state of a world gone awry.

But in the end, of course, Camus's vision was no different. When Dr. Rieux in *The Plague* claims that he is on the right track "in fighting against creation as he found it," he acknowledges the same reality that Russell does. The flaw is in the world as we find it. Evil is natural to our world. Describe it as we wish, fight it as we can, but what we confront is still the universe as it is. All the warm-blooded outrage and compassion in the world cannot mask the nature of things. Whatever we desire, the absurd is what we discover. We simply cannot get around it. Within the humanist view, as in the Eastern view, evil is normal and natural in the world as we know it.

For Charles Darwin and all who make evolution and natural selection central to their view of life, realism constantly tends to collapse into pessimism, whatever their individual protestations of joy and hope in life. And the reason is simple: not only is natural selection utterly blind to evil and suffering, but it favors the "selfish gene" and the survivalist ethic of "might makes right" that is the evil heart of oppression and abuse of power. No account of twentieth-century evil can ignore its close kinship to the dark side of Nietzsche's will to power.

In the preface to *Back to Methuselah*, George Bernard Shaw laments what he sees as the practical implications of natural selection. "When its whole significance dawns on you, your heart sinks into a heap of sand within you. There is a hideous fatalism about it, a ghastly and damnable reduction of beauty and intelligence, of strength and purpose, of honor and aspiration."

Coming to the same point from the opposite direction, H. G. Wells exults in the logic of natural selection but points out its callousness for all to see. Outlining his Darwinian utopia in *The New Republic*, he writes chillingly about how "inferior races" will be treated:

> Well, the world is a world, and not a charitable institution, and I take
> it they will have to go. . . . And the ethical system of these men of
> the New Republic, the ethical system which will dominate the world
> state, will be shaped primarily to favor the procreation of what is fine
> and efficient and beautiful in humanity—beautiful and strong bodies,
> clear and powerful minds. . . . And the method that nature has fol-
> lowed hitherto in the shaping of the world, whereby weakness was
> prevented from propagating weakness . . . is death. . . . The men of
> the New Republic . . . will have an ideal that will make the killing
> worth the while.

Writing as a self-professed "Devil's Chaplain" today, the biologist Richard Dawkins makes the same point, though less flamboyantly: "If there is mercy in nature, it is accidental. Nature is neither kind nor cruel but indifferent."

Ennobling Our Little Day

All these writers also agree on the second prominent feature of the Western secularist response to evil and suffering. Given the flaws and the evil and suffering in "creation as we find it," it is up to us to create and shoulder our own meaning and to ennoble life by working resolutely for what reform we can.

Here the Western secularist answer decisively parts company with the Eastern answer, as befits its character as the stepchild of the Jewish and Christian faiths. Evil and suffering are part and parcel of life—on that both secularism and Buddhism agree. But far from withdrawing, as the East does, the Western secularist answer is engagement—working to build, to fight, and so to leave the world a better place regardless of the final outcome.

Although Russell later rejected the lyrical, rhetorical style of "A Free Man's Worship," many were inspired by the essay's call to the free man to "ennoble his little day." United only by the "tie of a common doom," fully aware that life is "a long march through the night," and conscious that our comrades are vanishing one by one— "seized by the silent orders of omnipotent death"—we must still, says Russell, shed "over every daily task the light of love."

Here, the biologist Julian Huxley wrote in his *Essays of a Humanist*, is where the humanist's challenge and hope intersect. "Man is the product of nearly three billion years of evolution, in whose person the evolutionary process has at last become conscious of itself and its possibilities. Whether he likes it or not, he is responsible for the whole further evolution of our planet."

Dawkins seconds this goal with fervor.

> So, the Devil's Chaplain might conclude, Stand tall, Bipedal Ape. The shark may outswim you, the cheetah outrun you, the swift outfly you, the capuchin outclimb you, the elephant outpower you, the redwood outlast you. But you have the biggest gifts of all: the grace of understanding the ruthlessly cruel process that gave us all existence; the gift of revulsion against its implications; the gift of foresight— something utterly foreign to the blundering short-term ways of natural selection—and the gift of internalizing the very cosmos.

Questions explode in every direction after reading such paragraphs. Above all, we want to examine the evidence for the practicality of such hopes. Have the years since humanity discovered that it was responsible for evolution and the future of the planet shown a new maturity in avoiding evil and establishing good? Quite the contrary. Did each of these individuals—for instance, Bertrand Russell— live this altruistically himself? Not exactly. As his friends commented tartly, in his relations with other men's wives Russell had the morals of a goat.

In private Russell even expressed later reservations about his essay's ethic. "I wrote with passion & force, because I really thought I had a gospel," he said. "Now I am cynical about the gospel because it won't stand the test of life."

When Joseph Conrad wrote to congratulate him for the essay,

Russell told his mistress, Ottoline Morrell, that a sense of shame came over him. "No, the man who wrote that is not the man Conrad sees now—the affection he gives is not now deserved—the man who would face a hostile universe rather than lose his vision has become a man who will creep into the first hovel to escape the terror & splendour of the night."

Commenting on the essay twenty-five years later, Russell wrote, "Fundamentally, my view of man's place in the cosmos remains unchanged." But he qualified the scope of his call to altruism: "In times of moral difficulty and emotional stress, the attitude expressed in this essay, is at any rate for temperaments like my own, the one which gives most help in avoiding moral shipwreck."

For Camus the rub lay elsewhere. Although we rebel and fight courageously, the outcome is always—as Dr. Rieux in *The Plague* acknowledges—"never-ending defeat." The plague will always break out elsewhere. Evil will always stalk the earth again. After Dr. Rieux's friend Tarrou dies, the grief of the death chamber is at first a relief, but then it grows into a silence that "made Rieux cruelly aware that this defeat was final, the last disastrous battle that ends a war and makes peace itself an ill beyond all remedy."

Too Bad to Be True?

"It won't stand the test of life," says Russell. "Never-ending defeat," says Camus. Here we can see the modern world's grand challenge to the secularist family of faiths. These faiths appeal to society's intellectual elites (seen in George Steiner's description of agnosticism as "the established church of modernity. By its somewhat bleak light, the educated and the rational conduct their immanent lives"), but they hold little or no attraction for ordinary people. Bloodless as well as bleak, they are too cerebral for everyday life. This is a fatal flaw, and a central reason for the decline of atheism and the weakness of the secularist movement.

Russell prescribed his ethics "for temperaments like my own," but how many people are included in this sweep? How many of us, having been told about the bleakness of human prospects, will still adhere to the nobility of humanist ethics—especially if it appears that the author himself did not? Why should we care for others as ourselves? Would it not be just as consistent to eat, drink, and be merry, for tomorrow we die?

On Camus's tombstone are these words from *The Myth of Sisyphus*: "The struggle toward the summit itself suffices to fill a man's heart." But how many will find rebellion to be a satisfying reason for existence when we know from the beginning that we can never reach the summit? When we know that, like Sisyphus, we can never roll the stone to the top of the hill, that even our best, highest, and ultimate efforts can end only in final defeat?

Despite their courage, the bleakness of Russell and Camus is all too clear. Russell's friend and fellow humanist H. J. Blackham once admitted: "The most drastic objection to humanism is that it is too bad to be true. The world is one vast tomb if human lives are ephemeral and human life itself is doomed to ultimate extinction." Jean-Paul Sartre put it equally bluntly: "Atheism is a cruel, long-term business; I believe I have gone through it to the end."

Are secularism's bleakness and narrow appeal to elites signs of strength or weakness? Are these qualities proof of secularists' honesty and a badge of their unflinching realism, or are they an admission of secularism's ultimate inadequacy? Does the secularist view pass the requirement for realism? Does it live up to the requirement for hope? How does it pass the acid test of helping a mourner at a funeral? How does it answer the instinctive questions raised earlier? Again, in my judgment, secularism falls fatally short, but each of us must make up our minds for ourselves.

We each need an ultimate framework to give us meaning as we face evil and suffering. So the way lies open for the protagonist of the examined life to explore, but not to cheat. Exploring answers always means following the logic of an answer to the very end and seeing the difference that the answer makes. And as the record of the twentieth century shows, differences make a difference.

At the very least, secularists must enter the debate with their own candor and humility. Those who rejected one hell as quite beyond belief created several other hells—on earth—and ones even more incredible. Those who rejected a Grand Judgment at the end of the human story have replaced it with a vision of final conflagration and catastrophe. But will our delight in stage effects outweigh our passion for justice and a balancing of history's books? The second family of faiths must show how its promised future will be decisively different from the horrors of its recent past and what its envisioned outcome will mean for the longings of the human heart.

CHAPTER 12

PEOPLE OF THE CROSSED STICKS

Baroness Caroline Cox has been described as "the Mother Teresa of the war-torn poor." A nurse, scientist, and deputy speaker of Britain's House of Lords, she has, to many of the world's helpless, become "love in action" in human form and a powerful voice on behalf of the forgotten. Regardless of the color, creed, or race of the victims of war—those who have been maimed and raped, their families robbed, killed, or taken into slavery—she reaches out with food, clothes, and medicine. Often when she arrives, the people greet her with the words: "Thank God you've come. We thought the world had forgotten us."

A friend of mine once asked her to relate both her worst moment and her best during all her journeys of mercy. The worst? She thought for a moment, then described with brutal simplicity what it was like to enter a Dinka village after Sudanese government-backed soldiers had left, laden with human loot.

The stench of death was overpowering. More than a hundred corpses lay where they had been savagely butchered. Men, women, children, even cattle, had been cut down or herded into captivity to be carried north as slaves. Straw huts were ablaze, crops had been razed, and devastation and death confronted the eyes everywhere. Worst of all was the knowledge that the militia would return with their gunships and Kalashnikov rifles, and the area's villages would once again lie naked before the ferocity and bloodlust of the Muslim fundamentalists from the North. "*Genocide* is an overworked word," Lady Cox said, "and one I never use without meaning it. But I mean it."

And her best moment? It came, she said, right after the worst. With the raiders gone and the results of their cruelty all around, the few women still alive—husbands slain, children kidnapped into slavery, homes ruined, and they themselves brutally raped—were pulling themselves together. Their first instinctive act was to make tiny crosses out of sticks lying on the ground and to push them into the earth.

What were they doing? Fashioning instant memorials to those they had lost? No, Lady Cox explained, the crudely formed crosses were not grave markers, but symbols. The crossed sticks, pressed into the ground at the moment when their bodies reeled and their hearts bled, were acts of faith. As followers of Jesus of Nazareth in the Horn of Africa, they served a God whom they believed knew pain as they knew pain. Blinded by pain and grief themselves, horribly aware that the world would neither know nor care about their plight, they still staked their lives on the conviction that there was one who knew and cared. They were not alone.

Triple Reassurance

In the hour of their greatest need, these Dinka women had gone instinctively to the heart of the biblical view of suffering. To appreciate what they were doing, step back for a moment. There are many parts to the biblical response to evil; it includes the notion of *sin*, which is the ultimate localizing of evil in each of our hearts, as well as the central and decisive understanding of the person whom the Jews saw as the Adversary and Jesus called the Evil One—the human enemy par excellence. But rather than providing a full summary of the biblical position, let me take up just one theme: the unique and powerful biblical response to the challenge of the trilemma.

The challenge of evil, you remember, hits the believer in God from the Abrahamic family of faiths in the form of the deadly trilemma. In Augustine's version: "If God were all-good, he would only will good, and if he were all-powerful, he would be able to do all that he wills. But there is evil. Therefore God is either not all-good or not all-powerful, or both." In other words, the challenge of evil explodes on the believer with deadly force because it appears to make it impossible to hold together three cardinal truths of biblical faith: evil is evil, God is all-good, and God is all-powerful. Suddenly the three truths seem quite contradictory.

At first sight, all seems up for faith. It must surely be smashed to smithereens. Like massive hammer blows, the deadly trilemma smashes down on faith and pounds it against the so-called "rock of atheism"—life's terrible experience of evil and affliction.

But when the cry of pain dies away, faith is seen to endure and even to thrive. For faith in God has a source of unexpected resilience. Within it lies a threefold reassurance, both bracingly rational and comfortingly emotional, which gives it the strength to withstand the worst and still prevail. In an extraordinary manner, these three reassurances give faith the strength to counter the triple threat of the trilemma with precision and power. Together, like hands bonded in a firm and interlocking grip, these three reassurances allow the believer to keep the faith and ride out the storm of evil and suffering with assurance deepened rather than destroyed.

Oddly, faith's trick is to do the exact opposite of what we might expect—to relax or jettison one of the offending and seemingly contradictory truths. Give up the idea that evil is evil, that God is all-good, or that God is all-powerful, and the tension created by the contradiction dissipates—but so also does faith. If evil is not evil, what is the problem? And if God is not all-good or all-powerful, how does faith provide an answer? Rabbi Kushner's *When Bad Things Happen to Good People* and many modern believers take this tack: they give up belief in an all-powerful God, which is why their answers are so unsatisfactory. Without meaning to, such answers flatter to deceive in that they set out the problem of evil brilliantly but fail to provide an answer that satisfies intellectually and emotionally.

The biblical reassurances move in the opposite direction to this approach. With a paradoxical move that defies our expectations, they *reinforce* rather than reject the three cardinal truths, but they do so in a way that turns the objections inside out, so that these three unshakable truths become comforting rather than challenging.

Evil and suffering remain a mystery, of course. All the profoundest explorations of human searching agree on that and take it as the starting point of their responses. It is not that followers of the Jewish and Christian faiths are stumped by the problem of evil whereas others have found an answer. Some of the deepest questions baffle us all as human beings, Jews and Christians included. For all the passion and curiosity of our human answers and attempted answers, none of us finally knows "whence evil," nor why there is evil, nor why evildoers do evil. All these things are what the medievals called *insolubilia*—the insoluble things that are the untied knots and impenetrable codes of human existence.

It is also true that if we were to cave in and cry "mystery" every time we encountered anything incomprehensible, it would strongly suggest that faith is cowardly and irrational. But the mystery of evil is a mystery for all human beings. Evil remains as finally irrational as it is inscrutable, and the deep rationality of biblical faith is opposed to absurdity, not to mystery.

To be sure, other mysteries of the Christian faith, such as the threefold relationship of the Trinity, are illuminating mysteries—we do not finally understand them, but we understand so much else in their light. On the other hand, the mystery of evil—which the Apostle Paul calls "the mystery of iniquity"—often appears to be a darkening mystery. It makes life opaque and throws deep shadows on the best of our faiths, joys, and loves. But the three reassurances of the Bible are addressed precisely to that world of affliction and pain, simultaneously reinforcing its truths and subverting the objections made out of them, so that in the end the experience of pain and affliction leads toward faith rather than away.

Bifocal Vision

The first biblical reassurance addresses the first prong of the trilemma, the evil of evil: *the world should have been otherwise.* From the beginning of the Bible to its end, there is no shred of ambiguity about evil. Evil is totally, radically, and flagrantly counter to the character and purpose of God. It is disruptive and destructive by definition. It is both a perversion and a privation—the absence of good in something that by its very nature should be expected to have this good. Contrary to Leibniz, Alexander Pope, and all who believe this is the best of all possible worlds, whatever is, is emphatically *not* right.

A tree, a cow, or a rock without love is no less a tree, a cow, or a rock, but a human being whose heart is filled with the intent to harm rather than to seek another's good is disordered and decisively less of a human being. Evil is therefore in essence that which was not supposed to be, a rupture in the cosmic order of things, a cancer whose malignancy has spread to every part of life, a form of red-handed mutiny against life as it was supposed to be. Thus, unlike Eastern faiths, which view evil as ignorance, the Bible unequivocally grounds its view of evil in the consequences of free, responsible, culpable choice—or sin. Being informed is not enough; being transformed is what we need.

Importantly too, unlike both the Eastern and secularist views—which see evil as the very essence of existence, as part and parcel of what has always been—the Bible views evil, suffering, pain, and death as abnormal, as an alien intrusion rather than as something natural, precisely because their entry into the world is the consequence of free choice, not fate. Evil is therefore a parasite on a healthy body, an unwelcome gate-crasher at the party of life. For both the Jewish and Christian faiths, the ultimate problem therefore lies not in who we are but what we have done—in our disobedience rather than our existence.

John Milton expressed this well in *Paradise Lost*: when Eve sinned, the earth "felt the wound" and "gave a second groan" when Adam followed.

The author Garry Wills puts it in more modern terms: the biblical view of sin states simply that humanity "has a past."

In André Gide's line, man is "God's striving, problem child."

The roots of this conviction that the world should have been otherwise lie in the twin biblical doctrines of the creation and the fall. Created directly out of nothing by God, the world was and remains good. But it is also fallen. The entry of moral disobedience has left the world marred and broken. An illegitimate force is at work, which runs everything down and never renews, which degrades and never improves, which ruins and destroys and never creates.

The way I express the biblical vision is that it is characteristically bifocal. The world must always be viewed simultaneously through two different lenses: the perspective of creation and the perspective of the fall. Sometimes we see what it might have been. Sometimes we see only what it has become by being marred. Neither one lens nor the other provides focus by itself; only the two together bring clear sight. From the perspective of creation, evil need not have been. From the perspective of the brokenness of our world today, the world should have been otherwise.

This bifocal vision lies behind a defining feature of the biblical faiths and their significance for civilization—what C. S. Lewis calls their "two-edged character." The Christian faith, Lewis wrote, has a track record of being world-affirming and world-denying at the same time.

Because of its view of creation, the Christian faith—like humanism today and Confucianism in the past—openly affirms the world. It therefore builds hospitals, encourages the arts, pursues science, propels reforms, and is the most powerful animating force in history's most world-affirming civilization.

At the same time, because of its view of the fall, the Christian faith openly denies the world—as Buddhism and Hinduism do, al-

though for very different reasons—and therefore teaches the importance of fasts as well as feasts, self-denial as well as celebration, and
the glories of heaven as well as the grandeurs of the earth.

Christians have at times gone overboard on one side or the
other—some becoming too worldly and others becoming too other-
worldly. But the biblical position unashamedly stresses both sides together.

This bifocal vision carries a momentous implication for the biblical
response to evil and suffering. If suffering is the result of the fall rather
than of creation—a consequence of what we have done rather than of
what the world was created to be—then evil, pain, suffering, and death
are abnormal and alien, not normal and natural. As such, they are in-
criminating evidence of what almost all human beings feel in the face
of evil: the world should have been otherwise. In some definite but in-
definable way, human life is not on track. There could be no outrage
against wrong and no "crimes against humanity" if evil were completely natural and inhumanity were all that humanity is. But this is not
so in the biblical vision, and it is not so in our experience.

In his memoir *Errata*, George Steiner describes the outrage he
feels when wanton pain is inflicted on children and animals:

> At the maddening center of despair is the insistent instinct—again I
> can put it no other way—of a broken contract. Of an appalling and
> specific cataclysm. In the futile scream of the child, in the mute
> agony of the tortured animal, sounds the "background noise" of a
> horror after creation, after being torn loose from the logic and
> repose of nothingness. Something—how helpless language can be—
> has gone hideously wrong. Reality should, could have been, other-
> wise. . . . The impotent fury, the guilt which master and surpass my
> identity carry with them the working hypothesis, the "working
> metaphor," if you will, of "original sin."

In strong contrast to the Jewish and Christian position, Herodotus
tells us of the Thracians who mourned the birth of a baby, because of
the suffering it would endure through life, and rejoiced at funerals, be-

cause the pain of existence was over. Not to be born was the best thing; next best was to die young. "Those whom the gods love die young."

In a similar vein, the seventeenth-century writer Pedro Calderón de la Barca lamented, "Man's greatest offense is that he was born."

The philosopher Arthur Schopenhauer believed the same. In *The World as Will and Representation*, he wrote, "We have not to be pleased but rather sorry about the existence of the world; that its nonexistence would be preferable to its existence; that it is something that at bottom ought not to be, and so on."

Richard Wagner was no different. Deeply excited after reading Schopenhauer, he wrote to his friend Franz Liszt: "Let us treat the world only with contempt, for it deserves no better; but let no hope be placed in it, that our hearts be not deluded! It is evil, evil, fundamentally evil."

The playwright Samuel Beckett asserted similarly, "The major sin is the sin of being born."

All these pessimists, blaming suffering on human existence rather than human action, moved inevitably toward the Eastern position and its implication of radical renunciation of the world. Within the Eastern perspective, after all, birth is death and death is rebirth, so the task is to escape attachment and the constant turning of the wheel of suffering. Thus, Schopenhauer praised a Hindu holy man who in his attempt to move beyond desire even avoided lying down twice under the same tree in case he became attached to it.

Not so for the biblical faiths. As George Steiner shows, their logical thrust blasts in the opposite direction. "Life ought to be otherwise," say the Jew and the Christian. Outrage at what is wrong in life is the negative counterpart of wonder at what is beautiful in the world: both point to truths that transcend present reality. If things were not supposed to be this way, human beings may be caught in tragic situations in life, but the problem can be traced ultimately to human beings, not life. Or to use Camus's phrase, the problem is not in creation but in "creation *as we find it*"—its found condition being a later result of the fall rather than its original state.

Outrage at Death

Is this mere wordplay? Far from it. It is a sure foundation for the freedom to be human in the face of evil and suffering. I first encountered the human implications of this belief many years ago through an older and wiser friend in Switzerland. We were together when he heard the news that the son of a well-known Christian leader had been killed in a cycling accident. The leader had been devastated, but he earned the quiet admiration of all when he summoned up his strength, suppressed his grief, and preached eloquently on hope at his son's funeral. My friend quietly commented, "I trust he feels the same thing inside."

A few weeks later my friend received a phone call from the Christian leader. Could he come and talk to him? Several of us were there and welcomed him, and he went in to talk to my friend. But after a few minutes the rest of us left the house altogether. The chalet's walls were thin, and what we heard was not the hope of the preacher but the hurt of the father—pained and furious at God, dark and bilious in his blasphemy. After all, surely God had willed the death of his son.

My friend's response was not to rebuke him but to point him to the story of Jesus at the tomb of his friend Lazarus. The account in the Gospel of John says three times that Jesus was angry. One of the words used is the Greek term for "furious indignation"—the word the tragedian Aeschylus uses to describe warhorses rearing up on their hind legs, snorting through their nostrils, and charging into battle.

This was the reaction of Jesus of Nazareth when brought face to face with a loved one's death. The world that God created good and beautiful and whole was now broken and in ruins. In moments Jesus was going to do something about it, but his first response was outrage—instinctive, blazing outrage. Premature death is wrong, outrageously wrong, and clearly it was even worse in his eyes than in ours.

The freedom this view gives us is soul-stirring. Once you know in the depth of your soul that the world should have been otherwise, you are free to feel what it is human to feel: sorrow at what is heart-breaking, shock at what is shattering, and outrage at what is flagrantly all wrong and out of joint. Indeed, it is every bit as wrong not to be angry when we should be as to be angry when we should not be. To pretend otherwise is to be too pious by half, and harder on ourselves than Jesus himself was.

The death of a close friend prompted Larry Ellison, chairman of the Oracle Corporation, to exclaim, "Death makes me very angry. Premature death makes me angrier still." From the Jewish and Christian perspectives, such outrage is right, not wrong. This, as C. S. Lewis observed, brings us back to the paradox of the biblical faiths: "Of all men we hope most of death; yet nothing will reconcile us to—well, its unnaturalness."

No Other God Has Wounds

The second biblical reassurance addresses the second prong of the trilemma, God is all-good: *no other god has wounds.* At the very heart of the Bible is a God who cares and comes to the aid of those who look to him. In contrast to the Eastern religions, the biblical response to evil and suffering is one of engagement, not detachment. And in contrast to secularist beliefs, we are not on our own as we fight evil. Precisely because of a wisdom and strength greater than our own, those who combat wrong can have solid grounds for trusting in the final triumph of good over evil. Our individual prospects end only in death, and the cosmic prospects for the planet are a stay of execution only delayed somewhat by a few billion years. But Jewish and Christian confidence is not in science and human efforts. Even when we die, God keeps faith with us in the dust.

So for Jews and Christians to sing "We shall overcome" is not whistling in the dark but a commitment to justice based on confidence in its ultimate victory. This confidence grows directly from their vision of God. Far from being an "undifferentiated impersonal," a bare "ground of being," a "cosmic force," let alone blind chance or the laws of nature, the God who addresses his creatures in the Bible is personal as well as infinite.

In contrast to those who think religious belief is mere human projection, the God of the biblical story is not simply personal for us but personal in himself. He is personal because of his own nature, not because we need him to be personal. He is not made in our image; we are made in his. And there is no other ground for justifying the preciousness and inalienable dignity of each human being. Those who prize human rights without this root will find it a cut-flower ideal as disappointing as it is short-lived.

No one stands taller in Jewish history than Moses; the theme of God's personal involvement is powerful from the beginning of his mission to liberate his people. "Let my people go!" his command rings out to Pharaoh (and down the centuries to oppressed peoples everywhere). And behind the command: "I have indeed seen the misery of my people in Egypt," God said to Moses. "I have heard them crying out because of their slave drivers, and I am concerned about their suffering. So I have come down to rescue them from the hand of the Egyptians."

At the end of Moses's life, with the exodus and the crossing of the wilderness behind him, his wonder is deeper than ever. "What other great nation is so great," Moses asks rhetorically, "to have their gods near them the way the Lord our God is near to us whenever we pray to him?"

Whether the Torah pictures God as redeemer—the next of kin whose business is to meet every need, bear every burden, and pay every price—or as the one who promises to send his Messiah, the suffering servant, the God of the Jews is an intervening God. His heart is to step in on behalf of his people and on behalf of the poor and helpless, especially when they cry to him from under oppression.

For followers of Jesus, who believe that he *is* that kinsman-redeemer, that suffering-servant Messiah, faith centers on a scandal that no time can rub smooth and no triumph can ever soften: his death as a tortured criminal, spread-eagled and naked on the instrument of his execution, for our sake. The God whom Jesus shows on the cross is one who defeats evil by taking it to himself, letting it do its worst to him, and then overcoming it. No wonder the crucifixion of Jesus is the supreme pattern of innocent suffering in history.

It was this cross that took Dostoyevsky to faith through "the hell-fire of doubt." Gazing at the suffering of Jesus as he stood in front of Hans Holbein's *Descent from the Cross*, he realized that the painted scene was more than graphic realism. It was a window into the reality of the universe. If God's son suffered like this, there could be redemption in the world. As Alyosha says in *The Brothers Karamazov*, "I do not know the answer to the problem of evil, but I do know love."

It was this cross that kept alive Emily Dickinson's flickering faith despite her doubts. Jesus was the pioneer even in suffering and death: "All the other distance / He hath traversed first— / No New Mile remaineth." Or as she expressed it in another poem, the piers on which believers tread may be brittle, but God "sent his son to test the plank, / And he pronounced it firm."

It was this cross under which Dietrich Bonhoeffer sheltered as he waited for the hangman's noose in prison in Berlin for resisting Hitler. "Only the suffering God can help," he wrote.

It was this cross that Duke Ellington wanted over his bed as he lay dying. His Christmas cards, which he often sent out as late as July, were mailed early that year—in May. Their design was the same as the sign over his bed. Against a brilliant blue background, gold letters spelled G-O-D in a horizontal line with L-O-V-E placed vertically, forming a cross with a common O in the middle.

It was this cross that spelled out to the author Henri Nouwen "the compassionate God." After contemplating *The Crucifixion* of the Isenheim Altar by Matthias Grünewald in Colmar, France, for more than three hours, he wrote, "I had an inkling of the reaction of the plague-stricken and dying sufferers in the sixteenth century. On this altar they saw their God, with the same suppurating ulcers as their own." God liberates, Nouwen concluded, not by removing suffering from us but by sharing it with us. Jesus is "God-who-suffers-with-us."

Is it any wonder that for followers of Jesus it is only this cross that allows them to face the horrendous evils of the modern age without flinching? What other faith has at its heart a writhing body, torn flesh, shameful desertion and disgrace, anguished desolation, and a darkness that can be felt? But what other faith has a God who so takes evil into himself that the day of the death of all deaths becomes the day death died?

In the famous words of George Macleod of Iona:

> Jesus was not crucified in a cathedral between two candles, but on a cross between two thieves; on the town garbage heap; at a crossroad so cosmopolitan they had to write his title in Hebrew and in Greek and in Latin; at the kind of place where cynics talk smut, and soldiers gamble. Because that is where he died. And that is what he died about.

Or in the simple conclusion of John Stott, chaplain to Queen Elizabeth II, "I could never myself believe in God, if it were not for the cross. The only God I believe in is the one Nietzsche ridiculed as 'God on the Cross.' In a real world of pain, how could one worship a God who was immune to it?"

Unless God has wounds too, any mere sense of duty always flags in facing the worst evil, high-minded principles run out of breath, education and speculation become mere chatter, and sophisticated therapy is exposed as charlatan incompetence. Here is where the silence of the Bible over why God permits evil is outweighed by the Bible's stentorian shout about what God is doing about it. In the crucifixion of Jesus, sheer and utter evil meets sheer and utter love; unadulterated love wins out over unadulterated evil. No one can ever go so low that God in Jesus has not gone lower. The horrendous evil that looks as if it is the final obliteration of goodness and humanness becomes God's deepest identification with his creatures. There is hope for victims; there is even forgiveness for perpetrators. For those who know the cross, the pages of history are stained indelibly in blood with the evidence of the goodness of God.

In the words of the old African American spiritual, "Nobody knows the trouble I've seen; nobody knows but Jesus."

And in the philosopher Peter Kreeft's powerful phrase, "Jesus is the tears of God"—even for the age after Auschwitz.

The Resistance Leader Knows Best

The third biblical reassurance addresses the third prong of the trilemma, God is all-powerful: *the resistance leader knows what he is doing and victory day is coming.* Not only is evil truly evil and God truly good, but God is truly powerful. How can this third truth be reconciled with the other two? Is it rational to trust God when we do not know what he is doing? One of the most illuminating answers was put forward by the Oxford philosopher Basil Mitchell in his celebrated parable of the resistance leader.

Imagine you are in German-occupied France during World War II and you want to join the resistance movement against the Nazis. One evening in the local bar a stranger comes up to you and introduces himself as the leader of the local partisans. He spends the evening with you, explaining the general requirements of your duties, giving you a chance to assess his trustworthiness, and offering you the chance to go no further. But his warning is stern: If you join, your life will be at risk. This will be the only face-to-face meeting you will have. After this, you will receive orders and you will have to follow them without question, often completely in the dark as to the whys and wherefores of the operations, and always with the terrifying fear that your trust may be betrayed.

Is such trust reasonable? Sometimes what the resistance leader is doing is obvious. He is helping members of the resistance. "Thank heavens he is on our side," you say. Sometimes it is not obvious. He is in Gestapo uniform arresting partisans and—unknown to you—releasing them out of sight to help them escape the Nazis. But always you must trust and follow the orders without question, despite all appearances, no matter what happens. "The resistance leader knows best," you say. Only after the war will the secrets be open, the codes revealed, the true comrades vindicated, the traitors exposed, and sense made of the explanations.

The parable of the resistance leader is an apt picture of the anomalies and dilemmas of faith in the fallen world—in "enemy territory," as C. S. Lewis used to describe it. Evil is not a problem because God is too small, though doing his best, but because God is so great that we cannot be expected to know what he is doing. Can a littleneck clam understand a rocket scientist? No more can we fathom the unfathomable mysteries of God. Thomas à Kempis put it simply: "God is able to effect more than man is able to understand." Or as a Portuguese proverb expresses it, "God writes straight with crooked lines."

The trouble is that, being more like rocket scientists than littleneck clams, we press our questions anyway. Is God really on our side? How can we tell when he is in disguise? Why does he sometimes appear to be wearing the wrong uniform? Surely we need more than just *trust*. Can't we also *know*? His silence does not seem to square with his sovereignty. What if we have been duped, led into a trap, and betrayed? With faith, as with the French resistance, nothing is worse than the fear of betrayal.

In the thick of such wartime dilemmas, two issues are decisive for faith. First, are we truly able to trust the resistance leader? And do we have good reason to trust him? If there is no reason to be sure about the leader, then trust is a fool's gamble. But if there are good reasons to have confidence, then trust is warranted and the picture is changed. Knowing the one thing that matters, we can suspend judgment about everything else. *We do not know why God is doing what he is doing, but we know why we trust God, who knows why.*

There must be no sentimentality or confusion here—no blind, irrational "leap of faith." For his followers, Jesus is the fullest, clearest reason why we can know the answer to the two deepest questions of faith: "Is God truly there?" (his existence) and "Is God truly good?" (his character). Thus, Christians do not say to God, "I do not understand you at all, but I trust you anyway." That would be suicidal. Rather, they say, "Father, I do not understand you, but I trust you"— or more accurately, "I do not understand you *in this situation, but I un-*

derstand why I trust you anyway." It is therefore reasonable to trust even when we do not understand. We may be in the dark about what God is doing, but we are not in the dark about God. Thus, when he was racked with illness, the great French reformer John Calvin could say, "You are crushing me, Lord, but I am content that it comes from your hand."

The second decisive issue is whether we truly expect to win the war, for only then are the secrets opened, the explanations made clear, and the trust vindicated or not. But those are exactly the prospects opened up by Christian hope. Living between the first coming of Jesus, which is like D-day, and the second coming, which will be V-day, followers of Jesus can face the worst now because they are sure of victory then, and all the intervening struggles are seen in the light of that day.

That is the import of the remarkable vision of Julian of Norwich in the fourteenth century. From the vantage point of the end, she saw that all complaints and second-guessing would evaporate. Instead, there would be universal appreciation that "all shall be well, and all shall be well, and all manner of things shall be well." Those who prevail, she overheard, would even be thanked by God for what they went through. "Thank you for your suffering, the suffering of your youth." God knows what he is doing, and one day we all will too.

At the end of the twentieth century it was clear beyond doubt that all our human efforts to build a utopia had been botched and all we had produced was an apocalypse. The last century's secularists came closer to creating a hell than a heaven. But does this mean that we must join Voltaire's Pangloss and settle for the present as the best of all possible worlds? Or side with Carl Gustav Jung and try to integrate Satan and evil into God and the good? Or enlist with Albert Camus in a heroic rebellion that is doomed to never-ending defeat?

No. Jewish and Christian hope is nonhumanist. It is not all up to us. The resistance leader knows what he is doing. The night will end, and victory day is coming. There will be reasons and explanations enough on the day of celebration.

For the moment it is sufficient to press on in the fight against evil and hang on for the day when tears will be wiped away and suffering and injustice will be no more. For the biblical faiths, it has been said, hope is the new world a-coming, because this world is the next world a-building. All this and far, far more lies in the triple reassurance that is at the heart of the biblical response to evil and suffering.

After Auschwitz, many have claimed that it is no longer possible to believe in God—or to make love, or to write poetry. But the facts speak otherwise. The darkness of the heart revealed in Auschwitz must be faced with unblinking realism. But the truth is that even in Auschwitz more people deepened or discovered faith than lost it, and this is just the sharpest end of an important trend of thinkers returning to faith precisely because of modern evil, not despite it. For the biblical faiths, the depth and scale of modern evil is a sobering confirmation of their view of the darker side of humanity as well as a sharply lit reminder of the need for the very answers they bring.

Isn't There Something We Can Do?

The fifth basic question for exploring the challenge of evil is about doing something. When it comes to evil, Karl Marx's famous saying is apt—"Philosophers have interpreted the world in various ways. The point is to change it." Or as the philosopher Peter Kreeft wrote with feeling, in discussing Dostoyevsky's question about whether the world is worth the tears of a single child, "By the time you finish reading this book, ten thousand children will starve, four thousand will be brutally beaten by their parents, and one thousand will be raped."

The best words and ideas are never enough. They must be matched with compassion for those who suffer and with action to relieve pain, resist the evildoer, and rescue the victim. When children are crying, they need comfort, not a school lesson. When wives are abused, employees exploited, prisoners tortured, girls under ten trafficked for sex with pedophiles, and whole families coerced into bonded slavery, they need rescuing. Resistance is often associated with armed revolt, but in its wider sense it stands for every practical response to evil and suffering that meets the need and sets out to resist injustice and restore justice and well-being.

Yet here is the Achilles' heel of most current discussions of evil—they remain discussions. The gap between words and deeds, between theory and practice, is an age-old chasm.

With rare exceptions, most contemporary discussions of evil and suffering that take the philosophical questions seriously ignore the practical response, just as most people who take the practical issues seriously ignore the philosophical. But as the early Christian letter of James puts it famously, "Faith by itself, if it is not accompanied by action, is dead."

Second, understanding evil without responding to it feeds into the problem of the indifference of the bystander, which is one of the greatest reinforcements of evil in the modern world. Edmund Burke's famous remark shows that the problem is not new: "The only thing necessary for the triumph of evil is for good men to do nothing." But modern conditions make bystanders of us all, and thorny psychological and ethical questions confront anyone who sets out to care and act in the era of globalization.

Resisting evil is therefore a titanic task. And we must remember once again the important differences between the families of faiths, for practical responses to evil differ according to these different worldviews. The Jewish and Christian faiths, for example, have an unabashedly world-affirming stance, a commitment to justice, and a long tradition of reform movements. Hinduism, by contrast, is equally unabashed about its world-denying stance and has little interest in a matching tradition of reform. To engage the world in that way is thought by many devotees of Shankara's Hinduism to perpetuate captivity in the world of *maya*, or illusion.

In asking this fifth question—and the next one as well—we explore the response to evil and suffering of the biblical family of faiths, mainly because the Jewish and Christian faiths form the single strongest set of ideas that have shaped the West, including its unique tradition of reforms. People of other faiths are of course welcome to set out their own views of the essentials for standing against evil.

There are three key features to the biblical response to evil and suffering:

First, there is the acknowledgment that evil resides in each of our hearts. Such an acknowledgment includes both realism and a sense of personal responsibility, which are in clear contrast to the mistaken responses to evil that are widespread today.

The second key feature of a biblical response to evil is a commitment to forgive the evildoer appropriately, though without ever condoning the evil deed. Far from being weak or sentimental, such forgiveness is vital in showing that the past is not irreversible. This is the only hope for breaking the cycle of violence and opening the door to a very practical politics of the second chance.

The third feature is the commitment to take a practical stand against evil and injustice, whatever the cost. There are no recipes or formulas here, only stories, principles, and heroes. Yes, there are pitfalls when it comes to resisting evil—the well-intentioned do-gooder is not always the doer-of-good and may even be a doer of-evil. But the same two maxims shine through all the stories of human goodness in the face of evil: however large or small our influence, however horrendous or ordinary the evil we face, we can at least all answer for ourselves as individual forces for good "always ready to help" and one-person dissident movements drawing our lines in the sand and announcing resolutely, "But not through me."

CHAPTER 13

THE PROBLEM WITH THE WORLD IS ME

The night the two men met was a key link in the grand chain of events that shaped the twentieth century, though the links that led to their meeting are unknown, the place they met was uncongenial, and they themselves were unlikely prospects to have any chance to change their world, let alone the wider world.

About the one who played the most crucial part that night we know very little except his name, that he was Jewish and a doctor, and that he did not survive the night. In postrevolutionary Russia it would have been difficult for anyone connected with czarist Russia to gain a medical education, so people have guessed that he came from a Jewish family that had pinned its hopes on the revolution and that his family was secular, because his first two names—Boris Nicholaye-vich—reflected a Russian rather than a Jewish background.

What the crime was that took Dr. Boris Kornfeld to prison we do not know, but it was almost certainly a minor political crime because major crimes were punished by death, not imprisonment. And we can only guess what the process was that disillusioned him while he was in prison, though it is safe to assume that the barbed-wire brutality of Stalin's prison camps was a highly effective cure for the communism that had put him there.

What we do know is that Kornfeld was influenced by an unnamed fellow inmate who shared the faith that was the secret of his survival. On the one hand, Kornfeld's external conditions were likely to have been better than those of most prisoners because he was a doctor and doctors were in short supply in that harsh and remote region. No prisoner or prison guard wanted to end up in the hands of a doctor he had insulted or abused.

On the other hand, the inner wrestling of a man of his sensitivity and education was bound to be more intense. Like other prisoners, he hated and despised his captors and the vicious system they represented. He was as much an innocent victim of hatred and a hateful system as his Jewish ancestors had been under the pogroms of the czarist era. But he was also appalled by the hatred and the violence in his own heart, for hatred had spawned hatred and he was trapped by the very evil he despised. If victims hated victimizers with the hatred by which they were victimized, then hate would beget only more hate, and the whole world would become a concentration camp imprisoned and stoked by hatred.

It was at that point that Kornfeld found himself repeating the prayer taught him by his friend: "Forgive us our trespasses as we forgive those who trespass against us." They were strange words for him as a Jew, but they came from another Jew, and in the relentless grind of his daily work he found that they allowed him to face up frankly to the shocking evil in his own heart as well as the sordid evil all around—and to ask for cleansing.

Eventually the anguish in his heart overpowered the counterweight of his ancestors' persecution. Kornfeld came to the conviction that he must not just say the words of the Lord's Prayer but become a follower of the one who had taught it.

So it was that Kornfeld became a Christian and formed a resolve to make a stand against the system. And so it was that he refused to sign the forms that doctors signed routinely that became sentences of execution for the prisoners. And so it was that he even turned in the quisling fellow-prisoner orderlies who were stealing food and medicine from his patients in the hospital.

Such stands were preposterous in the camps of Stalin's day. In effect Kornfeld was signing his own death warrant. By not going along with the forms all the doctors signed routinely, he was challenging the authorities. By exposing the quislings among his fellow prisoners, he was breaking with the winks, nods, and betrayals that made the prisoners complicit in their own imprisonment. But he was not foolhardy, so he decided to take reasonable precautions—sleeping in the hospital, for instance, rather than the open barracks—but he would go about his life knowing that any moment could be his last. If he was at risk, he was also free because his conscience was free, and he was eager to share his newfound freedom and the faith that was behind it.

Two months later Kornfeld examined a prisoner who had been operated on for stomach cancer, and here is where the second man enters the story—a man infinitely better known now but then an equally unknown convict imprisoned equally unjustly for trivial criticism of the Soviet leader. Was it the young man's cancer and his brush with death? Or was it his special sensitivity as a teacher and writer and the deep sorrow and misery written all over his face? Kornfeld may not have known, but he started to tell the young man his story and could not stop, speaking as with the urgency of a dying man to a dying man.

All that afternoon and late into the night the two men talked. They were alone in the ward, and the light was off so as not to hurt the patient's eyes. At times the patient drifted back into semiconsciousness, but the ardent intensity of the doctor's story always jerked him back, and the patient somehow knew that he was hearing not only a fellow human's story but a life confession.

"On the whole," the doctor concluded when it was late at night and everyone else was asleep, "I have become convinced that there is no punishment that comes to us in this life on earth which is undeserved." Kornfeld was not suggesting that there is a one-to-one correlation between what we do and what we get, but rather, "if you go over your life with a fine-tooth comb and ponder it deeply, you will always be able to hunt down that transgression of yours for which you have now received this blow."

The patient could not see the doctor's face, but he was stirred to the depths of his soul—"there is such mystical knowledge in his voice that I shudder." The doctor's words were the last he said. They parted, and both went off to sleep. The patient was rudely wakened in the morning by the rush of running feet: it was the orderlies carrying the doctor's body. He had been murdered in the night, with eight blows of a plasterer's mallet to his head.

"And so it happened," the younger man wrote later, "that Kornfeld's prophetic words were his last words on earth, and those words lay upon me as an inheritance." In their light he reflected on his own experience and the character and purpose it was giving him. In their light he thought over the savagery of his jailers and their fate: "From that point of view they have been punished most horribly of all: they are turning into swine; they are departing downward from humanity."

But above all, the patient declared, Kornfeld's words, by throwing light on all his dark prison years, allowed him to say, "Bless you, prison!" and to carry away on his bent, almost broken back one essential experience: having learned "how a human being becomes evil and how good." Earlier, intoxicated by youth, he had felt himself to be infallible, and in that state he had become cruel and oppressive, convinced that he was always right and always good.

But now, wrote Alexander Solzhenitsyn, the Nobel Laureate and one-man dissident movement whose works from the heart of the Gulag helped blow away the might of Soviet tyranny, he knew a truth both deeper and more liberating:

> It was only when I lay there on rotting prison straw that I sensed within myself the first stirrings of good. Gradually it was disclosed to me that the line separating good and evil passes not through states, nor between classes, nor between political parties either, but right through every human heart, and through all human hearts.

I Am

Solzhenitsyn's famous words from *The Gulag Archipelago* throw light on the first of the three essentials for responding to evil from the perspective of the biblical family of faiths: whenever we confront evil, we must acknowledge the evil in our own hearts and take full responsibility for the evil we find there and its consequences. In short, a hallmark of Jewish and Christian responses to evil is their characteristic realism and responsibility.

The same potential for evil and proneness to evil is in every one of us. Our first responses to evil may legitimately be shock, grief, or outrage, but before we take action, our second response should always be an examination of our own hearts: me too? There but for the grace of God go I.

"If only there were evil people somewhere," Solzhenitsyn also wrote in *The Gulag Archipelago*, "insidiously committing evil deeds, and it were necessary only to separate them from the rest of us and destroy them. But the line dividing good and evil cuts through the heart of every human being. And who is willing to destroy a piece of his own heart?"

When the *Times* of London once asked several of Britain's leading intellectuals what they thought was the problem with the world, the celebrated Catholic journalist G. K. Chesterton sent back a postcard response: "I am."

The problem of the world is me. None of us is truly among the innocents. There are certainly differences between Jews and Christians over the accent they give to evil in human nature, just as there are differences within Jewish and Christian traditions. But they share a realism that is highly practical in combating evil because it directly confronts two of evil's most supportive allies: dualism and utopianism.

You Bad, Me Good

Dualism is the view that breaks the world into two camps: discerning evil in others and denying it in ourselves. Numerous errors stream out in its wake. We deceive ourselves by dividing the world falsely into "us" and "them," "good" and "bad," "black" and "white," "progressive" and "reactionary," by declaring that "we" are obviously good and free and progressive and "they" are obviously bad. At the end of the line, we project onto others the evils we do not admit in ourselves and so lose touch with reality.

Dualism and its twin brother, hypocrisy, are a special hazard of all who aspire to virtue, whether individuals or nations. As François de la Rochefoucauld pointed out, hypocrisy is the flattery that vice pays to virtue. It was therefore more characteristic of the Pharisees than the Sadducees, just as it is of the Victorians rather than the postmoderns, and the British and the Americans rather than the French and the Italians. "The hardest possibility Americans have to confront about themselves," the journalist Lance Morrow wrote about his own nation, "is always the thought that they may be evil. That is the thing they find most difficult to face."

Soon after Morrow made this comment, the world was witness to the publication of American soldiers' own trophy photographs of themselves having fun while they abused, sexually humiliated, and tortured prisoners at Saddam Hussein's infamous Abu Ghraib jail during the Iraqi war—and to other Americans' reactions to the worldwide outrage that followed.

Most of the explanations of these "un-American" atrocities carried out by all-American young people traced them back to such systemic problems as the stresses of war, the demands of intelligence gathering, and an administration policy of ignoring the Geneva Convention. But such atrocities also trace back to early military massacres, such as My Lai in the 1960s and the Philippines in the 1880s, not to speak of other egregious evils, such as the lynching of blacks in the 1930s and the shooting of the Digger Indians in the nineteenth century.

Clearly American exceptionalism does not extend to innocence.

And America's problem is more than a few "rogue soldiers" and the odd "bad apple," as anyone can tell who has looked at the brutal violence of American video games, the diseased fantasies of American rock stars such as Kurt Cobain, the classic sadomasochistic blend of torture and pornography that now flourishes in the dark recesses of the Internet, and other examples of violence in American popular culture, which has become the cultural sewer of the world.

The "America is great because America is good" school is in need of a sober revision. There was too much hypocrisy in the explanations of Abu Ghraib. Defensive comparisons did not work. It was not as bad as Saddam Hussein? The United States is judged by its own judgments of others; there is little honor in being outstripped in cruelty stakes by tyrants. Facile excuses were no better. "Following orders" was no excuse at Nuremberg, and if the soldiers were simply "untrained" and "badly supervised," what does that say for their natural state as young Americans? Neither did euphemisms serve. What the world saw was more than "abuse" and "humiliation"; by the very definitions of the human rights charters to which the United States is a signatory, the unspoken "T-word" had to be spelled out as the torture it was.

Abu Ghraib was a warning sign that, if not heeded, will not be the end of the story. The fatal combination of factors—America's securing dominance through her own power, America's always seeing her cause as virtuous because it is in the name of freedom, and America's insistence that her citizens are above and beyond international review—can lead only to the arrogance that befalls all dominant powers, and then to further cruelty and evil, which is the outcome of such hypocrisy.

Needless to say, we need not respond to the danger of dualism by swinging to the opposite extreme and espousing moral equivalence, as if all cats are gray. There are monsters and there are monstrous evils, and both are to be fought. But we are all liable to become hypocrites, whether standing for virtue or standing against vice, when we engage in dualism. In the stinging rebuke of Jesus to the virtuous-appearing Pharisees of his day, we become concerned about the splinter in our neighbor's eye but ignore the beam in our own. Or in Nietzsche's warning, "Whoever fights monsters should see to it that in the process he does not become a monster."

Creating Mankind Anew

Jewish and Christian realism also attacks the other ally that supports evil: utopianism. Belief in human perfectibility and progress inevitably denies evil in human nature and views history as the path to ever-upward improvement. As the last century demonstrates, the most murderous tyrannies in history were the fruit of ungrounded utopian confidence in politics, science, education, and psychology and in what they could do to improve human nature and society.

The utopian theme runs loud and clear from Stalin's Russia to Mao's China to Pol Pot's Cambodia. Even Nazism was utopian in Hitler's eyes: "Those who see in National Socialism nothing more than a political movement know scarcely anything of it. It is more even than a religion: it is the will to create mankind anew." Each of these movements was a human catastrophe that flowed directly from its zeal to make the world anew. Like all utopias, they could bridge the gap between the ideal and the real only through coercion and violence.

The Khmer Rouge called their revolution the "Year Zero"—history's radical new beginning. Mao exulted similarly that he was the artist who would paint a new vision of China: "A blank sheet of paper has no blotches, and so the newest and most beautiful words can be written on it, the newest and most beautiful pictures can be painted on it." In each case the dream sired the nightmare—the illusory hope of total reconstruction gave birth to cataclysmic destruction. An irrefutable lesson of the twentieth century is: "Beware utopianism."

Are there liberal forms of utopianism as well as totalitarian ones? More than a century ago the great historian Jacob Burckhardt warned of the danger that evil had become possible "mainly because there are good splendid liberal people who do not quite know the boundaries of right and wrong, and it is there that the duties of resistance and defense begin."

As if to prove his point, secular liberals and liberal Protestants began to trumpet their rejection of the traditional idea of evil altogether. "The doctrine of original sin," Reverend Shailer Matthews, the dean of the Chicago Divinity School, wrote famously in 1930, "was a theory of human behavior adequate to the scientific knowledge of St. Augustine's time, but overthrown by more recent research." This was written in the very decade when the dark architects of the Final Solution were conceiving their vile designs.

Vigilance against utopianism is one reason why Jewish and Christian realists oppose those who confuse the passion to flout boundaries with freedom. The very notion of freedom without virtue is utopian. Besides, in the biblical view, the evil, or sin, in each of us is already a form of transgression, so the attempt to do it again and make a virtue out of a vice is a double folly. In both the liberal and totalitarian cases, those who never see bad in human nature and only see good have a habit of creating worlds that are far from good and far too often bad. Justice and freedom may be fought for and won in the name of utopianism, but without realism they never last and are certain to degenerate into either chaos or tyranny.

The Golden Age of Exoneration

Responsibility, which is the other half of the Jewish and Christian views, is similarly out of step in the modern world, for we live in the golden age of exoneration. In most of the West we have seen a vast defusing of responsibility. Everything is now explicable in terms of our parents and our past, and so life becomes one long schooling in blaming, resenting, and suing, while always excusing ourselves.

Psychology is destiny, we are told. We cannot help ourselves. We are the products of our past. It is genetic. We are victims. Blend the language of the civil rights movement with the language of the therapeutic movement and you have an instant platform and a set of slogans for victim parties of all kinds. We can all be walking billboards for our own chosen grievance.

The darker side of this culture of exoneration can be seen in countries that have genuinely experienced horrendous evil. Here the stratagem is more understandable but also more lethal. In such countries, evil was truly evil, victims were truly victims, and there truly are lessons to be learned from the history of what happened. They must never be forgotten.

But what exactly should not be forgotten? When we learn the wrong lessons of history, evil is reinforced rather than restrained—particularly when we use the injuries of the past to serve the interests of the future and ignore the injustices of the present.

Hitler's Posthumous Triumph

After half a century of working to understand the Holocaust and its aftermath, Zygmunt Bauman warns that there are wrong ways to respond to injury and that we can learn the wrong lessons from the history of the most horrendous evils. The first error is to make a *cult of survival*. When wholesale slaughters occur, such as the Holocaust and the Armenian and Rwandan massacres, it is natural to think about how to survive and to focus on the good fortune of those who do. The danger comes, Bauman observes from his experience, when the idea grows of "staying alive as the sole thing that counts, as the supreme value that dwarfs all other values." Eventually the idea takes hold that life is about surviving, that to succeed in life is to outlast and outlive others, and that survival is the supreme value and the end of life itself: "Who survives wins."

Bauman warns all who flock to the cult of the survivor—whether through pondering horrendous evils or watching tawdry American "reality" TV shows—of the destination to which this obsession leads. Underwritten by Darwinian views of natural selection and the survival of the fittest, the idea of survival at all costs and by any means leads to an ugly, cynical struggle that is destructive of civilization and human values. In the end the survivor becomes the person for whom staying alive is everything and who is even prepared to kill others so as not to have others survive him.

The second error is to create an *aristocracy of victimhood*. A terrible lesson of massacres is that the perpetrators see themselves as victims and therefore victimize others. Those who are "more victimized than thou" believe they have social permission to avenge, whether they be Israelis, Palestinians, Serbs, Croats, Bosnians, or Kosovars. Thus, Bauman notes, we witness "the most widespread and iniquitous arguments brandished nowadays around the world in justification of recurrent new genocides: namely, a new round of victimization being needed to avenge the past cruelty as well as to defend the victims of past persecution against the repetition of their suffering." The result is a "socio-psychological device serving the systematic production and distribution of evil."

To make matters worse, Bauman says, we have not only direct victims playing the victim card illegitimately but an "aristocracy of victimhood"—people who claim the status of "victim by proxy" because they are members of groups descended from the victims. Some truly are the children of survivors, but others are part of a swelling number of "sons and daughters of the Holocaust" who are neither. The result is either a hereditary claim to sympathy or an entirely false claim that often masquerades as "a signed-in-advance certificate of moral righteousness" and reverses the fundamental principle of English-speaking law: that one is innocent until proven guilty.

In a world haunted by the ghosts of earlier evils—from empires to colonies to tyrannies to slavery to genocide and massacre—all descendants of earlier perpetrators of evil can be treated as guilty by association and therefore judged guilty in advance. These fictional culprits then become the foolproof alibi for whatever is done to them in return—"Look what the Nazis (or European colonialists, or white slave-owners, or male chauvinists) make us do."

The third error is to create a *brotherhood of martyrdom*. It is a banal truth, Bauman says, that violence breeds more violence: "Somewhat less banal, since not repeated enough, is the truth that victimization breeds more victimization." The lesson is then drawn that humanity is "divided into victims and the victimizers, and so if you are (or expect to be) a victim, your duty is to reverse the tables."

This twisted logic leads ultimately to terrorism, which is as totalitarian as communism and fascism but of a nonstate kind. It also raises victimhood to the level of fanaticism. Finally, it leads to suicide bombers who in the final twist of the logic assert through their own death both a claim to glory in their community and a renewed claim to victimhood in their martyrdom. Suicide bombers are therefore literally dying to die. They hold in their hands their ultimate weapon of destruction—themselves—and so play their part as devotees of the cult of death and destruction.

The problem, Bauman argues, can even be seen at the level of official state policy by nations and peoples once victimized as well as among desperate and disinherited individuals. His conclusion is sobering.

The pernicious legacy of the Holocaust is that today's persecutors may inflict new pains and create new generations of victims eagerly awaiting their chance to do the same, while acting under the conviction that they are avenging yesterday's pain and warding off the pains of tomorrow—while being convinced, in other words, that ethics is on their side.

This is perhaps the greatest of the Holocaust's curses and Hitler's posthumous victories.

There are certainly other reasons for our defused sense of responsibility today. One is the rise of squishy notions such as "collective guilt" and "national complicity." If everyone is guilty, then no one is responsible—but it is only when no one is responsible that terrible wrongs are done and everyone becomes guilty.

Another reason for nonresponsibility is the impact of living in a global world. For the first time in history we face an impossible, almost unbearable, gap between the sufferings we see and our ability to help. Even if we wanted to, even if we were the wealthiest people in the world, and even if we represented the richest nations on earth, our still-limited hands and all-too-limited pockets could no longer reach out to help all of those whom our technologically enhanced eyes can now see daily.

In an age of global communications this widening chasm between the technological and the moral is stretching us like a torturer's rack. For many, the impossible gap serves to justify heartlessness. For others, the outcome is compassion fatigue—the exhausted state of caring too little that follows the effort of caring too much.

Here I Stand

In the biblical view, each of us is still always responsible for our part. Even in a globalized world we are our neighbor's neighbor. Even in a bureaucracy, we are never helpless pawns but responsible agents who will have to give an account of ourselves to one who is higher than any boss. Even under the tyrant's threat of death, we are moral agents who can choose to disobey as well as obey. As the writer Mary McCarthy used to say, "If somebody points a gun at you and says, 'Kill your friend or I will kill you,' he is tempting you; that is all."

In the biblical view, there is no ducking the challenge of individual responsibility. As Søren Kierkegaard wrote, the significance of the Christian faith for a society "ought to be to do everything to make every man eternally responsible for every hour he lives, even for the least thing he undertakes." To be sure, we are only responsible for what is ours to give and say and do. No more and no less. Those with more—whether better health, higher intelligence, fatter bank balances, wider social influence, stronger friendships and family ties, or greater energy—are responsible for more. But none of us is without responsibility. To be a human is to be responsible.

In *Genealogy of Morals*, Nietzsche describes the search for responsibility as "the task of breeding an animal entitled to make promises." In an age of low accountability and quick alibis, it is no easy task to vouch for ourselves, to stand behind everything we do, and to fulfill our promises. But along with being realistic about human nature, taking responsibility is essential for resisting evil.

"Who stands fast?" Dietrich Bonhoeffer asked under the looming shadow of the swastika. Only the responsible person, he answered, and then he raised the question that every generation must answer for itself: "Where are these responsible persons?"

CHAPTER 14

THE POLITICS OF THE SECOND CHANCE

"What should I have done? What could I have done? What would you have done?" In most situations those questions have an excuse-making ring. That certainly is not the case with the famous Jewish Nazi hunter Simon Wiesenthal. Courage and responsibility are at the very center of his life. He has described his passionate sense of pur-pose like this: "When history looks back I want people to know the Nazis weren't able to kill millions of people and get away with it." Yet those are exactly the questions he raises in his searing, haunting World War II memoir, *The Sunflower*.

When imprisoned in a concentration camp in Lemberg, Poland, Wiesenthal and other prisoners were marched one day into town for a manual labor project at a military hospital that had once been the Lemberg High School, where Wiesenthal had studied. He was pulled aside from the work detail by a nurse, who took him to a private sick-room and left him alone with an obviously dying German in a bed.

"I have not much longer to live," the sick man whispered in a barely audible voice. "I am resigned to dying soon, but before that I want to talk about an experience that is torturing me. Otherwise I cannot die in peace."

The awkwardness between the two men was palpable. One was on the verge of death, swathed in bandages, badly burned, in heavy pain and breathing heavily, but weighed down by a desperate desire to unload his conscience before he breathed his last. The other, the last Jew in his life, was tense and suspicious, still sensing a trap and sizing up the dying man before him in the half-light and fetid atmosphere of the ward.

"I must tell you of a horrid deed—tell you because . . . you are a Jew." And so he did. The twenty-one-year-old former Catholic had betrayed his family and joined the SS—only to degenerate into a killer who committed ghastly acts of murder, including the burning alive of several Jewish families.

The contrast between the two men was deep. "Here lay a man in bed," Wiesenthal wrote later, "who wished to die in peace—but he could not, because the memory of his terrible crime gave him no rest. And by him sat a man also doomed to die—but who did not want to die because he yearned to see the end of all the horror that blighted the world."

Once the German groped for Wiesenthal's hand, but he withdrew it out of reach. Once Wiesenthal stood up to go, but was held fast by the cold, bloodless hand. Eventually the dying man sat up painfully in bed and put his hands together as if to pray or plead, but he was unable to get any words out. Wiesenthal was in no mood to help and remained silent.

"I know that what I am asking is almost too much for you," the young German said, "but without your answer I cannot die in peace." Again there was no response.

"At last," Wiesenthal said, "I made up my mind and without a word I left the room."

Fortunate to survive the Holocaust, Wiesenthal has spent the rest of his life tracking down Nazi criminals of all sorts—hunting them down, hearing witnesses describe them, providing evidence against them, and watching how they behaved when tried. Few of them, he admits, were born murderers and vicious criminals. Most were the "ordinary people" who carried out heinous crimes under orders. But very few showed remorse, except the regret that witnesses had survived to report their deeds. So he always wondered about the young Nazi in the hospital. Was he truly one of the exceptions, or was his repentance a deathbed confession that might have been different had he survived?

Also, Wiesenthal reflected later, there are many kinds of silence. So he has asked himself whether his was right or wrong. But that leads him to the grand question that still challenges his heart and mind, which he wants to share with the readers of *The Sunflower* so that their consciences can be challenged too: "Was my silence at the bedside of the dying Nazi right or wrong?"

Wiesenthal realizes that there are those who can appreciate his dilemma and endorse his decision and that others are "ready to condemn me for refusing to ease the last moments of a repentant murderer." But let everyone who enters the debate be in no doubt. "The crux of the matter is, of course, the question of forgiveness. Forgetting is something that time alone takes care of, but forgiveness is an act of volition, and only the sufferer is qualified to make the decision."

Who Are We to Say? . . . But We Do

"Forgiveness is an act of volition, and only the sufferer is qualified to make the decision." That sentence is a conversation-stopper. If only the sufferer is qualified to make the decision, the rest of us would have to listen in on a debate among a dwindling handful of Holocaust survivors. We would have nothing to say because we have not suffered what they suffered. But Wiesenthal cannot have meant that literally or he would not have invited so many friends and distinguished leaders to give their opinion. And their debate leads directly to the second essential element for responding to evil according to one tradition in the biblical family of faiths: whenever we confront evil, we must forgive the person who has wronged us even as we condemn the evil or take steps to counter it.

When it comes to forgiveness, we encounter a new twist in the discussion. Here there is a huge difference not only between the biblical faiths and others but within the biblical faiths themselves. Jews and Christians, who have next to no daylight between them on so many issues, have markedly different views of forgiveness, at least as represented by public voices today.

"Politically I do not want to hear anything of forgiveness!" Jean Améry, a fellow survivor, wrote back to Wiesenthal. "I refuse any reconciliation with the criminals."

"The crimes in which this SS man had taken part," wrote Rabbi Arthur Hertzberg, "are beyond forgiveness by man, and even by God. . . . The God who had allowed the Holocaust did not, and does not, have the standing to forgive the monsters who carried out the murders."

"No one can forgive crimes against other people," the philosopher Abraham Joshua Heschel argued. "It is therefore preposterous to assume that anybody alive can extend forgiveness for the suffering of any one of the six million people who perished. According to Jewish tradition, even God Himself can only forgive sins committed against Himself."

"When an act of violence or an offense has been committed," Primo Levi responded, "it is forever irreparable."

"I find myself indifferent to the wounded Nazi's plea for forgiveness," answered Joshua Rubinstein, director of Amnesty International. "Simon was merciful enough with him. For Simon to grant him forgiveness as well would have been a betrayal of his, and his family's, suffering, and all the suffering around him."

"God Himself does not forgive a person who has sinned against a human being," Rabbi Dennis Prager wrote, "unless that human being has been forgiven by his victim. Therefore, people can never forgive murder, since the one person who can forgive is gone, forever."

Unforgivable, forever irreparable—the most chilling response of all was from the man who replied, "I would have silently left the deathbed having made quite certain that there was now one less Nazi in the world." But three themes emerge from the broad chorus that differ decisively from a Christian understanding: First, even God cannot forgive where humans have not forgiven first. Second, only the injured party can forgive, so murderers are unforgivable. And finally, to forgive is dangerous because forgiving is condoning.

The Christian responses to Wiesenthal were varied too, but the overwhelming voice was strong and clear. Cardinal Frank Koenig, formerly archbishop of Vienna, declared boldly in favor of forgiveness: "The question of whether there is a limit to forgiveness has been emphatically answered by Christ in the negative."

Two practical lines of argument emerge in support of this basic position. One is that forgiveness frees the past for both the one who forgives and the one who is forgiven. As the historian Martin Marty comments, "Forgiving and being forgiven are experiences that allow me to be free for a new day." Beyond all slogans and hype, forgiveness is the only reliable foundation for a true second chance in life.

The other argument is that forgiveness frees the future. Responding as the chairman of South Africa's Truth and Reconciliation Commission, Archbishop Desmond Tutu recounted how he was overwhelmed by the willingness of many survivors of the apartheid regime to forgive their oppressors and torturers. "This magnanimity, this nobility of spirit, is quite breathtakingly unbelievable. I have often felt I should say, 'Let us take off our shoes because at this moment we are standing on holy ground.'"

"It is clear," Tutu concluded, "that if we look only to retributive justice, then we could just as well close up shop. Forgiveness is not some nebulous thing. It is practical politics. Without forgiveness there is no future." Not only for individuals but for nations, forgiveness is the secret of a politics of the second chance.

Unsentimental and Unrelenting

It would be absurd to suggest that forgiveness is uniquely a Christian virtue or that Christians have been consistent exemplars of forgiveness. But unquestionably—one might say, almost uncomfortably—forgiveness is a radical and highly distinctive feature of the teaching of Jesus of Nazareth, and in a world of evil an essential but costly form of love.

Arguably, forgiveness is the single, clearest, greatest contribution of Jesus of Nazareth to world affairs. "The glory of Christianity," said the poet William Blake, "is to conquer by forgiveness." If the acknowledgment of personal responsibility explains the first half of Oscar Wilde's famous maxim, forgiveness underscores the second: "Every saint has a past, and every sinner a future."

Buddhists, by contrast, sometimes teach forgiveness, but as a step on the path toward right mindfulness and detachment from caring about the injuries of life, whereas for Christians it is supremely an act of love by one human being for another and part of loving our neighbors as ourselves. Or again, many humanists are truly generous and forgiving, but their secular worldview could as easily justify a Darwinian struggle of the survival of the fittest. The teaching and example of Jesus, by contrast, are unambiguous about forgiveness, and any refusal to forgive is a blatant affront by his followers to their master.

Jesus is quite unsentimental about forgiveness. Since God is greater than all, including evil, he is never defeated by evil and there is no evil so great that God cannot forgive it—not as a matter of justice but of grace. In the picture drawn by the eighth-century B.C. Hebrew prophet Isaiah of Jerusalem, sins that are blood-crimson red can be white as fresh fallen snow. How can such grace square with justice without either violating righteousness or condoning evil, and without allowing grace to degenerate into cheap grace? Like Isaiah, who set out a vision of a servant sent by God to suffer for others, Jesus deliberately went forward to his own death, seeing it as the sacrifice that would satisfy the demands of justice and open the door to a wide offer of mercy.

Starting with this radical view of God's mercy and the evil we can be forgiven, Jesus is wildly lavish in welcoming and forgiving the rejects and outcasts of society—those whom others despise, exclude, and will never forgive. At the same time he is sternly uncompromising with his followers about their duty to show similar mercy to all who injure them in return.

Once Jesus was asked to approve a limit beyond which things had surely gone too far and no one could reasonably be expected to forgive any longer. The Pharisees of his day put the limit at seven times. Jesus responded by telling a story of a hard-hearted debtor. This man was forgiven millions but was so stingy to a colleague in return that he refused to forgive a paltry debt of pennies; he was then in turn dragged off to jail to serve the sentence for his original unpaid debt.

In other words, nothing that anyone can ever do to us will equal what we have done to God, and he has offered us forgiveness completely and freely. Our duty, then, is to forgive as we have been forgiven and to show that we have been forgiven by being willing to forgive others in our turn. Do they deserve it? Did we? More sobering still, Jesus teaches his followers that if they do not forgive others as they have been forgiven, they forfeit the forgiveness that God has given to them.

No wonder Saint Augustine called the famous line in the Lord's Prayer "the terrible petition": "Forgive us our trespasses as we forgive those who trespass against us." If we pray that prayer and fail to forgive our fellow human beings as we have been forgiven, we are actually asking God not to forgive us.

Anyone who examines the actual teaching of Jesus on forgiveness finds it anything but soft and sentimental. Indeed, his terms of discipleship are stern and demanding. As C. S. Lewis points out, the command to love our enemies and forgive those who have injured us is even more unpopular than Jesus' call to chastity. "Everyone says forgiveness is a lovely idea, until they have something to forgive, as we had during the war. And then, to mention the subject at all is to be greeted with howls of anger. It is not that people think it is too high

and difficult a virtue: it is that they think it is hateful
temptible. 'That sort of talk makes them sick,' they say."

Confusions and Counterfeits

In a day when faith for many has become a soft and amiable affair that
is intellectually vague and ethically undemanding, we must begin by
distinguishing forgiveness from its surrounding confusions. First, true
forgiveness has nothing to do with sentimentality. "Forgiveness,"
Mark Twain said, "is the fragrance that the violet sheds on the heel
that has crushed it." But this, though a beautiful comment on the possible effect of forgiveness, utterly fails to capture the sacrificial act of
will that is its central thrust.

Second, true forgiveness has nothing to do with utilitarianism or
cynicism. "Always forgive your enemies," Oscar Wilde quipped.
"Nothing annoys them so much." "Forgive your enemies," President
Kennedy once said, "but never forget their names." By contrast, those
who forgive—or "forth-give"—give up their own personal and emotional right to any further case against the one who has injured them.
They may still bring them before the bar of the judgment of the law.
But if they do, it is for the sake of justice rather than revenge, and
their hearts should be clear of all sense of personal vengeance and retaliation.

Third, true forgiveness is not the same as condoning. In a century
of horrendous evil, the recurring fear of this confusion is understandable. But to forgive is not to excuse evil. It is not to deny wrong. It is
not to tolerate the intolerable or lie down under the outrageous. It is
to call a spade a spade, and evil evil, and to allow the full horror of its
magnitude and outrage to sink in on every level—and then to be willing to dismiss the grounds of our own personal vengeance toward the
evildoer. In other words, forgiveness confronts the evil as evil, and the
wrongdoer as guilty, but refuses to retaliate and so refuses to play
evil's game and let evil have the final say.

Fifth, true forgiveness is not cheap grace. "God will forgive me. It's his job," wrote the poet Heinrich Heine. But for Christians, such presumption entirely misses the depth of God's ultimate sacrifice that makes possible the immediate sacrifice of our human acts of forgiveness. Equally, when Christians themselves go around saying, "I forgive you," to those who have injured others and not them, they spray religious language indiscriminately and cheapen forgiveness for themselves and others.

Forgiveness is love, and like love it may be costly. "One forgives to the degree that one loves," said La Rochefoucauld. Without love, forgiveness would be pointless sentiment; without forgiveness, love would be forlorn yearning.

Sixth, true forgiveness is not a matter of virtue and strength. "The weak can never forgive," said Gandhi. "Forgiveness is the attribute of the strong." But with due respect to other faiths, this view is not the forgiveness taught and demonstrated by Jesus. Others may see forgiveness as the virtue of a strong person, heroically prevailing over baser instincts that cry out for revenge and passing out forgiveness in a grand act of noblesse oblige. Christian forgiveness, however, is the gratitude of the humble person reciprocating, willing and eager to pass on to others, even at great cost, the unexpected and overwhelming grace that has been passed on to him.

Seventh, true forgiveness is different from reconciliation while at the same time it is an opening offer of peace. Many people refuse to forgive because they claim the other party shows no sign of repentance and no desire to be reconciled. I have heard this well-worn argument from both sides in conflicts such as the "troubles" in Northern Ireland, but it rests on a misunderstanding. It takes two to be reconciled, but only one to forgive. Yet that first act of forgiveness by the party that has been wronged or injured may be the break in the logjam that leads to full reconciliation between both parties. Even if rebuffed, it is still a step of obedience, an act of love, and a removal of the barriers from one side of the divide.

Vengeance is reactive and automatic; forgiveness is active and chosen. At the very least, the choice to forgive takes one party out of the Corsican blood feud cycle—or the Irish sectarian vendetta—that now need spiral down no further for lack of response.

With All My Heart

Talk of forgiveness is idle unless it spurs real victims to forgive real evildoers who have done them real injuries, which is all too common in a world of mounting domestic, ethnic, and sectarian hatred—cold, black, implacable hatred that freezes over individual hearts and communities and catches millions of victims in its arctic grip.

What is hate but the terminal condition of victims victimizing and being victimized all over again so often that cause and effect, past and present, are fused together in an orgy of despairing rage? And what is forgiveness but the strongest form of love that can reverse the irreversible and destroy the baggage of centuries; break the vicious cycle of action and retaliation, injury and vengeance, oppression and terrorism; and free fellow human beings from the consequences of their disastrous actions in the past? As Martin Luther King declared—and as he and national leaders as diverse as Abraham Lincoln and Nelson Mandela have shown in practice—such forgiving love is "the only force capable of transforming an enemy into a friend."

"Who is the greatest hero among heroes?" Rabbi Nathan asked. "He who turns his enemy into his friend."

In the dark months after the collapse of Germany in 1945, people everywhere were trying to piece together their devastated lives after the catastrophe of the Nazi years. There was a desperate shortage of food and shelter, but mercy and hope seemed in even shorter supply. One who was trying to bring them to Germany was a middle-aged Dutch watchmaker, Corrie ten Boom, who with her sister Betsie had been imprisoned in Ravensbrück concentration camp for harboring Jews. "I had come from Holland to defeated Germany," she wrote in *The Hiding Place*, "with the message that God forgives."

One day in Munich she had given her stump speech, and the audience members, their beaten-down faces still solemn, were leaving in silence, not quite daring to believe. And it was then that she saw him, working his way forward against the others. With a rush, his overcoat and brown hat changed back to a blue uniform and a skull-and-cross-bones cap, and she was back in the concentration camp, walking past him naked along with her sister, who later died there—one of the cruelest guards of all.

"A fine message, fraulein! How good it is to know that, as you say, all our sins are at the bottom of the sea!" Since Ravensbrück, he went on, he had become a Christian. God had forgiven him for the cruel things he did there, "but I would like to hear it from your lips as well, fraulein. Will you forgive me?" And he put out his hand for the second time.

For what seemed hours, time stood still. Ten Boom knew she had to do it. She had been forgiven and she must forgive. But she could not. She had spoken so glibly of forgiveness, and "Betsie had died in that place—could he erase her slow terrible death simply for the asking?"

An icy cold clutched her heart, but knowing that forgiveness is an act of the will, not an emotion, she prayed, "Help me!" and stuck out her hand, woodenly and mechanically. "And as I did, an incredible thing took place. The current started in my shoulder, raced down my arm, sprang into our joined hands. And then this healing warmth seemed to flood my whole being, bringing tears to my eyes."

"I forgive you, brother!" I cried. "With all my heart."

In Victory, Magnanimity

Rare, costly, difficult—no one should minimize the steep price of personal forgiveness or discount the fact that the consequences of forgiveness flow far beyond personal relationships. From lawyers to police officers, judges, generals, presidents, and prime ministers—people in positions of authority whose hearts are free through forgiveness are then freed in turn to serve the ideals of their office selflessly rather than using ideals such as honor, truth, and justice to mask the fact that they are really serving the interests of their own injured hearts or groups.

Nor should we discount the importance of national acts of forgiveness, such as amnesties and debt relief. Our Western roots include the Jewish notion of the Year of Jubilee, the periodic time of release and restoration that underscores the fact that without forgiveness some types of freedom will never be possible. Ours is a world that has traveled far down the road of hatred and now sees that many of its unforgiving responses to evil are not only ineffective but counterproductive. From the excessive and vengeful reparations exacted from Germany after World War I to the high-minded laws against hate crimes passed today, many of them have only made the situation worse.

"We never get rid of an enemy," Martin Luther King said, "by meeting hate with hate; we get rid of an enemy by getting rid of enmity."

Winston Churchill drafted the inscription for a plaque in a French town honoring the soldiers of the Great War and also used it as the motto for his histories of the Second World War. "In war, resolution; in defeat, defiance; in victory, magnanimity; in peace, goodwill."

For leaders of nations as well as common citizens, there can be a magnanimity of spirit that forgives the injuries of the past, a generosity of heart that knows the moment to go beyond what is deserved, and a grandeur of vision concerned with higher goals than getting even. Without the realism that was the theme of the last chapter, such virtues can become weak and easily abused. But no one has accused leaders such as Lincoln, Churchill, King, and Mandela of being cowards or saintly unrealists. Along with realism and courage, these virtues are crucial in responding to evil and an essential foundation for a world desperately longing for genuine second chances and the opportunity to begin all over again—again and again.

CHAPTER 15

THE COURAGE TO STAND

Was it because he himself was the father of twin girls? Or was it be-cause so many of the victims were children and the problem of evil has always been most horrifying when it is children who are abused, raped, and murdered? What finally moved a brilliant young Harvard-and Chicago-trained lawyer to switch careers and devote his life to fighting for justice for the oppressed was his encounter with two little girls who survived the terrible massacre in Kbuye, Rwanda, in 1994.

Gary Haugen was in Kbuye soon after the massacre, directing the United Nations' genocide investigation, on loan from the U.S. Depart-ment of Justice. It was the last mass-grave site he had to inspect before he flew home to be with one of his own daughters who had been diagnosed with meningitis.

Kbuye had suffered two horrendous slaughters, one in the cathe-dral and the other in the local stadium. On the one hand, Haugen wrote later, "it was a filthy, stinking job, but it had to be done." On the other hand, what undid him was not the nameless, faceless, de-caying body parts but the painful glimpses into the uniqueness of each victim, expressed in such objects clutched in death as wedding pictures and Bibles with loving inscriptions—"For as difficult as it was to imagine, each crumpled mortal frame had indeed come from a mother, one single mother who somewhere in time had wept tears of joy and aspiration over her precious child."

After a day spent picking through the sad remains of the thousands who had died, Haugen was suddenly overwhelmed at the moral immensity of the task and the contrast of the two little girls who had survived, though with the livid reminder of the slashes across their necks and heads.

> Through it all they were the picture of courage, sadness, and sweetness. . . . I was pierced again with the true identity of the rubbish I had been forced to wallow in all day. These two little girls—they were the rubbish. Though "fearfully and wonderfully made" (like my own two little girls at home), the awfulness of evil, the remoteness of Rwanda, and the lifelessness of death had conspired to very nearly rob these little ones of their human face.

Earlier, Haugen had been sent to the Philippines by the Lawyers Committee for Human Rights to investigate why the new democratic government that followed Ferdinand Marcos had not successfully prosecuted any of the police and military for human rights abuses.

Cory Aquino, the new president, was a human rights activist—her own husband had been murdered by her predecessor's henchmen—but she had not been able to stop the killing, raping, and torture of innocent civilians. Just before Haugen went to investigate, the world news had carried the story of the Lupao massacre, the Philippines' equivalent of My Lai. Soldiers of the Fourteenth Infantry Battalion, on a hunt for communist guerrillas, had murdered seventeen unarmed civilians, including six children, and wounded eight more. But to everyone's surprise, the court-martial had acquitted them all. "Twenty witnesses failed to testify," the presiding officer said, "which resulted in insufficiency of evidence."

Haugen was puzzled. The trial was inside the military headquarters in Manila, so it was understandable that the witnesses might have been afraid to appear, but he knew that people who had seen their own family members killed were usually passionate enough to insist that the truth be told. What he discovered, however, was quite differ-

ent. As the transcript of the trial showed clearly, the villagers had tes-
tified. With great courage, they had traveled to Manila, given their evidence, and identified the murderers—only to have the soldiers
change their testimony several times, give various phony alibis, and
get off scot-free, despite the dedication to human rights of the president and her administration.

The turning point in the investigation came in talking to the survivors themselves. "As usual," Haugen said, "it was all rather busi-
nesslike until I let my eyes meet theirs. Especially Merissa's—a
beautiful eight-year-old girl whose hand had been shot off by the soldiers' high-powered weapons." Even the local attorney, who knew the
story inside out, was moved all over again: "He just couldn't stand
thinking about what Merissa had been through."

Champions for the Oppressed

Two days after arriving home from his Rwanda assignment, Haugen
was riding to work in a bus in northern Virginia. Everything was
comfortably normal in its American suburban way, but all of a
sudden he was seized with the urge to shout out, "Excuse me, friends,
but did you know that less than forty-eight hours ago I was standing
in the middle of several thousand corpses in a muddy mass grave in a
tiny African country called Rwanda?" He was not out to shock them,
he said, but to affirm to himself that the whole terrible experience
had been real.

Instead of shocking his fellow suburban commuters, Haugen did
something that is sounding a bell around the world: he founded the
International Justice Mission in 1994 to stand up against the abuse of
power and provide advocacy and rescue for the oppressed of the
world who have no champion to speak for them. Building a strong
corps of public justice professionals—lawyers, criminal investigators,
diplomats, government relations experts, and so on—IJM documents
abuses and seeks relief for victims of oppression, either directly or in

partnership with local advocacy groups and international human rights organizations.

Three themes blaze through all the work of IJM. First, our modern world is groaning under the weight of thousands of countless unspeakable daily acts of oppression and brutality. Somewhere between the mounting but still relatively unusual personal acts of horrendous abuse, such as domestic violence, in the West and the monumental evils of the world-shaking horror of Auschwitz and the Chinese Cultural Revolution, there is a middle-level belt of regular, daily violence and brutality that is every bit as real, as evil, and as devastating to its victims. In a thousand unreported ways these abuses are happening daily, somewhere, and are simply accepted as part of the wallpaper of "the way the world is."

Trafficking in persons, for example, has become the human rights issue of the twenty-first century: more than half a million men, women, and children are trafficked each year—each human being coerced forcibly and each one traded as a commercial commodity. And then there are the millions forced into chattel slavery or bonded slavery (with more people in slavery today than in the worst days of the transatlantic slave trade four hundred years ago); the millions of young girls and women (some as young as four or five) forced into prostitution and abused daily by Western pedophiles and others; the countless numbers arrested and held without charge, subjected to illegal seizure of lands, forced migration, political intimidation, racial violence, state-sponsored torture, terrorism, and police corruption—not to speak of the murder of street children and of the children pressed into war. These are people so abused by power, Haugen says, that they know law only as injustice and run *from* the police, not to them.

Second, all these diverse forms of brutality and oppression grow from the same core—abuse of power. In its turn, abuse of power relies on two tactics: coercion and deception. On the one hand, all these abuses are forms of the strong compelling the weak and defenseless to act against their free will, whether by force or by the threat of force. Sometimes the force is naked, as when thugs flout the law and use physical violence to impose their will. Sometimes the abuse is masked, as when thugs act with impunity and apparent legality at the behest of corrupt legal authorities who are the real power behind the abuse. Sometimes again the abuse is mantled in the highest authority of the state, or justice itself, and becomes state policy.

On the other hand, all these abuses depend on deception and surround themselves with a bodyguard of lies. Typically, such deceptions begin by obscuring the evil: "Nothing is wrong and no one is being hurt." But when the deception becomes undeniable, coercion is used again, this time to obstruct the rescue—so that force is used to protect the deception that was originally used to obscure the oppression. The net effect is that oppressors lie in order to mask their evil but spin such a tangled web of lies that we all get used to there being such lies. Thus, even when we hear the truth, we reject it: we know that not everything is what it seems, so we suspect ulterior motives and end up cynical, apathetic, and not knowing whom to believe. Nothing is more dangerous to such deceptions than hard questions and exposure to the sunlight of truth.

Third, IJM members share two powerful convictions: that their passion for justice is the natural and necessary expression of their faith in a God who requires justice for the poor and the oppressed, and that they stand in a long line of similar people of faith who for three thousand years have made courageous stands against one form of evil or another.

As such, Gary Haugen and the International Justice Mission are a perfect present-day demonstration of the third essential for responding to evil: *the courage to make a stand for justice and against oppression.*

The Gift of the Jews

If Jews and Christians sometimes have differences over the first two essentials—in describing the evil in our human hearts and in disagreeing over the place of forgiveness in responding to injury—they are

closest and boldest in their united affirmation of justice. As both biblical faiths see it, this is a part of their world-affirming character. But
far more importantly, it is the direct expression of their view of God.
God, as we encounter him in the scriptures, is a God of justice. He
seeks justice, he hates injustice, he is on the side of the victims of injustice, he is adamantly opposed to those who perpetrate injustice,
and all who live before him must in their turn seek justice and have
the courage to stand against injustice. As the sublime prophet Isaiah
of Jerusalem declared simply, "The Lord is a God of justice."

In this view, our world is emphatically not the best of all possible
worlds. But the vision of a better world is not an escapist dream or an
opiate, as critics have charged. It is the model and the source of a
transcendent critique that motivates those who spend their lives resisting what is wrong and making this world a better place.

This clarion call to justice has sometimes been muted or even lost
altogether. It may also be distorted—twisted into its opposite so that
Jews and Christians become agents of terrible injustice, as the Christians often were in the religious persecutions of the medieval world
and the Jews sometimes have been in the political repressions of the
modern world. But from the Torah to the prophets to the New Testament to the blood-red stories of reform movements in Western civilization, the passion for justice is unquenchable and irrepressible.

Some years ago at a forum for political and business leaders near
Washington, D.C., an Asian leader introduced himself by saying, "I
am here as a Hindu seeker after Jesus." After the initial surprise had
registered, he explained that he had begun this search when he was
dismayed to see how few from his country had gone to the rescue of
their countrymen after a massive earthquake. Christians, by contrast,
had been in the forefront of the practical response, and when he had
looked into the Western tradition of giving and caring, he had discovered where it came from and was now on a search to learn more for
the sake of his country in the future.

The Western tradition of reform is just as distinctive as the Western culture of giving and caring. No other civilization has anything
that comes close. Many have nothing that moves in that direction at

all, and some have imported and transplanted copies of the Western reform movements. But the distinctiveness of the Western reform movements is perhaps even more overlooked and taken for granted than Western giving and caring. These movements are also decisively grounded in the Jewish and Christian faiths, or—if you like—the Christian mediation of the Jewish faith that Benjamin Disraeli called "Judaism for the multitudes."

Moses's challenging cry to Pharaoh, "Let my people go!" has been echoed by liberators and would-be liberators down the centuries until the words have become legendary. And having been liberated that way, the Israelites were expected to honor justice at the center of their national way of life. "Do not deprive the alien or the fatherless of justice, or take the cloak of the widow as a pledge," Moses said, laying down God's law. "Remember that you were slaves in Egypt and the Lord your God redeemed you from there."

The lion's roar of the Hebrew prophets is therefore an outcry against a freed people rejecting the justice they had been given and a heart's cry for them to return. And what was justice? Far from being paralyzed by fancy complications, the prophets were plain and blunt: justice was the righting of wrongs and injustice was the inflicting of wrongs.

"Have you murdered a man and seized his property?" Elijah thunders to King Ahab after his abuse of royal power in the act of land grabbing.

"You are the man!" Nathan quietly says to King David, rebuking him to his face for his adultery with Bathsheba and the murder of her husband.

"They sell the righteous for silver, and the needy for a pair of sandals," Amos charges Israel indignantly in the eighth century B.C. "They trample on the heads of the poor as upon the dust of the ground and deny justice to the oppressed."

"He looked for justice," Isaiah pronounces about God in his opening charge against Judah, "but saw bloodshed; for righteousness, but heard cries of distress."

Will God be pleased with ritual and ceremony? Micah asks famously, "He has showed you, O man, what is good. And what does the Lord require of you? To act justly and to love mercy and to walk humbly with your God."

"Now listen, you rich people," the apostle James writes in the first century, continuing the same tradition. ". . . The wages you failed to pay the workmen who mowed your fields are crying out against you. The cries of the harvesters have reached the ears of the Lord Almighty. . . . You have condemned and murdered innocent men who have not opposed you."

The Blood-Red Tradition of Reform

Like an active volcano, this same tradition has erupted repeatedly down the centuries.

"He who lives for himself only and overlooks all others, is useless," John Chrysostom, the golden-tongued preacher, thundered, castigating the careless wealthy in Constantinople in the fourth century. "He is not even a man, he does not belong to the human race."

"In the name of Christ, stop!" cried the little Turkish monk Telemachus in the Coliseum in Rome in the fifth century. Nearly three-quarters of a million gladiators had died to serve the Roman bloodlust, and the furious crowd stoned him to death too for disturbing their entertainment. But it was the last time, and with their consciences now pricked, they banned the gory spectacle for good.

"I am the voice of one crying in the wilderness," cried out Antonio de Montesinos, the Dominican priest who in 1511 first challenged the Spanish exploitation of the Indians.

> This voice says that you are in mortal sin and will die in it because of the cruelty and tyranny that you use against these innocent people. Tell me, by what right or justice do you hold these Indians in such cruel and horrible slavery? . . . Are these Indians not men? Do they not have rational souls? Are you not obliged to love them as you love yourselves?

"It is certain that judgment will fall upon this land," declared Bartolomé de las Casas, another Dominican monk who is often described as the conscience of the sixteenth century and who dared to argue before the Holy Roman emperor Charles V on behalf of the same Indians.

> For he who fails to fulfill the highest duty bears the heaviest guilt. Therefore God's anger will fall upon this land. . . . And if those who rise from the ruins accuse the Lord, and ask why he has brought this misery upon the land, I shall arise from the tomb to testify to God's justice. I will answer the accusers. . . . Terrible punishment follows terrible crime!

"Our conquest there, after twenty years, is as crude as it was the first day," Edmund Burke protested to the House of Commons in a blistering attack on British colonial rape and pillage in India in 1783. Often caricatured as a dyspeptic conservative, Burke's lifelong theme—or "great melody," in the words of W. B. Yeats—was the abuse of power and the "harrying of peoples," whether in America, Ireland, France, or India. "Every rupee of profit made by an Englishman is lost forever to India. . . . Were we to be driven out of India this day, nothing would remain, to tell that it had been possessed, during this inglorious period of our dominion, by anything better than the ourang-outang or the tiger."

"We can no longer plead ignorance," cried William Wilberforce, the greatest reformer in history, at the climax of his first great speech, in 1788, in what would be a forty-seven-year fight against slavery.

> We cannot evade it. We may spurn it. We may kick it out of the way. But we cannot turn aside so as to avoid seeing it. For it is brought now so directly before our eyes that this House must decide and must justify to all the world and to its own conscience. . . . Let not Parliament be the only body that is insensible to the principles of natural justice. Let us make reparation to Africa, as far as we can.

"God has always led me of Himself," Florence Nightingale wrote in 1851 as she wrestled with what it meant to break with her family and social conventions and set out to reform nursing and health care.

"The first idea I can recollect when I was a child was a desire to nurse the sick. My day dreams were all of hospitals and I visited them as often as I could. I never communicated it to anyone. It would have been laughed at."

"The name of Lord Ashley would forever stink in the nostrils of men," one of his enemies said. But when the "poor man's earl" died in 1855, the streets of London were packed with thousands of poor people whom he had helped with his tireless reforms of the evils of early industrialized factories. One group of his Ragged School boys held a banner that read, "I was a stranger, and you took me in."

An Unjust Law Is No Law at All

Space precludes a full roll call of the heroic individuals and groups who have had the courage to ask "why" and "why not" and then to break with the status quo and vested interests of their day and stand for a higher view of justice and human dignity. In our own day the most famous Christian stands against evil are unquestionably Martin Luther King Jr. and Alexander Solzhenitsyn. But the former illustrates the problems as well as the principles of making such a stand in our day.

Martin Luther King's "Letter from Birmingham Jail" is rightly praised as a prophetic message of America's civil rights movement, but it is also a testament to the reforming passion of the Christian pastor and man of faith who wrote it. Written with a white-hot intensity, it manages to achieve a universal voice and at the same time carries a host of highly specific contemporary applications. The passage that is crucial to a Christian understanding of reform comes in King's answer to the liberal clergy who had charged him with inconsistency. Was he calling for lawbreaking or not? "One may well ask," he wrote, "how can you advocate breaking some laws and keeping others?"

King's response goes right to the heart of the view of reform made possible by the biblical faiths: "The answer lies in the fact that there are two types of laws: just and unjust. I agree with St. Augustine that an unjust law is no law at all."

There is a right to break unjust laws, King asserted. "One who breaks an unjust law must do so openly, lovingly, and with a willingness to accept the penalty." Such a lawbreaker is not evading law, but giving a bigger picture, a wider portrayal of law. "I submit that an individual who breaks a law that conscience tells him is unjust and who willingly accepts the penalty of imprisonment in order to arouse the conscience of the community over its injustice is in reality expressing the highest respect for law."

Behind King's argument is the same bifocal vision of the biblical family of faiths that we explored earlier. Wherever human injustice comes up short in contrast to divine justice, the challenge to remedy and rectify is not only permissible but required.

"Am I not a man and brother?" Wilberforce and Josiah Wedgwood asked on behalf of African slaves. And in the savage gap between justice and injustice lay their passion to reform.

Who Says?

This straightforward principle of reform has become controversial today, because in our era of exploding pluralism we have a clash of competing moral principles. Commenting on the courageous stand of Las Casas and his allies against the cruelty of the conquistadors, the Peruvian novelist Mario Vargas Llosa noted that "they fought against their fellow men and against the policies of their own country in the name of the moral principle that to them was higher than any principle of nation or state." He then continues more provocatively: "This self-determination could not have been possible among the Incas or any of the other pre-Hispanic cultures. In these cultures, as in the other great civilizations of history foreign to the West, the individual could not morally question the social organism of which he was a part."

That is no longer the case, because the leverage for such critique has been transposed from a Jewish and Christian key to other keys, including the secularist key. The challenge is therefore no longer that of asserting a transcendent moral principle against the inertia of the status quo, but of asserting one moral principle against another, or several others. One person's reform may well be another person's reactionary position, and we are left with the question: who says?

Homosexuals, for example, often argue that the fight for their rights is today's equivalent of yesterday's fight to abolish slavery, whereas those who disagree would see their demands as a step backward toward earlier cultures, such as Sparta, which elevated homosexuality but devalued women.

Does this mean that we are left to interminable culture-warring between the disciples of some monistic universalism on one side ("Our way is the one way") and the disciples of multicultural relativism on the other side ("Whatever")? The alternative to this dismal prospect would be to encourage a third position: examined pluralism. Each individual and community is free to assert its principles and argue its position, based on freedom of conscience, but always remembering two requirements.

First, a right for one is a right for another, so any right we demand for ourselves should be a right we also defend for all others—even those with whom we differ most strongly. This would mean we conduct public debate with a disciplined appreciation of the rights, responsibilities, and respect of others in the debate.

Second, we are not subject to radical relativism so long as each claimant is prepared to assert and argue for the "good" by which he or she judges what is good or bad, just or unjust, progressive or reactionary. Such "goods" can no longer merely be asserted. They are no longer self-evident, except to those who believe them. They must be justified with arguments that are publicly accessible and persuasive to others if they are to compel assent in a pluralistic society.

Thus, even reform has been made more complicated by the conditions of our modern world. But this must never become one more excuse for swelling the crowd of bystanders—for shrugging our shoulders and allowing evil to pass unchallenged. In a world of rampant evil, the stakes are too high and the lessons of the recent past are too clear.

Let no one have any doubts where people of the biblical family of faiths stand. While human life lasts, those who live their lives by the Jewish and Christian faiths will always assess the changing conditions of succeeding generations and societies under the aspect of eternity and God's justice. Wherever the gap between just and unjust laws reemerges, the task of reform must begin again. The work of reform will never be complete; it will always have new tasks to perform— though to counter the danger of arrogance that this might suggest, we must add that the first and last focus of any reform must be the reformers. If reform is to be convincing and truly humanizing, reformers must reform themselves, and only then set about the task of reforming what is wrong.

Why Can't I Know
What I Need to Know?

The sixth basic question for exploring the challenge of evil concerns our inability to account for evil when we feel we really must be able to. In other words, the line between what we know as human beings and what we cannot know is one we simply cannot cross.

When it comes to evil and suffering, our passion for inquiring into the why of things, our insatiable curiosity and desire to make sense of every experience of life, gets us into trouble. At the very moment when our questioning is most insistent, it comes up against a mystery that is utterly and unfathomably impenetrable. There is quite simply no complete and fully satisfying human answer to all the whys and wherefores of evil. Yet never is our desire to know more intense and our inability to know more frustrating and agonizing.

Not surprisingly, when we come to the deepest mysteries of evil and suffering, this impasse prompts a disastrous move: we follow our hearts instead of our heads and insist on trying to account for the unaccountable. Most experiences of evil leave unanswered questions, and death does above all. For death means that, whatever we have achieved and whatever point we have reached, our accounts are cut off mid-page. For all but the privileged few, the termination of our lives does not coincide with the termination of our labors or our longings. We die with tasks left undone, hopes unfulfilled, relationships unrealized, questions unanswered, debts unpaid, good deeds unrecognized, and less than good deeds unpunished.

Through the sixth basic question we examine the most common strategies used to break out of this impasse and look at how each in turn fails to answer the real issue at stake. Worse still, in trying to account for the unaccountable, we can fall into the trap of turning our accountings into accusations—either of ourselves or of others.

To question life is the glory of being human, but to insist on a precise accounting of the unaccountable—whether in our own lives or in those of others—is to be cruel and insensitive as well as plain wrong. The mystery of evil in this world is impenetrable. The real question is how we face the mystery. If ever we do not know, we are always better off to say nothing.

CHAPTER 16

DON'T KNOW, DON'T SAY

"I am falsely accused." "If it was the last moment I was to live, God knows I am innocent." "I am wronged. It is a shameful thing that you should mind these folks that are out of their wits." The anguished appeals of Sarah Good, Elizabeth Howe, and Martha Carrier fell on deaf ears before they were hanged at the Salem witch trials in New England in 1692. But they are a haunting reminder that few things in life are more terrible than to feel we are falsely accused.

It would be a mistake to think that such waves of hysteria are a thing of the past. From earlier fears about communists to current allegations of sexual abuse, witch hunts are a recurring feature of modern life, each one justified according to the reason of the times and bringing in its train similar sorry features—a genuine problem inflated into a societywide obsession, runaway fears, uneasy imaginations, overzealous investigators, a tidal wave of lawsuits, false accusations, uncorroborated charges, manipulated testimony, frenzied media coverage, and a trail of besmirched characters and ruined lives.

We Shall Remain Ignorant

We risk a terrible equivalent of the witch hunt when our attempts to account for evil and suffering lead us to make accusations. This happens when, in seeking to account for the experience—in searching for the why that allows us to bear the how—we explore ways of accounting that are false, and therefore cruel, because they end in having to accuse someone: ourselves, someone else, or even God.

The root of the problem is our human passion for questioning that does not know when to stop. As "the animal that asks and asks," we press our questions until they get us into trouble because we refuse to be silent in the face of mystery. We balk at the limits of what we know.

To many people, the notion that anything is truly unknowable is an insult to human intelligence. What others count as unknowable they call simply unknown so far. The light of reason, they confidently believe, will one day shine into the darkest and most impenetrable recesses of experience. But testimony to a deeper view of an inscrutable mystery is strong and ancient, as is testimony to its companion truth—humility.

"Do not seek to know more than is appropriate," wrote the great Augustine. "Absolute truth is beyond our grasp," wrote Nicholas of Cusa in the fifteenth century. A century later Montaigne wrote, "A man can be only what he is and can imagine only according to his reach." Pascal, in many ways his faithful echo only a little later, wrote similarly in *Pensées*: "Let us then know our reach. We are something and not everything. . . . Our intelligence occupies in the order of things the same place as our body in the extent of nature."

This theme carries down, more muted but still clear, into the modern world. In *Paradise Lost*, John Milton wrote: "Heaven is too high for thee / to know what passes there; be lowly wise." At the end of an 1872 lecture, "On the Limits of Science," Émil du Bois-Reymond, a celebrated scientist, finished with one emphatic Latin word, *Ignorabimus*, or "We shall remain ignorant." To say so is to practice not know-nothing obscurantism but humility. There are certain insoluble problems in life, mysteries that neither science nor human intelligence of any kind can solve, and wise thinking acknowledges the boundaries of these mysteries.

This impasse is hard enough to accept in general. But when we come to evil and suffering, the urge to know why makes it impossible and we press our questions regardless. If only the final accountings were fair and obvious in this life. But they rarely are. If only reason and justice could sign off together on the final verdict on our days on earth. But they rarely do. And in the case of unimaginable suffering or untimely death, the mismatch is such that we cannot accept the verdict of life. Our experiences explode our explanations, so we cry out for a fuller explanation. We demand an answer that goes beyond straightforward accounting.

Goethe's Faust speaks for us all when he cries out, "All I see is that we cannot know! This burns my heart."

"What is the use of grief?" Thomas Jefferson asked in anguish after losing his wife and several members of his family. As an Enlightenment thinker, he believed he had worked out the answers to many of life's questions to his own satisfaction, but no economy he could see explained the grief of loss.

There is no full, satisfying answer to the deepest questions. Life always raises more questions than our minds can answer. Oceans of ink have flowed in search of answers to evil, but no human mind has ever figured it all out. The essential mystery remains and always will. If there had been a simple answer, it would have been found by now Whatever answers we each believe to be true will still face further questions that they do not answer completely.

But at this point, when our questions hit the wall, there is an obvious solution. We can say that the experience in question, even our lives as a whole, are simply too short and too small to allow us to do the sums properly. We must therefore take a wider view and bring in more factors. Perhaps that will give us the perspective to understand our situations better and find an explanation for our suffering. Those who think like this—who search for a wider perspective to provide an accounting that can satisfy the human heart—employ one of three common strategies.

Going Backward

The first strategy is the answer of the Eastern faiths—to stretch the accounting period backward by positing an unknown past that explains the evils and sufferings of the present. If we believe in reincarnation, each of our lives is part of a long series of lifetimes. What we have done in a previous life thus explains the apparent injustices we are facing in this lifetime. The explanation lies in our karma. Where there is suffering, there must have been sin.

"Just as a calf will find its mother among a thousand cows," runs a traditional Hindu saying, "so your sins will find you out among a thousand rebirths."

"The acts done in former births never abandon any creature," the Mahabharata says sternly. "Since man lives under the control of karma," he adds, "he must always be alert to ways of maintaining his equilibrium and of avoiding evil consequences."

"Men of devout faith," cried Nicheren, the thirteenth-century Japanese leader who expounded Buddhist teaching, "because you committed countless sins and accumulated much evil karma in the past, you must expect to suffer much retribution for what you have done."

Such tough-mindedness is a world away from the soft sentiments of today's "boomer Buddhism" and New Age thinking, but is it satisfying? Logically, yes. By tracing a strong, sharp line between our previous deeds and our present fate, it is coolly logical. But that is the rub. Is it emotionally satisfying? Does even the most ardent Hindu and Buddhist really think we are responsible today for every detail of our fate? Do we really believe that the success of today's superathlete, megabillionaire, or business titan is the karma reaped from previous lives? Were we Westerners so much more virtuous in previous incarnations that we deserve our prosperity, more so even than the peoples of Asia, who followed Hinduism and Buddhism so ardently? More importantly, do we really believe that the abused child, the battered wife, and the tortured dissident are reaping injustice as their karma? The thought revolts the mind, not to speak of the heart.

Going Wider

The second possible strategy, represented by the Stoics, is to stretch the accounting period wider by considering the broader considerations of suffering that offset its immediate costs. Thus, Stoics were able to achieve a detachment from their emotions that allowed them to remain indifferent to both pain and pleasure, while others have endured suffering as a means to greater virtue and more mature character.

"Happy the man who can endure the highest and the lowest fortune," Seneca wrote. "He who endured such vicissitudes with equanimity has deprived misfortune of its power."

And again, "It is a proof of nobility of mind to despise the injuries."

And again, "There is nothing in the world so much admired as a man who knows how to bear unhappiness with courage."

"If you are distressed by anything external," the emperor Marcus Aurelius wrote in his *Meditations*, "the pain is not due to the thing itself but to your estimate of it; and this you have the power to revoke at any moment."

And again, "When thou art above measure angry, bethink thee how momentary a thing a man's life is."

And again, "Thou must be like a promontory of the sea, against which, though the waves beat continually, yet it both itself stands, and about it are those swelling waves stilled and quieted."

Such thinking allowed Stoics to face evil and suffering with as much courage as anyone in history. Seneca even said, "Great men rejoice in adversity just as brave soldiers triumph in war." After all, "it is a proof of nobility of mind to despise injuries"—a sentiment Marcus

Aurelius echoed in deeds as well as words. "Here is a rule to remember when anything tempts you to feel bitter: not 'This is a misfortune,' but 'To bear this worthily is good fortune.'"

The modern world is hardly congenial for full-blooded Stoicism. Its appeal is limited in a generation that is as soft and narcissistic as ours. But the Stoic insistence on overcoming suffering by gaining detachment through a wider perspective is a thread running through many modern responses to suffering. A good perspective and a sense of proportion—these are the thoughtful person's aspirin.

"Nothing that grieves us can be called little," Mark Twain wrote in "Which Was the Dream?" "for by the eternal laws of proportion a child's loss of a doll and a king's loss of a crown are events of the same size."

"Happiness is good for the body," Marcel Proust wrote, "but it is grief which develops the strengths of the mind."

Asked what she had learned from all the scandals, divorces, and sickness in her life, the actress Ingrid Bergman answered simply: "The tears you have shed make you into a human being, and that is much to be grateful for."

Going Forward

The third strategy, natural to all three Abrahamic faiths, is to stretch the accounting period forward into an unknown future beyond death and to speculate on the meaning of the suffering from God's point of view. "God has allowed you to suffer for such and such a reason," we are told. "God's purpose for you is this, that, or the other." After all, deeds and consequences that do not balance in this life will be balanced in the life "hereafter" and the world that is to come, so clearly that is the way to make sense of things. Dante's *Divine Comedy* is a classical Christian expression of this belief, but similar views can be found in the Talmud and the Qur'an.

There are important differences between these strategies. The Eastern one is the most precise in the way the explanation of suffering automatically provides its meaning and purpose. There is a one-to-one clarity here: you are suffering, you have sinned, so your suffering is the result of your karma.

By contrast, the second strategy puts less weight on explanation and more on outcome and purpose, and the third approach typically says next to nothing about explanation and everything about a final outcome that will include the understanding of purpose—in hindsight.

Some people find these explanations satisfactory. But for others who have probed them more deeply, there is one common flaw in all three strategies: they are speculation. We really do not know. The fact is that there is only one explanation that would satisfy us here and now as we suffer, and that is the one we do not have and cannot have—a full explanation of why we are suffering here and now. So we are caught in the impasse again. Our demand for an immediate accounting is a recipe for frustration. It leaves us hammering on a door that simply does not open. It condemns us to demand answers to questions that appear to be denied us. How then are we to face this mystery in life?

Every Sufferer's Brother

There is one bracing lesson we see in the story of Job, the world's classic sufferer and the one in whom all sufferers know that they have at least one brother who understands their pain: say no to false accountings. We misunderstand the book of Job if we view it as the Hebrew attempt to give an answer to the problem of evil. To see it that way is to miss the point and cheapen the story. The book is harrowing enough in translation, but in the original, the novelist Herman Wouk says, "the craggy, sometimes tortured Hebrew eerily calls up the agony of a just man on the rack of an unjust experiment, performed by Satan with the incomprehensible permission of God."

At the very least, the book of Job is more about God than it is about an answer to evil. But in all the mystery of Job, one lesson is clear. If we do not know the meaning of the suffering, we should not pretend we do. To say something when we know nothing is not only wrong but cruel—and an insult to God, not just to our fellow humans.

George Steiner captures the awe and the sublime heights of the Hebrew poem when he writes that he can just about picture Shakespeare returning home for lunch or supper after working on *King Lear* or *Twelfth Night* and remarking casually that his work had gone well or badly, and then inquiring about the price of cabbages, but that he cannot begin to imagine any such mundane event in the life of the one who wrote down God's great speeches out of the whirlwind. What it must have taken to hear those words and see those images is unimaginable. So to reduce the book to a how-to answer to the problem of evil is an insult to its immensity. In Job, it is not we humans who are given answers to satisfy our curiosity. The book that starts out with our questions for God ends with God's questions for us.

But again, the one thing is clear: if we do not know the answers, it is better not to say. Job's agony is not just physical. He is racked by a moral dilemma. As his crises mount, is he to trust God and suspend judgment on why all this is happening to him? Or as the child of an age that believed in a one-to-one correlation between sin and suffering, is he to press God for an explanation for his sufferings in order to clear his name before his notorious "comforter" friends who accuse him of wrongdoing?

At first Job passes the test with honors. Disasters hit him, his children are killed, and his future is ruined, but his character remains firm and his faith undeterred. "Throughout all this Job did not sin; he did not charge God with unreason." Job does not know why, but he knows why he trusts God who knows why.

But agony piles on agony. His wife encourages him to curse God and die, and his friends accuse him pitilessly. In the face of it all, Job's silent trust seems like an admission of guilt. On the one hand, his chosen style of defense reaches new heights of unrivaled courage and faith ("But in my heart I know that my vindicator lives and that he will rise last to speak in court"). On the other hand, it leads him at times into the bitter blackness of self-pity and doubt. God eventually rebukes

Job for defending himself in a way that accuses God ("Dare you deny that I am just or put me in the wrong that you may be right?").

What is pivotal is that Job's mistake turns out to be the mirror image of that of his faithless friends, though for a better reason. All of them err by starting from the faulty one-to-one accounting of sin and suffering that was common at the time: if someone suffers, it must be the result of his or her sin. This false accounting leads Job's friends to an equally false accusation: Job is suffering, so he must have sinned. They have no idea of the unseen dimensions of the contest.

On the other hand, this false accounting leads Job to a false demand for a one-to-one explanation from God. He has no idea of the unseen dimensions either, so to defend himself from what he knows to be false—"I am not who you think me to be"—Job demands from God a one-to-one explanation of his suffering. And when he does not get it, he dares to try to clear his own name by accusing God himself of injustice, not knowing either God or what is really at stake in the story.

In the end, rather than getting an answer from God, Job encounters God himself, which is his answer. But it is Job's friends, not Job, with whom God is angry. Speaking piously when they were ignorant, they became self-righteous and cruel as well as quite wrong. False accounting for evil always ends in falsely accusing someone, whether someone else, ourselves, or God. When we are with anyone who is suffering, we should never give words without love, and we should never give answers without knowledge.

Do any of us have a complete explanation for the long bloodstained record of human suffering? Do we have an explanation that covers the death of a beloved child as well as the slaughter of nameless millions? Forget for a moment the evils of Genghis Khan, Torquemada, Hitler, and Stalin. Do you have an explanation to cover the evils of even a single day? And do you have an explanation that stills all other explanations? Evil can be unbearable as well as unspeakable, and the pressure to account for it will always be insatiable. But if ever we do not know, we should not say. Silence itself is eloquent sympathy.

Isn't There Any Good
in All This Bad?

The seventh question for exploring the challenge of evil examines the silver linings in the darkest of experiences. In all but the very worst experiences of evil and suffering, some good is discernible, and this is often clearest not to sympathizers on the outside but to those at the center of the suffering. At its strongest, the claim by people of faith is that suffering, far from being an obstacle to faith and knowing the love of God, is the pathway on which these are experienced most richly.

No account of evil would be complete without this point. It is often a precious, if hard-won, fruit of pain, and we need to guard it carefully from misunderstanding and abuse. It is not a point to be made cheaply.

Many major "goods" have been attributed to suffering—for instance, its ability to get our attention (to be "God's megaphone," as C. S. Lewis put it), forge deeper character, and arouse compassion. In asking the seventh question, we should notice that recognizing such silver linings helps us to steer between two equal and opposite extremes—either exaggerating or dismissing the positive side of suffering.

One extreme, exaggerating the positive benefits of suffering, is more traditional. It can be seen in various schools of thought that have an admirable record of responding to suffering constructively. For example, the Stoic philosophers argued that one of the ways of detaching themselves from suffering was to see the essential goodness in the world. "From everything that happens in the universe," Epictetus wrote, "it is easy for a man to find occasion to praise providence."

Easy to praise providence? For those who follow Adorno and can no longer write poetry after Auschwitz, it would be harder still to praise providence. Epictetus was no stranger to atrocities, but the ancients were writing before the era of death camps and genocide. The same objection applies to the many different views of life, in one way or another, as a "vale of soul-making"—the idea that the world was created as a test course to deepen our characters and bring us to maturity. The phrase "vale of soul-making" was coined by John Keats in writing to his brother and sister in 1819. "Do you not see how necessary a world of pains and troubles is to school an intelligence and make it a Soul? . . . Call the world if you please 'The vale of Soul-Making.'"

The trouble with such views is that they are too sunny for the world after Auschwitz. Whatever horrendous evils do for our character or compassion, is anyone prepared to say that they have been deliberately designed to be for the victims' schooling in life? And if so, what sort of providence would have conceived of such a plan?

Those who exaggerate the positive side of suffering usually do so to try to explain why evil has happened in the first place. But what is correct as an observation—suffering has such and such good effects—is incorrect as an explanation. It is often said, for instance, that suffering deepens character. That is demonstrably true. A master of the universe in the business world may learn to be patient after suffering a stroke that leaves him dependent on the care of others. A

Hollywood starlet may grow less vain after scarring her face in a car crash and realizing that people value her for more than her glamour.

But that is not to say that deeper character is the purpose and explanation of suffering. It is only its dark gift. To suggest otherwise to the sufferer is cruel and wrong. The evil behind the suffering may be as malevolent and senseless as ever. But in a raging storm—perhaps even one of life's "perfect storms"—there may still be a silver lining in the clouds.

The opposite extreme, excluding any notion of the positive side of evil and suffering, is more modern. The much-quoted lines of the Greek tragedian Aeschylus are more typical of the ancient view:

> *Pain that cannot forget*
> *Falls drop by drop*
> *Upon the heart*
> *Until in our despair*
> *There comes wisdom*
> *Through the awful grace of God.*

The bleaker, modern view can be seen in the position of those who want to respond to evil realistically, and especially to do full justice to the magnitude and malevolence of contemporary evil. For example, the French philosopher Emmanuel Levinas views suffering as a combination of ultimate evil ("diabolical horror" and "undiluted malignity"), ultimate destructiveness, and ultimate passivity ("a pure undergoing"). He therefore sees no possibility of any purpose at all in suffering, whether from trust in God or from faith in secular progress. Suffering is intrinsically senseless and useless. In Levinas's chilling words, it is all "suffering for nothing."

Yet in spite of himself, even Levinas sees a silver lining in the worst of evil. He rules out giving evil any meaning through faith in God or in human progress. But he warns that if we see the "fundamental malignancy" of twentieth-century evil as the last word on life, then we descend to a nihilism that amounts to "finishing the criminal enterprise of National Socialism." Instead, we can at least

respond to the "useless suffering" of others with compassion that
renders their suffering meaningful for us.

Levinas's conclusion is meager, even desolate. Such compassion is
"meaningful in me, useless in the Other." But while this silver lining
is small, it is unmistakably a silver lining—from one of the darkest
storms the world has ever seen. And many other silver linings are
stronger and clearer still.

CHAPTER 17

"GODDAMNIT!" AND OTHER UNWITTING PRAYERS

"Biographies of writers," W. H. Auden once declared, "are always superfluous and usually in bad taste. A writer is a maker, not a man of action. . . . His private life is, or should be, of no concern to anybody except himself, his family, and his friends." Auden, who was the most influential English-speaking poet of his age, therefore dismissed literary biographers as "gossip writers and voyeurs, calling themselves scholars." He even proposed that writers publish their work anonymously, so that readers could concentrate on the writing rather than the writer. After he died in 1973, his executors found in his will the request that his friends burn his letters "to make a biography impossible."

But to paraphrase Shakespeare, the gentleman doth protest too much. Even if philosophy and poetry cannot be reduced to biography, the link between life and work is too close to sever, and no one is a clearer example than W. H. Auden himself. Take, for instance, the illuminating incident that undermined his facile early philosophy and helped to forge the faith of his mature years.

Utterly Wrong for Some Reason

Auden came to America as a refugee from all that menaced Europe in the 1930s, typified the very day he arrived by the news that Barcelona had just fallen to Franco's fascist forces. On September 1, 1939, Hitler invaded Poland, and Auden, in New York City, wrote a famous poem named after the date.

Auden was not a religious believer, and he had not been since he left school, where the religion he encountered was "nothing but vague uplift, as flat as an old bottle of soda water." The conviction had grown in him that "people only love God when no one else will love them." But as World War II broke out, he knew he had to "show an affirming flame" and make some stand for freedom. As he expressed it in the closing lines of his poem "September 1, 1939": "All I have is a voice / To undo the folded lie."

Eager to follow events in Europe, and living in a day before television, Auden regularly went to his local cinema to watch the documentary news. Two months after writing the poem, he was in a cinema in Yorkville, then a largely German-speaking area of Manhattan. There he saw *Sieg im Poland*, a documentary of the Nazi invasion of Poland. When Poles appeared on the screen, members of the audience cried out, "Kill them! Kill them!"

Auden was horrified. At the time his philosophy of life was a broad blend of liberal-socialist-democratic opinions, following an earlier intellectual odyssey through the dogmas of Freud and Marx. But one thread had always linked his successive convictions—a belief in the natural goodness of humankind. Whether the solutions to the world's problems lay in politics, education, or psychology, once these problems were addressed, humanity would be happy because humanity was good.

But as he watched the SS savagery onscreen and heard the audience's brutal response, Auden suddenly knew differently. With an intuitive flash he knew, beyond any question, that he was encountering evil and that it had to be condemned categorically.

Auden was not alone in facing up to evil because of the war.

Among others coming to the same realization were the philosopher C. E. M. Joad and the Nobel Prize–winning novelist William Golding. "This view of human evil which I adopted unthinkingly as a young man," Joad wrote, "I have come fundamentally to disbelieve. . . . A view which regards evil as the by-product of circumstances, which circumstances can, therefore, alter and even eliminate, has come to seem intolerably shallow."

"Before the Second World War," Golding wrote to explain how he conceived of his novel *Lord of the Flies*,

> I believed in the perfectibility of social man . . . but after the war I did not because I was unable to. I had discovered what one man could do to another. . . . I must say that anyone who moved through those years without understanding that man produces evil as a bee produces honey, must have been blind or wrong in the head.

For Auden it was the second part of his realization that stopped him in his tracks. "There had to be some reason," he was suddenly aware, why Hitler was "utterly wrong."

Auden was profoundly shaken by his experience in the cinema and reflected on it over the next few weeks. His earlier facile confidence in human goodness and in human solutions to human problems had collapsed, and his thinking opened up two troubling issues he knew he must answer. One was how to account for the undeniable evil he had encountered in the cinema, and the other was how to justify the absolute condemnation with which he had responded instinctively.

After all, there were no "absolutes" in his universe or in the thinking of any of his friends. To judge anything as absolutely wrong was naive and impossible. Philosophers had undermined absolute judgments through relativism. Psychologists had thrown them over in favor of nonjudgmental acceptance.

Auden shared his dismay with his friends. "The English intellectuals who now cry out to Heaven against the evil incarnated in Hitler have no Heaven to cry to," he told one friend. Clearly, liberalism had a fatal flaw.

"The whole trend of liberal thought," he wrote the next year, "has

been to undermine faith in the absolute. . . . It had tried to make
reason the judge. . . . But since life is a changing process . . . the attempt to find a humanistic basis of keeping a promise, works logically
with the conclusion, 'I can break it whenever I feel convenient.'"

The only remedy, Auden concluded, was to renew "faith in the absolute." He posed the challenge in another poem written soon after
his visit to the Yorkville cinema:

> Either we serve the Unconditional
> Or some Hitlerian monster will supply
> An iron convention to do evil by.

The New Eleventh Commandment

The issue Auden confronted more than half a century ago is one that
millions of us in Western society face today. From time to time we
encounter greater or lesser instances of something wrong and are
confused and uncertain how to respond. Who are we to judge anyone
else? And how on earth do we pronounce judgments without being
judged ourselves? But for all but the few, there also come those times
when we find ourselves face to face with instances of unmistakable
evil and then—automatically and intuitively—we condemn them as
wrong. Whether the instance is rape, murder, or terrorism, deep
down we know these are categorically, unreservedly, and absolutely
wrong, regardless of the purported intellectual inconsistencies.

I would argue that when people feel this way, they are right. And
that their intuition, in the face of real evil, that real evil requires an absolute judgment is one of the silver linings of the dark experience of
evil.

We all know the general sources of our modern hesitation to
judge evil. On the one hand, there is the social reality of the world we
live in—a world of exploding pluralism. "Everyone is now everywhere," it is said with only a little exaggeration. So the effect of our

travels around the world, our media-enhanced awareness of everyone else in the global village, the massive movement of peoples that is diversifying the most homogeneous societies, and the infinite array of offers held out by our modern consumerism, is to make us aware of choice and change as never before—and therefore of the relativity of our own choices.

The result is that certainties have evaporated, authorities have eroded, and seemingly permanent traditions and apparently rocklike convictions have softened into preferences and lifestyle options. So who are we to judge others if we just happen to have "our values" rather than "their values"? And worst of all, in light of our newly deepened sensitivity to the injustices of the past, would it not be "ethnocentric" or "racist" to assert that our values are superior to anyone else's? Ours then is a world in which "Thou shalt not judge" has become the new eleventh commandment, and tolerance the last undisputed virtue.

On the other hand, over the last two centuries a determined cadre of thinkers has assaulted traditional views of truth and of right and wrong, leaving the widespread impression that it is no longer possible to believe in such things. Some, like Karl Marx, argued that there is no objective truth and that the only way to judge a belief is by the results it produces. Others, like Friedrich Nietzsche, argued that all notions of absolute truth are examples of "perspectivism": there are many eyes, he argued, so there are many truths and no possibility of any single or absolute truth. Worse still, claims to truth mask what are, in reality, the interests and agendas of power. Truth and virtue are really power games, so to judge others as evil is not a moral evaluation but a power bid and a challenge to a duel. The net result is an erosion of any objective truth by which to stand against manipulation and the abuse of power.

Cries to Heaven, Cries for Hell

hat, face to face with raw and naked evil, our relativism, nonjudg—ntalism, tolerance, and fears of ethnocentrism count for nothing. Absolute evil calls for absolute judgment. Instinctively and intuitively, we cry out for the unconditional to condemn evil unconditionally. There is a right and wrong that at times we cannot avoid knowing.

"I decline utterly to be impartial between the fire brigade and the fire," Winston Churchill said.

"There are things which are bad, and false, and ugly, and no amount of specious casuistry will make them good, or true, or beautiful," said William Haley, the legendary editor of the *Times* of London on the day of his retirement.

Or as Geoffrey Warnock, the Oxford philosopher, stated categorically: "That it is a bad thing to be tortured or starved, humiliated or hurt, is not an opinion: it is a fact. That it is better for people to be loved and attended to rather than hated or neglected, is again a plain fact, not a matter of opinion."

Even atheism gets suspended at such times. Have you ever heard an atheist exclaim, "Goddamnit!" and really mean it? All too often those words are an empty oath, but when they are wrung from the heart in the face of something profoundly wrong, they can be a passionate, if unwitting, prayer—or what Peter Berger calls a "signal of transcendence" or "argument from damnation." It is an experience, he writes in *A Rumor of Angels*, in which "our sense of what is humanly permissible is so fundamentally outraged that the only adequate response to the offense as well as to the offender seems to be a curse of supernatural dimensions."

Instinctively we realize that failure to judge certain evils as evil is not just a theoretical failure in understanding justice but a fatal deficiency in our humanity. It is an outrage that cries out for further response: "Not only are we constrained to condemn, and to condemn absolutely, but, if we should be in a position to do so, we would feel constrained to take action on the basis of this certainty."

This conviction was precisely what moved Dietrich Bonhoeffer to join the plot to kill Hitler—despite the theoretical toils of certain misgivings as a pastor and teacher of ethics: "If I see that a madman is driving a car into a group of innocent bystanders, then I can't as a Christian simply wait and comfort the wounded and bury the dead. I must try to wrest the steering wheel out of the hands of the madman."

Berger points out that because we view such condemnation as "absolute and certain," we give our judgments the status of necessary and universal truth and that "we must look beyond the realm of our natural experience for a validation of our certainty." Looking beyond in this way, we make another discovery: "Deeds that cry out to heaven also cry out for hell."

In the debate over the execution of Adolf Eichmann, chief architect of Hitler's Jewish extermination program, Berger notes the general feeling that "hanging is not enough." But what would have been enough? As I write, the same powerful feelings are pouring out after the suicide of a notorious mass murderer in a British prison. A life sentence was too good for him, many people said earlier. Letting him cheat justice by taking his own life was too good, they are saying now. But hanging would have been too good for him too, they say. So what would have been "enough" for the perpetrator of such deeds?

In the case of horrendous human deeds, Berger continues, no human punishment would ever be "enough": "The doer not only puts himself outside the community of men; he also separates himself in a final way from a moral order that transcends the human community, and thus involves a retribution that is more than human."

In short, there are deeds that demand not only condemnation but damnation. The evidence that God exists, Winston Churchill once said, was "the existence of Lenin and Trotsky, for whom a hell was needed."

Victors' Justice or Something More?

The issue of what is assumed in judging horrendous evil is a question for nations, not just individuals. If postmodern thinkers sometimes talk as if it were impossible to make any valid judgments at all, some Western leaders talk as if there were no relativity at all—as if the principle of transcendent universal justice were self-evident, firmly established, and universally accepted.

Speaking at the time of the first Gulf War in 1990, former prime minister Margaret Thatcher declared that if anything happened to the Western hostages, "we could do what we did at Nuremberg and prosecute the requisite people for their totally uncivilized and brutal behavior. . . . They cannot say, 'We were under orders.' That was the message of Nuremberg."

Detailing the crimes of Saddam Hussein at the same time, the first President Bush said the same: all "those crimes are punishable under the principles adopted by the allies in 1945 and affirmed by the United Nations in 1950."

Yet little more than half a century after the Nuremberg trials of the Nazi war criminals, it is questionable whether the Western democracies have the moral certainty and assurance to conduct such a trial today as more than an assertion of Western power. On the one hand, Western thinkers have stripped away the intellectual underpinnings of such a higher view of justice. On the other hand, Western armies have committed their own atrocities, such as My Lai and the torture of Iraqi prisoners, and the United States, one of the original judges at Nuremberg, has pressed to exempt its own citizens from such an international court of criminal law.

Does this mean that Western talk of the rule of law is only a form of victors' justice? It was not always so. Earlier understandings were far more searching.

For the great African American reformer W. E. B. Du Bois, the issue was crystal clear and the appeal was to the absolute justice of the God of the Bible, whose justice would not be denied forever and whose authority was accepted by most Americans at the time. "All men know," he cried, "that there are in this world here and there and again and again great partings of the ways—the one way wrong, the other right, in some vast and eternal sense." Thus, in September 1922, after a white mob had raged through Atlanta murdering two dozen blacks, he wrote his impassioned "Litany at Atlanta": "Doth not this justice of hell stink in Thy nostrils, O God? How long shall the mounting flood of innocent blood roar in Thine ears and pound in our hearts for vengeance. . . . *Keep not Thou silent O God!*"

In our pluralistic world such an explicit appeal to the divine justice of the God of the Bible would not be possible between nations, but the cry still rises for a transcendent justice that assumes it. Hannah Arendt, for example, pointed out what the Nuremberg trials assumed about the perpetrators.

> What we have demanded in these trials, where the defendants had committed "legal" crimes, is that human beings be capable of telling right from wrong even when all they have to guide them is their own judgment, which moreover happens to be completely at odds with what they must regard as the unanimous opinion of all those around them.

In other words, the Nuremberg judgments asserted that the doers of the deeds in question were wrong, regardless of the legality of the deeds at the time, regardless of the orders the doers had been given, regardless of the near-universal acceptance of the practices by others, and regardless of the fact that the doers would not have been judged for these deeds had their nation won and not lost the war. But where is such judgment grounded?

Zygmunt Bauman and others have shone light on the assumption of transcendence in the judgments themselves. There can be no war criminals, and no right to try, condemn, and execute anybody, he argues, unless there is some justification for deciding that certain behavior is criminal over and above the laws and customs of a particular society.

And there would be no way to conceive of the punishment of such behavior as anything more than the vengeance of the victors over the vanquished . . . were there no supra- or non-societal grounds on which the condemned actions could be shown to collide not only with a retrospectively enforced legal norm, but also with moral principles which society may suspend, but not declare out of court.

But again, where is such justice grounded?

Keeping the Dream of Justice Alive

Not surprisingly, one of the consequences of twentieth-century evil has been a renewed appreciation of the importance of transcendence for making judgments, an appreciation sometimes found in unexpected quarters. The Marxist-leaning Frankfurt School, for example, even praised traditional religion for keeping alive the possibility of transcendence. Only if certain truths transcend present reality can we hope to protest the world as it is and to improve on it.

It was enough, some had said, that Auschwitz established a new moral imperative: to act so that Auschwitz should never happen again. But that powerful-sounding argument is hollow. It begs the question: how do we act so that Auschwitz never happens again? And there the need for transcendence raises its head again.

Once again the logic of this impulse points toward the Jewish and Christian faiths. Far from being servile lackeys to the status quo, Judaism and the Christian faith are now credited for keeping alive the dream of justice that transcends all wrong. After all, as Max Horkheimer wrote in words that echo the biblical insistence that the world should be otherwise, "What is religion in the good sense? The not-yet-strangled impulse that insists that reality should be otherwise, that the spell will be broken and turn toward the right direction."

The same groping for transcendence is evident in Rafael Lemkin's desperate search in the early 1940s for a word to capture the full moral horror of the horrendous evil he was to term "genocide." Somehow, as Samantha Powers recounts the story in *A Problem from Hell*, his new word "had to chill listeners and invite immediate condemnation." So on one of the almost indecipherable pages of his notebooks he "scribbled and circled 'THE WORD' and drew a line connecting the circle to the phrase, penned firmly, 'MORAL JUDGMENT.'"

"His word would do it all," Powers writes. "It would be the rare term that carried in it society's revulsion and indignation. It would be what he called 'an index of civilization.'" In short, it had to be a one-word judgment and signal of transcendence.

Once again we are back to *homo quaerens*, the animal that asks and asks. Why does real evil summon up absolute judgment, and how do we follow the direction in which it points? Why do we insist on judging absolutely even though we know that we too will be judged by the standards by which we judge others? What does it say of our humanity that, at such moments, we know we have no alternative? What does it show about our need to go beyond our humanity to justify and fulfill our humanity?

The answers to these questions would take us back to the fourth question and our assessment of the different explanations for evil. In my view, they point indisputably beyond the Eastern and secularist answers and in the direction of the biblical family of faiths, and for cogent reasons. The situation is not that reason has faltered so we must lean on faith, but that reason has pointed beyond itself to answers that only faith can fulfill. Whatever our conclusion, such answers are vital to our humanness and our future. Even raising them shows us a silver lining in the worst of evils.

CHAPTER 18

THE RAINBOW
THROUGH THE RAIN

No one would ever accuse Philip Hallie of being a Pollyanna. He was a scholar and a philosopher, but no one had grown up or lived farther from the tree-lined, white-picket respectability of suburbia or the urbane, pipe-wreathed comforts of a faculty club. He grew up, in fact, in one of the toughest neighborhoods in Chicago in the Roaring Twenties and lived on the West Side in a tenement building that he and his brother called "the Cockroach Building."

Crime and violence were all around Hallie as a boy. He saw the small-time gangster John Dillinger shot, killed, and carted away on his block, and he was often bullied and beaten up simply because he was Jewish. Eventually he escaped from this world through a combination of his own sharp intelligence, his love of books, and the help of an inner-city Christian mission near his home. But while he had left that world behind, its lessons and memories never left him. His early years had been a harsh schooling in the rough and arbitrary cruelty of life where there is no respect for law.

The desperate conditions in Europe in World War II and the gruesome revelations of the Nazi death camps underscored these lessons even further. Returning from the army, he graduated from college and did doctoral studies at Harvard and Oxford on the writings of David Hume and Montaigne, then became a professor of philosophy and devoted himself to a lifelong study of the Holocaust.

Philip Hallie's major work was *The Paradox of Cruelty*, a highly acclaimed study that demonstrates his signature blend of unflinching observation, rigorous intellectual analysis, and deep imaginative empathy. But this intense preoccupation with cruelty, coming on top of his childhood experiences and his military service in Europe, slowly began to drag him deeper and deeper into depression.

One spring evening in 1974, five years after the book was published, Hallie was so restless and frustrated that he knew he had to get away from his family. Angry and frightened himself, he was angering and frightening those around him. Before, he had always been able to walk his way out of such moods, so he set off to walk the mile to his office, even though there was nothing there for him to do. For more than a month he had not slept well, and his feelings of anger, bitterness, and fury had mounted until he embarrassed himself by suddenly trembling with rage or withdrawing into moody silence over a trifle. He had even thought of suicide and of his wife managing better without him, but those thoughts gave him no peace either.

When he reached the office, Hallie threw open the windows and looked out over the lights of the Connecticut River Valley. The walk had only made him feel worse. He could not get out of his mind an image of a white-coated Nazi doctor bending over a naked Jewish or Gypsy child, coldly cutting off a toe or a finger or an ear without anesthesia. His reaction was intense fury.

> I wanted to tear the head off the man, and I wanted to pick up the child and run with him or her out of the killing camp. But I could do nothing. . . . I could do nothing about them but think my murderous, useless thoughts. And shadowing even these shadowed thoughts was my fear that this busy monster, mankind, would do such things again, now that we have learned how.

Hallie was overwhelmed when he realized what all his years of study had done. "I had learned that you cannot go down into hell with impunity. You must pay an entrance fee, and an exit fee too. I had found myself consciously imitating the victimizers by yearning to victimize them too." But there was worse still:

> The deepest torture I experienced was the shame I felt for my occasional objectivity. Sometimes as I studied the records, the reports, the photographs, the letters, I found myself consciously imitating those monsters who could watch all this without a qualm. I was looking at it all with a cold eye so that I could analyze it.

Sitting at his desk, Hallie realized that he was looking despair in the face. More than fifty years of life had shown him that he tended to become what he was fascinated by. "Now I was staring into the face of cruelty and I was becoming cruelty itself. . . . Life was hellish, not only for me but also for the people who needed me and wanted to love me." His eyes raked the bookshelves in front of him and lingered on the volumes that covered the history of France. He had always believed there was no answer to cruelty except sheer force, and as he knew well, even the forces of good were often cruel in their combat with cruelty.

One type of force, however, had always been different: "The mere thought of the Resistance had always been a tonic to me." So Hallie reached out to the shelf with books on the Resistance and his hand fell on a slim volume of essays he had never noticed before. He started reading about a little town called Le Chambon-sur-Lignon. He immediately realized why he had not heard of it. The town's resistance was nonviolent, and his army days had taught him to be interested only in violent resistance.

Hallie started reading the essay listlessly but then was pulled up short. "When I got to the bottom of the third page of the article my cheeks started itching, and when I reached up to scratch them I found that my cheeks were covered with tears. And not just a few tears—my cheeks were awash with them."

Heart-Cracking Goodness

Hallie was stunned, though his first reaction was to think that he was crying out of despair. But as he thought about it, he realized that he had not cried for years. His long and intense study of horrendous cruelty had hardened his heart until he was quite beyond tears, perhaps even incapable of crying. And what had cracked his heart open? The patent goodness of these simple Huguenot people who, at the risk of their lives, had opened their village and their homes to shelter thousands of Jewish children from their Nazi predators.

Fascinated, Hallie read on and then sat back to ponder his tears. What was it in this story of a tiny village on a high plateau in the mountains of central France that had made him weep? "What had wrung these tears from me, body and soul, the way you squeeze a grape, seeds and all, to get its juice, though the seeds make the juice bitter?"

"Much of my joy came from sheer surprise," Hallie wrote. But the more he thought, the more he saw that the deepest reason of all was "the rarity of pure goodness." Those tears were "an expression of moral praise."

Hallie's account throws a soft, clear light on another silver lining of evil: it highlights the contrast with goodness. As his story shows, and the experience of many others would confirm, hearts that are hardened by evil are often sprung open by goodness.

In his posthumous autobiographical novel *The First Man*, Albert Camus tells of a priest catching him making a face at another pupil in his class, calling him up, and hitting him with all his strength, then sending him back to his place. "The child stared at him, without a tear," Camus wrote, "(and for all his life it would be kindness and love that made him cry, never pain or persecution, which on the contrary only reinforced his spirit and his resolution) and returned to his bench."

Eleonore Stump, whose story we followed earlier, argues that the same faculty of intuition that allows us to recognize the difference between degrees of evil also allows us to discern goodness. "We recognize acts of generosity, compassion, and kindness, for example,

without needing to reflect much or reason it out. And when the goodness takes us by surprise, we are sometimes moved to tears by it."

Stump points out that we have no words to describe the different
grades of goodness as we do for evil, so she uses the words "true goodness" to capture the contrast with real "wickedness." Repeatedly we
weep when we are surprised by such true goodness. Partly we weep
because of the surprise. Partly we weep because of the unexpected
grace of the gift. Partly we weep because of the savage contrast with
the surrounding experience. But mainly we weep because of the sheer
heart-stopping wonder of the beauty of true goodness itself.

Could it be that there is a mystery to goodness that is even deeper
than the mystery of evil? Certainly, like a diamond flashing in a pile of
dirt, it is often set off even more brilliantly in contrast with surrounding evil. In the topsy-turvy relativism of our modern world, there are
those who turn everything upside down, inside out, and the wrong
way round. Good they make bad, right wrong, and true false, until
many people are so confused they cannot tell the difference and see
everything as gray or a matter of spin.

Can goodness be made fashionable again, not discounted as prim,
uptight, and puritanical? There is comfort, if slim comfort, in the
knowledge that when we begin to reap the harvest of evil that such
relativism is sowing, goodness will once again be seen for what it is.

Whoever Saves a Single Life

It was some time later that the full significance of what he had experienced came home to Hallie. He had researched and written the full
story of Le Chambon in *Lest Innocent Blood Be Shed*, and he was in
Minneapolis lecturing about the tiny village that rescued five thousand Jewish children and was the safest place for Jews in German-occupied Europe. A woman with an obviously French accent stood up
at the back and asked if the village was the one in Haute-Loire. "Ah,"
she said. "You have been speaking about the village that saved all
three of my children."

There was a moment of utter silence before the mother went on to thank him for telling the beautiful story, so that her American neighbors who lived so far from the scene could begin to understand. "The Holocaust was storm, lightning, thunder, wind, rain, yes," she said. "And Le Chambon was the rainbow."

"Everybody in that audience," Hallie commented quietly, "knew what the rainbow meant in the ninth chapter of the Book of Genesis: *hope*."

It was as if he suddenly saw a world and historical force that was truly strong enough to be the counterpoint to evil. On one side were the swirling forces of evil and darkness: "During every moment of our lives on this planet strong teeth are crushing tender flesh and bones. Big fish continue to eat little fish, and all predators are more powerful than their prey. I could not forget the Cockroach Building, or those feet of John Dillinger pointing upward and jutting out of the police meat wagon near the Biograph."

But on the other side were the indomitable pastor and his wife, the villagers of Le Chambon, and all the children they rescued from death—and all the numberless host of similarly "just men" across the centuries and the continents. But to Hallie, it was not so much another side as a realm of peace in the eye of a hurricane. The Chambonnais "who did not hate and did not kill in order to make life thrive, pushed back the walls of the eye of the hurricane until the murderous winds seemed so far away as to be unreal."

Philip Hallie was unquestionably a Jew rescued by the villagers of Le Chambon long after the war just as much as the thousands of Jewish children had been earlier—in his case from depression and despair. "Whoever saves a single life," the Talmud says, "is as one who has saved an entire world." No good person would ever wish evil and suffering on anyone, but there is often a silver lining in the worst of evil and suffering: it is precisely then and there that the rainbow shines through the rain and evil is thrown into perspective by the goodness that shines over against it.

BUT NOT THROUGH ME

Never again . . . never again . . . never again . . . never again. Like a lighthouse bell tolling through the fog, these words sounded out with monotonous regularity to keep us from the rocks through all the twentieth-century atrocities. No sacred liturgy has been intoned more solemnly. No impassioned warning has cried out more urgently. But no solemn embargo has been breached more routinely and so often.

"To Woodrow Wilson," wrote Henry Morgenthau confidently, dedicating his 1918 book on the Armenian genocide, "the exponent in America of the enlightened public opinion of the world, which has decreed that the rights of small nations shall be respected and that such crimes as are described in this book shall never again darken the pages of history."

But they did.

Out of the memory of the Holocaust, President Jimmy Carter declared in 1979, on receiving the final report of the President's Commission on the Holocaust, "We must forge an unshakable oath with all civilized people that never again will the world stand silent, never again will the world fail to act in time to prevent this terrible crime of genocide."

But they did.

"Like you, I say in a forthright voice," said President Ronald Reagan to the International Convention of B'nai Brith in 1984, " 'never again!' "

But it still happened again.

Speaking "as a World War II veteran, as an American, and now as President of the United States," President George H. W. Bush told guests at the Simon Wiesenthal Dinner in Los Angeles in 1991 that his visit to Auschwitz had left him with "the determination, not just to remember, but to act."

But when the time came, those were only words.

"If the horrors of the Holocaust taught us anything," said William Jefferson Clinton, chiding President Bush over his Bosnia policy, "it is the high cost of remaining silent and paralyzed in the face of genocide."

But he remained silent and paralyzed during the Rwanda rage.

"Even as our fragmentary awareness of crimes grew into indisputable facts," President Bill Clinton said at the dedication of the U.S. Holocaust Memorial Museum in 1993, "far too little was done. We must not permit that to happen again."

But the very next year he did far too little too.

"Is another Holocaust possible? I often asked my students that question," Elie Wiesel wrote in *A Jew Today*. "Most answered yes; I said no. By its dimension, its scope, the Holocaust was a unique event; it will remain so. I explained to them that the world has learned a lesson. . . . I was wrong. What happened could happen again."

"If there is one thing sure in this world, it is certainly this," wrote Primo Levi in *Survival in Auschwitz* in 1958. "That it will not happen to us a second time."

"It happened, therefore it can happen again," Primo Levi wrote in *The Drowned and the Saved* twenty-eight years later. "This is the core of what we have to say. It can happen, and it can happen anywhere."

Has there ever been a time when it was more urgent to face up to our human capacity for evil? With all the shameful record before us, no longer can we say we do not know. No longer are we living on the far side of ignorance and nonresponsibility. Pleas of innocence have lost their grounds. Each time evil has surfaced, certainly since World War II, most of the world knew well enough what was going on and still turned away. The unimaginable and unbelievable has become believable and routine. With the few grand exceptions, we have all been bystanders, the liberals among us as well as the conservatives, our activist governments as well as our passive fellow citizens. More than 100 million human beings have been murdered, and most of us have "passed by on the other side of the road."

After twenty-five years in Soviet jails, an Estonian dissident was released into the care of his only surviving relative, his sister. Picking him up, she warned him that the family knew nothing of all he had experienced and that she did not want him to bring politics into their family affairs. Aghast, he ordered her to stop the car, got out, and said: "You don't know me and I don't know you. Good-bye."

"The struggle of man against power," the novelist Milan Kundera wrote, "is the struggle of memory against forgetting." But clearly our problem is more a moral issue than a matter of mental recall. One writer sardonically summed up the sorry parade of broken commitments and public indifference in the last century: "'Never again' might just as well be defined as 'Never again would Germans kill Jews in Europe in the 1940s.'"

Checks and Balances for a Reason

What lessons do we learn from this lamentable story? The very word *lesson* may sound grandiose when matched against the enormity of evil, for human answers are always beggared by evil itself—though once again, to find words is to begin to come to terms with the unspeakable.

One of the main lessons is to reconsider the significance of evil for our understanding of public and international life, though this topic would require a book in itself. I would simply argue here that living with our deepest differences is one of the world's critical problems and that one of the overlooked keys to solving it is to give religious liberty its due place in public life. People of different faiths—including secularism—might then relate to public life constructively and to each other civilly.

At the very least, we must shed Enlightenment prejudices about religion and consider the facts more objectively. We must reject the hoary myth that "religion is the problem," as well as the fallacious idea that the answer is a public square denuded of all religion. As we have witnessed again and again, religion of one kind or another has provided a rationale for evil, but so also has its opposite. The quality and tone of public discussion would improve immeasurably if secularists were to acknowledge that their faith is one faith among others and talk openly of their own failures—on the one hand, directly inspiring utopian evil, and on the other, failing to provide humanistic values strong enough to resist modern evil.

As the global public square emerges, there are two particular errors we cannot afford. One is to replace the religious establishments of the past with a secularist establishment or semi-establishment. The other is to create a two-tier global public square in which the cosmopolitan liberal secularists form the top tier of the global elites and all religious believers are relegated to the second rank. In a truly diverse world, neither of these options for the public square is just and neither is workable.

Understanding the role of religion in world violence today is not an all-or-nothing or black-and-white issue. The peril of religion grows directly from its promise, just as the promise of secularism grows from the peril of religion—which is why both must be respected and harnessed wisely. No force on earth gives deeper and more personal ultimate answers to the human search for meaning and belonging than faith. Religion is truly the master key to history, both for nations and for individuals. "To be religious," Albert Einstein said, "is to have found an answer to the question, 'What is the meaning of life?'" "To believe in God," Ludwig Wittgenstein wrote similarly, "is to see that life has meaning." "Religion," said Lord Acton, "is the key of history."

The very power and preciousness of faith in defining reality and ordering life is what can make religion a problem, as we see today in its inflammatory action in conflicts between Hindus and Buddhists in Sri Lanka, between Serbs and Croats in the former Yugoslavia, between Protestants and Catholics in Northern Ireland, between Muslims and animists in Sudan, and between Jews and Muslims in the Middle East.

But this is only half the story, and we must remember that the world also owes to religion such towering masterworks as the Ten Commandments, Dante's *Divine Comedy*, Chartres Cathedral, Bach's *Saint Matthew's Passion*, William Wilberforce and the abolition of slavery, Dostoyevsky's *Brothers Karamazov*, and Roger Williams's revolutionary writings on religious liberty for people of all faiths and for people with no faith.

This promise and peril make it all the more imperative to handle religion wisely in public life, but that is currently not the case in the United States or in much of the Western world. The time has come to say no decisively to both the "sacred" and the "naked" public squares and to embrace the challenges of forging a truly "civil" public square in which people of all faiths and none are free to enter and engage in public life within a shared agreement about the rights and responsibilities they are willing to accord to people of all other faiths.

Utopianism is unquestionably a great menace too, especially in its ideological and totalitarian forms, such as communism. And it is utopianism, not religion, that needs repudiating utterly. Are we on the verge of seeing secular liberalism provide a fertile breeding ground for evil because of its own ungrounded optimism? This could happen partly because of its nonchalance about the seriousness of evil—and therefore about the need for any ethical and cultural restraints—and partly because its own values, such as human rights, depend on traditional beliefs and have no sufficient foundation of their own.

Liberals in the Old World were disillusioned at the beginning of the twentieth century. At the end of World War I, Henry James wrote to a friend: "Black and hideous to me is the tragedy that gathers and I'm sick beyond cure to have lived to see it. You and I, the ornaments of our generation, should have been spared this wreck of our belief that through the long years we had seen civilization grow and the worst become impossible."

Will liberals in the New World soon experience a similar disillusionment a century later? In her memoir *Hope Against Hope*, Nadezhda Mandelstam pointed to the same flaw in modern liberalism that Auden had come up against: "We have seen the triumph of evil after the values of humanism have been vilified and trampled on. The reason these values succumbed was probably that they were based on nothing except boundless confidence in the human intellect."

Executioner, Victim, and Spectator All at Once

But let me say more about three lessons on a personal level.

First, *we must come to grips with the nature of our own humanity and the evil evident in our hearts and in our world*. Those who do evil, from Auschwitz to Abu Ghraib, are the same species as we are, and an unavoidable lesson of the past century is that we cannot afford to entertain utopian views of human nature that ignore our human capacity for evil.

For all the glory of humanness, we human beings also have a problem. We do not always seek the good of our fellow human beings, all too often we have clear intent to do harm, and sometimes we must acknowledge an uncontrollable hate and even a shameful love of dominance and cruelty. What Nietzsche called "the festival of cruelty" is a feature of the human, not of the animal world.

Is the problem simply ignorance, or is it a matter of a faulty upbringing, an inadequate education, or imperfect political systems? Is it enough, as the postmodern philosopher Richard Rorty advises, just to "pick ourselves up and try again"? Or is the problem worse? And do we once again have to take a closer look at the great religious answers to what the philosopher Isaiah Berlin called the "crooked timber" of humanity?

In his *Two Memoirs*, John Maynard Keynes accused Bertrand Russell of comments about life that were "brittle" because he had "no solid diagnosis of human nature underlying them." In other words, Russell was the victim of the unfounded optimism of the Enlightenment.

Shallow suburban views can be as utopian as the wildest political ideology. When the film of *The Diary of Anne Frank* was released in 1959, the last shot depicting Anne swaying in the fog in a concentration camp uniform was cut because it was "too tough in audience impact." The real Anne had written, "I simply can't build up my hopes on a foundation consisting of confusion, misery, and death." Her film counterpart said in conclusion—as the real Anne had written in her diary, but much earlier in her ordeal, "In spite of everything, I still believe that people are really good at heart."

Really good at heart? Dare we say that now, or are our hearts black and white like a zebra's stripes? And if so, what is the blackness of our black stripes, and where does it come from? Is the evil in our hearts a matter of ignorance or of a neutral tendency mistakenly chosen? Or is the problem worse because there is such a thing as sin? Can we even claim to be serious about understanding human nature if we have not weighed the evidence of human evil?

One of the most remarkable claims of concentration camp survivors is that they became aware of the ubiquity of evil. Though surely this group above all would angrily reject any notion of moral equivalence between perpetrator and victim, this was not the case when it came to their view of humanity as a whole. As Solzhenitsyn came to realize, "The line dividing good and evil cuts through the heart of every human being." Or as Elie Wiesel reflected after Auschwitz, "Deep down . . . man is not only executioner, not only victim, not only spectator; he is all three at once."

Our Neighbor's Neighbor

Second, *we must each consider our own response to the evil of our times.* Are we who live in the more developed parts of the world to retreat into a cocoon of privilege while the storm rages elsewhere—for the unfortunate people in Burma or the Sudan, for instance? Can we

...s with talk of compassion fatigue because we now see ...we can do anything about? Are we to join those who ...of what they know by taking refuge in apocalyptic fic-...end-of-the-world speculations? Are we to live in idleness because we can rationalize our rejection of the failures of idealism and do-goodery?

Emmanuel Levinas looked back on the last century as a whole and asked a question of us all: "Is humanity, in its indifference, going to abandon the world to useless suffering, leaving it to the political fatality—or the drifting—of the blind forces which inflict misfortune on the weak and conquered, and which spare the conquerors, whom the weak must join?"

My own conviction as a follower of Christ is that we each walk the earth to fulfill God's call. We are therefore entrepreneurs of our lives, and each and every one of us is responsible for making the most of our talents and resources, exercising our callings, engaging fully in making a difference in our spheres of influence, and doing our utmost to help our neighbors in their need—including relieving their suffering and taking a stand against the evil that oppresses them.

As such, within our definite limits we are each responsible. None of us can save the world, and to try to do so would be to flirt with despair. Our tiny circles of influence are limited, some less so than others, but for all of us that influence is significant. And when we each exercise our responsible significance, and the significance of each of our callings overlaps with those of others, the ripples we make together can spread far and wide.

So we can help more suffering people than just those we can help face to face. We can give to causes we could never visit. When we do not have the money to make such contributions, we can write letters, we can vote, and in a myriad of other ways we can influence events. And both first and last, we can pray for people and places we could never afford the time and money to visit and could never touch in any other way.

That is the only way I know to emulate the citizens of Le Chambon and be "always ready to help" and to follow Solzhenitsyn in daring to say, "But not through me." That is the only way I know to measure up to Dostoyevsky's challenging maxim: "We are all responsible for all, and for all men before all. And I more than all the others." Whatever others do or do not do, whatever the opposition, whatever the cost, we can each make our own stand and declare in our own way, "But not through me."

Wind and Fire

Third—and most importantly of all—*we must each decide for ourselves the faith by which we live, and the faith by which we understand and respond to evil and suffering.* Rarely has evil been so powerful, so blatant, and so destructive as in our modern world. And our language to describe evil and our ethical will to resist it have rarely been so uncertain and so confused. At a time when there has never been as much intellectual prejudice against an open discussion of the full range of possibilities for a truly "examined life," Edmund Burke's admonition remains timely: "The only thing necessary for the triumph of evil is for good men to do nothing."

It is time and past time for a searching review of where modern thinking about evil has brought us. What does it mean that our technology and our inhumanity are reinforcing each other dangerously? Why have so many secularist answers proven even more ineffectual than the views they were touted to replace? Should the accumulated weight of failed answers and powerful intimations lead us to a fresh consideration of long-discarded answers?

One thought in closing: is it really the case that evil is "the rock of atheism," as the unthinking mantra goes, and that, "after Auschwitz, there can be no God"?

Far from it. Many who make this claim were not in Auschwitz themselves, and the testimony of those who were there is different. In his last book, *Man's Search for Ultimate Meaning*, Viktor Frankl wrote from firsthand experience that the opposite was the case: "The truth is that among those who actually went through the experience of

Auschwitz, the number of those whose religious life was deepened—in spite, not to say because of this experience—by far exceeds the number of those who gave up their belief."

Just as a weak flame is blown out easily by a small breeze, so a weak faith, Frankl observed, may be extinguished quickly when it encounters evil and suffering. But real faith is more like a strong flame—a storm only fans it into an inextinguishable blaze.

"The unexamined life is not worth living," Socrates said famously. Or as Epictetus put it even more strenuously: "A life not put to the test is not worth living." If ever it is our lot to come face to face with evil and suffering, neither evil nor suffering need be the rock of atheism, but they will both be the supreme challenge to show whether we are living an examined life, and whether we are doing so by the power of a tested faith.

Is the unexamined life truly not worth living? Taken at face value, Socrates' claim would condemn many, and not surprisingly, he is quoted far more than followed. But what we can say is that only the unreflective and the uncaring can afford to lead unexamined and untested lives today. For a reflective person, life must be examined, and it is almost certain to be tested. Evil is neither one test among others nor one mystery among others. It is the supreme test and the profoundest mystery in light of which all other tests and mysteries will be judged.

Our challenge today is not to resort to faith as a crutch because reason has stumbled, but rather to acknowledge that reason, in its long, arduous search, has come up short and that where it has stopped it has pointed beyond itself to answers that only faith can fulfill. In the face of the horror of the unspeakable, only such faith can provide the best truths to come to terms with evil, the highest courage to resist evil, the deepest love to care for those caught in its toils, and the profoundest hope of the prospect of a world beyond evil, beyond hatred, beyond oppression, and even beyond tears.

As ever, the choice is ours, and so also will be the consequences.

SELECTED BIBLIOGRAPHY

Améry, Jean. 1980. *At the Mind's Limits: Contemplations by a Survivor on Auschwitz and Its Realities*, translated by Sidney Rosenfeld and Stella P. Rosenfeld. New York: Schocken Books.

Arendt, Hannah. 1978. *The Life of the Mind*. New York: Harcourt Brace Jovanovich.

———. 1963. *Eichmann in Jerusalem: A Report on the Banality of Evil*. New York: Viking Press.

Bauman, Zygmunt. 2000. *Modernity and the Holocaust*. Ithaca, N.Y.: Cornell University Press.

Bayley, John. 1999. *Elegy for Iris*. New York: St. Martin's Press.

Becker, Ernest. 1975. *Escape from Evil*. New York: Free Press.

———. 1973. *The Denial of Death*. New York: Free Press.

Berger, Peter. 1969. *A Rumor of Angels: Modern Society and the Rediscovery of the Supernatural*. New York: Anchor Books, 1990.

Bierce, Ambrose. 1906. *The Devil's Dictionary*. New York: Dover Publications, 1993.

Bobbitt, Philip. 2002. *The Shield of Achilles: War, Peace, and the Course of History*. New York: Anchor Books.

Camus, Albert. 1995. *The First Man*, translated from the French by David Hapgood. New York: Alfred A. Knopf.

———. 1955. *The Myth of Sisyphus, and Other Essays*, translated from the French by Justin O'Brien. New York: Alfred A. Knopf.

———. 1948. *The Plague*, translated from the French by Stuart Gilbert. New York: Alfred A. Knopf.

Chesterton, G. K. 1909. *Orthodoxy*. London: John Lane.

Courtois, Stéphane, et al., eds. 1999. *The Black Book of Communism:*

Crimes, Terror, Repression, translated by Jonathan Murphy and Mark Kramer. Cambridge, Mass.: Harvard University Press.

Dawkins, Richard. 2003. *A Devil's Chaplain: Reflections on Hope, Lies, Science, and Love*. Boston: Houghton Mifflin.

Dostoevsky, Fyodor. 1880. *The Brothers Karamozov*. New York: Penguin, 2003.

Emerson, Ralph Waldo. 1903. *The Complete Works*. New York: AMS Press, 1979.

Frankl, Viktor. 2000. *Man's Search for Ultimate Meaning*. Cambridge, Mass.: Perseus.

Freud, Sigmund. 1930. *Civilization and Its Discontents*, translated by Jean Riviere. New York: J. Cape and H. Smith.

Glover, Jonathan. 1999. *Humanity: A Moral History of the Twentieth Century*. London: Jonathan Cape.

Gourevitch, Philip. 1998. *We Wish to Inform You That Tomorrow We Will Be Killed with Our Families: Stories from Rwanda*. New York: Farrar, Straus, and Giroux.

Hallie, Philip. 1969. *The Paradox of Cruelty*. Middletown, Conn.: Wesleyan University Press.

Hume, David. 1779. *Dialogues Concerning Natural Religion*, edited and with an introduction by Stanley Tweyman. Ann Arbor, Mich.: Caravan Books, 2000.

Huxley, Julian. 1964. *Essays of a Humanist*. New York: Harper & Row.

Kaplan, Robert D. 2002. *Warrior Politics: Why Leadership Demands a Pagan Ethos*. New York: Random House.

Kreeft, Peter. 1986. *Making Sense Out of Suffering*. Ann Arbor, Mich.: Servant Ministries.

Kushner, Harold S. 1981. *When Bad Things Happen to Good People*. New York: Schocken Books.

Levi, Primo. 1988. *The Drowned and the Saved*, translated from the Italian by Raymond Rosenthal. New York: Summit Books.

———. 1986. *Survival in Auschwitz and The Reawakening: Two Memoirs*, translated by Stuart Woolf. New York: Summit Books.

Lewis, C. S. 1961. *A Grief Observed*. San Francisco: Harper San Francisco, 2001.